CIRCULATING THE CODE

CIRCULATING THE CODE

Print Media and Legal Knowledge in Qing China

TING ZHANG

UNIVERSITY OF WASHINGTON PRESS

Seattle

Circulating the Code was made possible in part by the UW Press Authors Fund.

Composed in Minion Pro, typeface designed by Robert Slimbach

24 23 22 21 20   5 4 3 2 1

Printed and bound in the United States of America

UNIVERSITY OF WASHINGTON PRESS
uwapress.uw.edu

LIBRARY OF CONGRESS CATALOGING-IN-PUBLICATION DATA
Names: Zhang, Ting (Legal historian), author.
Title: Circulating the Code : print media and legal knowledge in Qing China / Ting Zhang.
Description: 1st. | Seattle : University of Washington Press, 2020. | Includes bibliographical
   references and index.
Identifiers: LCCN 2019041164 (print) | LCCN 2019041165 (ebook) | ISBN 9780295747163
   (hardcover) | ISBN 9780295747156 (paperback) | ISBN 9780295747170 (ebook)
Subjects: LCSH: Da Qing lü—Publication and distribution. | Legal literature—Publishing—
   China—History. | Law—Study and teaching—China—History. | China—History—Qing
   dynasty, 1644–1912.
Classification: LCC KNN82 .Z484 2020 (print) | LCC KNN82 (ebook) |
   DDC 349.5109/03—dc23
LC record available at https://lccn.loc.gov/2019041164
LC ebook record available at https://lccn.loc.gov/2019041165

The paper used in this publication is acid free and meets the minimum requirements of American National Standard for Information Sciences—Permanence of Paper for Printed Library Materials, ANSI Z39.48–1984.∞

For my parents, Zhang Qiang and Zhang Suhua

CONTENTS

ACKNOWLEDGMENTS

During the research and writing process of this project, I received enormous help from various people, institutions, and libraries. First and foremost, I owe William T. Rowe and Tobie Meyer-Fong a deep debt of gratitude for their generous help, thoughtful guidance, and heartwarming encouragement. Their erudite knowledge of Qing China and their excellent advice have shaped the ways I have researched and written this book. I am also grateful to Sarah Schneewind, Mary Ryan, Erin Chung, Cynthia Brokaw, Li Chen, James Gao, the anonymous readers of the manuscript for University of Washington Press, and fellow members of the DC area Modern China Reading Group, who read most chapters or the whole manuscript, raised insightful questions, and provided valuable advice. I also want to thank my editor, Lorri Hagman, for her efficient work and wonderful suggestions.

In the course of my research, I have made use of a number of libraries, archives, and online databases, including the National Library of China, Library of Congress, First Historical Archives of China, C. V. Starr East Asian Library of Columbia University, Harvard-Yenching Library, HathiTrust Digital Library, and the libraries of the University of Tokyo, the National Committee for the Compilation of Qing History, the University of California, San Diego, Johns Hopkins University, and the University of Maryland. I am indebted to the wonderful staff at these institutions. Special thanks are due to my friends Liu Wenpeng, Wang Yuanchong, and Emily Mokros, who helped me get access to important databases and to collect and photocopy some important primary sources.

This research was assisted by generous fellowships and grants from a number of agencies. They include the Henry Luce Foundation/ACLS Program in China Studies, the Doris G. Quinn Foundation, the Chiang Ching-kuo Foundation, the China Scholarship Council, the China and Inner Asia Council of the Association of Asian Studies, the University of Maryland at College Park, and Johns Hopkins University.

Many people have commented on chapters or on related conference papers, asked meaningful questions, and offered critical advice. They include Jonathan Ocko, Madeleine Zelin, Wu Yanhong, Chiu Peng-Sheng, Benjamin Elman, Matthew Sommer, Melissa Macauley, Kai-wing Chow, Shuang Chen, Wang Zhiqiang, Robin Yates, Lisa Mar, Stanley Chodorow, Taisu Zhang, Weiting Guo, Yun Xia, David Crowe, Janet Chen, Meghan Cai, Michael Bryant, Timothy Waters, He Bian, and Nancy Park. I am also grateful to Antoine Borrut, Ahmet Karamustafa, Philip Soergel, Peter Wien, Sarah Cameron, Madeline Zilfi, Holly Brewer, Andrew Schonebaum, and my other colleagues at the University of Maryland for their help and support. Thanks also go to my fellow students and friends at Johns Hopkins: Ke Ren, Zhang Ying, Yang Jin, Zhu Xiaolei, and Li Yao. They made the research and writing process a lot more fun and my life happier.

My deepest gratitude is to my family. My parents, Zhang Qiang and Zhang Suhua, are always confident in me and encouraged me to pursue a career as a historian. They and my parents-in-law, Wang Xianghua and Huang Cunrong, provided tremendous support and helped with childcare when I was researching, teaching, and writing. I am grateful to my grandmother, Liu Shuqing, who provided me with a comfortable place to stay and cooked for me every day when I was collecting primary sources for this project in Beijing. My two children, Meilan and Yilan, arrived when I was writing and revising the manuscript. They brought endless fun and joy to our lives. Finally, my husband, Wang Jianwu, has shared all my frustrations and happiness throughout the writing of this book. This work could not have been done without his love, encouragement, and support.

CHRONOLOGY OF DYNASTIES AND QING REIGN PERIODS

Shang	ca. 1600–1046 BCE
Zhou	1046–256 BCE
Qin	221–206 BCE
Han	206 BCE–220 CE
Age of Disunion	220–589
Sui	581–618
Tang	618–907
Five Dynasties	907–960
Song	960–1279
Liao	907–1125
Jin	1115–1234
Yuan	1271–1368
Ming	1368–1644
Qing	1644–1911
Shunzhi	1644–1661
Kangxi	1662–1722
Yongzheng	1723–1735
Qianlong	1736–1795
Jiaqing	1796–1820
Daoguang	1821–1850
Xianfeng	1851–1861
Tongzhi	1862–1874
Guangxu	1875–1908
Xuantong	1909–1911

CIRCULATING THE CODE

INTRODUCTION

IN THE SUMMER OF 1695, A FARMER NAMED DU HUAILIANG IN Liaocheng County, Shandong, turned himself in to the county magistrate. He reported that he had just caught his wife and her lover having sex in his house and that he had known for a long time something "fishy" was going on with his wife and this other man, Chen Wenxian. He testified that on the night in question, when he was sleeping in the courtyard to guard his cattle, he heard noises coming from his bedroom. He quickly got up, picked up a hatchet, and rushed into the room, where he found his wife in bed and Chen, stark naked, trying to get away. Naturally, he was outraged, he explained to the magistrate, so he blocked the door and hacked his wife and Chen to death.

The magistrate launched an investigation and went to Du's house to collect evidence. He personally examined the two corpses and questioned the neighbors. As a result of his extensive investigation, he discovered that Du had made up the whole story—and the truth was even more sordid. Du had been having an affair with Chen's wife—not the other way around—for three years. Deeply in love, Du wanted to live with Chen's wife, and after she ended their illicit relationship, Du desperately wanted to get her husband and his own wife out of the way so that he could reconcile with Mrs. Chen and live openly with her. He knew about a legal loophole that excused homicide by a husband if he caught his wife and her lover in flagrante delicto. According to the Qing Code, "If a wife or concubine commits adultery with another man and her own husband catches the adulterers at the place in the very act of adultery and immediately kills both of them, there is no punishment."[1] Du was a farmer and had probably received little formal education. But obviously he knew something about the law. He lured Chen to his house for a visit and got him drunk. He then killed his guest with a hatchet and hacked his own wife to death. He took off their clothes to make it look like they had been having sex when he killed them. Du later confessed: "I hoped that if it seemed as though I had killed them while they were committing adultery, I wouldn't be charged with a crime."[2] Du's hope was in vain because Mrs. Chen's confession implicated him, and the magistrate was smart enough to see through his scheme. The magistrate sentenced him to be beheaded according to a provision in *The Great Qing Code* on the crime of premeditated murder.

Qing legal records contain a surprisingly large number of cases like this one—cases that suggest that ordinary people, as well as officials judging them, were quite familiar with the law. These cases raise several major questions about legal knowledge and Qing society: How were Qing officials—such as the magistrate in Du's murder case—informed about the laws? How did commoners—such as the murderer Du—know about the law? In what forms—and in what venues—did legal information circulate? How did legal knowledge influence people's actions and decisions? Did the Qing state try to control the dissemination of legal information? What were the cultural, political, and judicial implications of the circulation of legal knowledge?

Scholars have usually assumed that most Qing subjects knew little about the law, as there was no easily recognizable system of legal education. Scholars have also assumed that the Qing state monopolized the production and circulation of accurate legal information and kept the common people in the dark, with little access to precise and up-to-date legal knowledge. These assumptions date back to the Orientalist roots of social science. For example, Max Weber argued that Qing officials received no professional legal training and knew nothing about the law. The Qing legal system was a total disaster because it was run by "amateur officials" with little legal knowledge, in contrast to western Europe's efficient legal system run by "professionals."[3] Similarly, Wejen Chang's "Legal Education in Ch'ing China," the most comprehensive English-language study to date of Qing legal knowledge, argues that the Qing state disappointingly lacked formal legal education for both officials and the common people.[4] As a result, he concludes, Qing officials had no workable legal knowledge, and the common people could get only fragmented and imprecise ideas about law through sources such as lowbrow novels, plays, and operas.

This narrative about nonexistent legal education and legal knowledge accords with the once dominant assumption that the traditional legal system of China had failed. Qing laws and legal institutions had lacked "separation of power, due process, respect for individual rights, and civil law," in sharp contrast to the "dynamic and progressive" law and legal system of modern Western Europe. Qing law was viewed as "a tool of autocratic control," and most of the populace found the law and the legal system too intimidating to turn to when they had problems.[5] In recent years, however, based on newly opened local legal archives, scholars have challenged this narrative about the traditional Chinese legal system, especially on the level of judicial practice. They have found that Qing society was more litigious than previously thought, so it was not unusual for people to turn to the court to resolve their disputes. The cost of litigation was not as intimidating as scholars previously thought, and local magistrates often sentenced cases according to the statutes and substatutes of *The Great Qing Code*.[6] Many of these "new Qing legal history" studies imply that both officials and the common people were more or less familiar with law and legal procedure. But none of these studies has explained how officials and commoners got access to legal knowledge. Even as law has gained presence, the narrative of deficient legal education and legal knowledge has not been seriously challenged.

During the Qing, most reliable legal information circulated in book form, but historians of print culture usually focus on the Song and late Ming periods, when there were important technological breakthroughs and when many elegant editions were produced. The publishing history of the Qing period has long been ignored because of the perception of stricter government censorship, the diminished quality of books and illustrations, and the decline of lavish publishing centers in the Jiangnan area.[7] However, as historian Cynthia Brokaw argues in her pathbreaking work on Qing printing history, these declines accompanied a sharp rise in the quantity of printed books, a much broader reading audience, lower prices of books, and an expanding publishing industry in other areas of the Qing empire.[8] Brokaw's important work is however, focused on Sibao, a rural printing center in Fujian, which published few legal books. In recent years, some historians begin to examine several genres of legal imprints, such as official handbooks (*guanzhenshu*) and litigation masters' secret handbooks (*songshi miben*), but none has systematically analyzed the impact of commercial printing revolution on legal culture.[9]

This book explores the production, circulation, and reception of legal knowledge in Qing China. It focuses on the flow of legal information through both textual and oral channels and the role of legal information in the formation of early modern Chinese legal culture. Drawing on methodologies used in recent scholarship in the fields of print culture and legal history, it demonstrates that the late Ming commercial publishing revolution (ca. 1550s), which continued in the Qing, had a huge impact on the way legal information traveled. Before the late Ming, most books related to the state's laws were published by official publishing agencies, and accurate legal information was by and large confined within the government. Beginning in the late Ming, however, more and more commercial publishing houses engaged in compiling, printing, and selling legal books, including the Code—the most authoritative legal text in the judicial system. As a matter of fact, the Qing period witnessed a publishing boom in books related to the law.

Analysis of the archives of the Wuyingdian Imperial Publishing House and other official publishers shows that the Qing state did not provide enough usable editions of *The Great Qing Code* (Da Qing lü jijie fuli *or* Da Qing lüli) to its judicial officials. The imperial editions of the Code were expensive, updated slowly, printed in a limited number, and issued only to high-ranking officials. Among 131 editions of the Code that I have found, only eleven were published by official publishing houses. Official editions could not meet the demand of officials and commoners who wanted—and needed—to get precise legal knowledge from the Code. In this context, commercial editions flourished and filled the gap. Most Qing legal books were commercially printed and sold freely on the book market, available to anyone who could afford them.

Commercial publishers and non-official editors played a leading role in supplying judicial officials with access to printed, up-to-date editions of the Qing Code. Careful comparison of imperial editions and commercial editions shows that, surprisingly, commercial editions of the Code were not simply reprinted copies of the imperial editions. Commercial publishers and editors reorganized the text of the Code and included additional legal information that was not authorized or approved by the imperial government, such as private legal commentaries, administrative regulations, and case precedents. By the 1800s, based on popular editions published in Hangzhou, commercial publishers had established their own standard format for compiling and publishing the Code, a format quite different from that of imperially authorized editions. These commercially printed Hangzhou editions quickly dominated the book market and became the most widely used and authoritative texts in the Qing judicial system and society. All commercial editions of the Code published after the year 1800 discarded the design of imperial editions and closely followed the content and printing format of these Hangzhou editions.

The commercialization of legal knowledge enhanced the judicial authority of private legal commentaries and case precedents, which were printed along with the imperially promulgated statutes in commercial editions of the Code. Qing officials frequently referred to private commentaries and case precedents when making judicial decisions. County magistrates, such as in murderer Du's case, who received little formal legal training and were not given imperially authorized copies of the Code could easily buy commercial copies and locate specific provisions when sentencing a case, thanks to the reader-friendly arrangement of texts in commercial legal imprints. Easy access to the laws encouraged officials to make judicial sentences based on the Code more frequently.

Quite different from the old image that the state paid little attention to its officials' legal education, this research shows that the Qing government established specific and effective regulations regarding officials' legal training. The Qing rulers especially emphasized such education for newly appointed county magistrates. Although the state did not itself provide formal legal education to officials, it encouraged new officials to buy and read legal books, including the Code, various administrative regulations, official handbooks, and legal treatises, after they passed the civil service examinations and waited for appointment to official posts. The state also established legal examinations for new officials and required new magistrates to pass these examinations before being actually appointed. Officials also placed great emphasis on reading legal books and acquiring useful legal knowledge, noting that it was important and necessary for officials to equip themselves with legal knowledge in order to survive as judges and administrators in this legally sophisticated society.

The commercial printing revolution also made the law more accessible to those outside the official bureaucracy. A new genre of legal imprints called "litigation masters' secret handbooks" became popular among non-elite readers. These popular legal handbooks demystified and translated complex laws and legal terms into easy-to-understand formats such as rhymed songs and questions and answers. These books compiled legal information useful for commoners and taught it together with litigation skills. Law and punishments in popular handbooks presented law as a tool, a weapon that anyone could use and even abuse to achieve his or her own ends. In other words, popular legal handbooks popularized and vulgarized the laws, empowering readers and encouraging them to use (and abuse) law and the judicial system to solve their problems. The history of popular legal handbooks in late imperial China provides us another salient example on how the book market and commercial publishers challenged state control.

The Qing state and its officials made serious efforts to provide the common people with accurate legal knowledge from the Code through the community moral and legal lecture system. Such knowledge, including many statutes and substatutes regarding important civil and penal laws that commoners would encounter in their lives, was taught orally, with the goal of warning people not to commit crimes and thus promoting public order and morality. The Qing state not only promoted such lectures in China proper but also held similar lectures in frontier regions where the majority of populace were non-Han ethnic groups. Through disseminating orthodox legal information, the Qing state intended to establish judicial authority, stabilize control, and transform (or "acculturate") local customs in frontier regions. Qing people had unprecedented access to written laws and punishments in the form of texts, speeches, and lectures, thanks to commercially printed editions of the Code, popular legal imprints, and the community lectures.

The popular dissemination of legal knowledge, however, was a double-edged sword. On the one hand, information about the law, particularly punishments, could frighten people into behaving properly. Officials viewed the law as an essential means of moral indoctrination and crime prevention, but legal knowledge was also powerful and potentially "dangerous." When people knew the laws well, they were more likely to use them to pursue their own ends. Some Qing ruling elites worried that people might be too familiar with the laws and become litigious, which would disturb social stability and add to the workload of the already overburdened judicial system. In other words, there was tension between the state's interest in disseminating information and its fear that legal knowledge would lead people to manipulate and abuse the law. This tension was rooted in ambiguity and ambivalence about the law in the Confucian classics. While *The Rites of Zhou* (Zhouli), for example, articulated that a benevolent government should publicize its laws and punishments and let everyone in the realm know them, other classical texts indicated Confucian distaste and distrust for the law, legal knowledge, and litigation.[10] Such tension and ambiguity influenced Qing officials' attitudes toward and the state's policy on the publication of law books and community legal cultures, and also affected (and more often undermined) the state's capability and willingness to control the dissemination of legal knowledge.

This study challenges the previous assumptions that the state monopolized accurate legal knowledge, and that neither officials nor the common people knew much about the laws. It demonstrates that the commercial printing revolution in early modern China fundamentally transformed the judicial system and legal culture. Thanks to commercial legal imprints and community lectures, legal knowledge was widely available in the Qing, and both officials and commoners had ready access to it. The book market, rather than the Qing state, led the production and dissemination of accurate legal information. The Qing judicial system depended on the market for timely information. By publishing and circulating legal books, especially *The Great Qing Code*, commercial publishers and editors redefined the legal system and introduced new sources of judicial authority. Commercial legal publications also transformed popular views of the law and fostered popular legal awareness in Qing local society. The flourishing trade in commercial legal imprints contributed to the formation of a new legal culture in early modern China; features of this culture included the free flow of accurate legal information, the rise of non-official legal experts, a legally savvy population, and a high litigation rate in local society.

Three important genres of legal imprints are central to this study:

Published legal books: I have documented and studied 131 different editions of *The Great Qing Code* from several major libraries around the world.[11] Many of these editions were previously unknown or unexamined. I have also examined more than sixty-five editions of litigation masters' secret handbooks, fifteen manuals for community legal lectures, and many official handbooks. These legal books provide valuable information on their compilers, editors, revisers, publishers, printers, and target readers from titles, prefaces, general editorial regulations, and paper and printing quality. The printing format, structure, and content of these books also provide clues about how legal information was transformed during the process of communication and dissemination.

Sources regarding the legal publishing industry: These consist of documents about official and commercial legal publishers, such as the archives of the Wuyingdian Imperial Publishing House in Beijing, documents about some provincial publishing houses in the late Qing, and memoirs of bibliophiles. These documents have plentiful information regarding the daily operation, printing process, costs, profits, book prices, and circulation channels of official and commercial publishers in the Qing.

Documents related to government policies on law and legal knowledge: Examples include imperial edicts, official memorials, and administrative regulations. These sources reveal the state's changing regulations on and officials' complicated attitudes toward the dissemination of legal information in the bureaucracy and society. Legal case reports from the archives of the central government and some county-level archives illustrate how the dissemination of legal information impacted people's legal decisions and judicial practice.

1 QING LEGISLATION AND IMPERIAL EDITIONS OF *THE GREAT QING CODE*

QING LEGISLATORS MADE GREAT EFFORTS TO PROMULGATE UP-to-date laws for the bureaucracy and society. At least eight imperially authorized editions of the Code were compiled and published, as well as more than twenty editions of the *Expanded Substatutes of the Great Qing Code* (Da Qing lü xuzuan tiaoli). Qing rulers had a more flexible attitude than rulers of previous dynasties on modifying laws, especially substatutes, to adapt them to social and political changes.[1] Qing laws were frequently updated with a large number of new substatutes. Law-making matters, of course, but the circulation and reception of law matters as much as the legislation process itself. After all, laws cannot be effectively implemented unless they are effectively communicated. Active legislation requires an efficient dissemination system. This was especially true for the Qing, a vast empire that had numerous judicial officials working in the huge bureaucracy.

THE PUBLICATION AND CIRCULATION OF DYNASTIC CODES BEFORE THE QING

Codified law has a long history in the Chinese legal system.[2] Judicial officials at all levels used the codified law as a standard and authority to judge cases and pass sentences. Because the codified law was one of the symbols of the emperors' political authority as well as a tool of imperial control over state and society, the authority to compile and issue the dynastic Code belonged to the throne. The state was also responsible for issuing the validated Code and other regulations widely enough that the members of bureaucracy could implement and follow them. Before the late Ming period (1550s–1644), the state by and large monopolized the production and circulation of legal codes. For example, the central government of the Northern Song (960–1127) articulated its exclusive right to print books related to laws, strictly banning the private and commercial printing of legal books.[3] An imperial edict issued in the Qingyuan period (1195–1200) states: "Whoever privately prints the penal Code, statutes, regulations, ordinances, or classified statutes is to be punished by 100 blows of the heavy bamboo."[4]

Compared with the Song rulers, Ming emperors were more open-minded about the commercial publication and the circulation of the Code in society. The main concern behind the strict restrictions on private publishing of books in the Song was the potential divulgence of government secrets to its rivals. This concern was greatly alleviated in the Ming. The Ming government thus took a much more relaxed attitude toward private and commercial publishing activities than the Song did.[5] Viewing the codified law as a fundamental tool to transform social customs and restore Chinese culture and society that had been "damaged" under Mongol rule, the Ming rulers were enthusiastic about promoting the Code and other laws to their subjects, including both officials and commoners.[6] The imperial court and the central government were still the major publishers of the Code, but many local administrations began to be involved in the printing and publishing of the Code, commentaries, and legal handbooks. In the late Ming period commercial publishing boom, some private and commercial publishing houses began to publish law books. However, judicial officials and official publishers still played a leading role in editing and publishing the Ming Code and other books that convey the dynastic laws.[7]

THE CODE AND THE QING JUDICIAL BUREAUCRACY

As a part of the Qing bureaucracy, the structure and procedures of the judicial system were highly centralized and well-regulated. The judicial bureaucracy operated on four main administrative levels. On the lowest level, there were approximately 1,450 counties. As "father and mother officials" (*fumuguan*), county magistrates took the responsibilities of almost all major aspects of local governance in their jurisdictions, playing the most important role in the local judicial administration. They usually took charge of the initial investigation, conducted hearings, prepared reports, and suggested sentences of legal cases filed in county courts. Above the county level, there were about 180 prefects, whose main judicial responsibility was transmittal of cases from county-level to provincial-level courts. Serious criminal cases were usually reviewed and retried at the provincial level. Each of the eighteen provinces in China proper had a judicial commissioner (*anchashi*)—a full-time judicial official who took charge of the provincial court. The provincial courts' judgments required ratification by the governor or governors-general, who usually prepared reports submitted to the central judicial bureaucracy for review. At the central level, there were three main judicial offices: the Board of Punishments (Xingbu), the Censorate (Duchayuan), and the Court of Judicial Review (Dalisi). At the top of the Qing judicial bureaucracy, these three high courts reviewed legal reports from provincial courts, made or suggested judicial sentences, and occasionally retried serious cases.[8]

One of the most important methods of the central government's control over the judicial bureaucracy on local and provincial levels was the automatic judicial review of all serious cases that involved a sentence heavier than bambooing (*chizhang*). At the bottom level of the judicial bureaucracy, county magistrates could make final judgments and carry out sentences over only minor cases. All other cases involving sentences of penal servitude (*tu*), exile (*liu*), and death (*si*) were required to go through the strict judicial review process at various stages of the judicial ladder: from county, to prefecture, to province, to the central government, and in many cases, to the emperor.[9] Although the automatic judicial review was not a Qing innovation, only the Qing seriously and effectively enforced it throughout the entire judicial system. Since the late Kangxi period, the central government established a detailed list of administrative sanctions for officials who committed mistakes in dealing with legal cases.[10] In the judicial review process, if officials assigned unjustified penalties (e.g., by citing improper statutes or substatutes) or violated standard judicial procedures (e.g., by using unacceptable torture instruments during a trial), they endured punishments including administrative fines, demotion, cashiering, or even corporal penalties.[11]

Suggesting a wrong sentence based on an inappropriate statute or substatute was a common mistake that led to administrative sanctions in the judicial review process. Qing laws strictly required officials to sentence legal cases based on statutes or substatutes from the Code. Article 415, "Citing Laws and Orders in Deciding Cases," read: "Every official who is deciding a case must cite the statute of the law or the substatutes; any violation (i.e., failure to cite) will be punished with 30 strokes of the light bamboo."[12] Although county magistrates did not always follow this law when sentencing minor cases in county courts, the law was rigorously enforced in all major cases that required judicial review in upper-level courts.[13] The core principle of late imperial Chinese law was to "let the punishment fit the crime." The Code attempted to foresee all kinds of possible variations of any given crime and to subscribe specific punishments for each specific crime. The aim of this differentiation was to maximize justice by allowing the law to fit as closely as possible with every foreseeable circumstance of a crime.[14] In judicial practice, however, it was challenging for officials to find a "perfect" statute or substatute from the Code because scenarios of true crimes were often beyond the stipulations of the laws.

That Qing laws were constantly changing also increased the difficulty of choosing a matching statute or substatute for a crime. The main content of the Code was composed of statutes and substatutes. Statutes (lü) were usually fundamental legal principles, which were "the codification of moral truths retaining eternal validity irrespective of time or place."[15] The Qing rulers seldom changed or revised the statutes, and the number of statutes was reduced only from 459 to 436 between the early Qing and 1740.[16] After 1740, however, the number and content of statutes remained largely unchanged until the late Qing legal reforms in the early twentieth century. Compared with the statutes, substatutes (li) were more specific and often ad hoc, reflecting changing imperial policies and social environment. The Qing rulers frequently revised, modified, added, or removed substatutes. The number of substatutes greatly increased over the course of the dynasty, from 449 to 1892.[17] New substatutes generally came from three sources: imperial edicts, officials' suggestions or court decisions (especially collective decisions made by the Board of Punishments) as approved by the emperor, and more often, specific case precedents (cheng'an).[18] Since substatutes were more concrete, updated, and practical than statutes, judges usually preferred to make their decision based on a substatute if a statute and a substatute were both applicable to a case.[19] Qing law required that officials make legal sentences based on the updated laws. According to article 43, "Deciding a Punishment according to Newly Promulgated Laws": "Every law comes into effect the day it is promulgated."[20] If an official cited an outdated statute or substatute to sentence a case, he could be sanctioned.

Judicial officials were under enormous pressure because of the demanding requirement to choose appropriate and updated statutes or substatutes when sentencing legal cases, the strict regulations in the judicial review process, and the potential harsh sanctions if any mistake was made. Most judicial officials received little or no formal legal training. The most important channel for officials to learn the laws and make judicial decisions was through reading a variety of law books, including the Code, collections of case precedents, and legal treatises. As the most authoritative book in the legal world, the Code was of ultimate importance to those working in the judicial system. Judicial officials and their legal advisors needed to look through the Code carefully to find and cite proper and updated statutes and substatutes in order to make judicial sentences, especially for the cases that would be scrutinized through the review process. The proper functioning of the extensive and highly regulated judicial bureaucracy required effective dissemination of usable editions of the Code and other updated legal information.

EARLY QING LEGISLATION AND OFFICIAL PUBLISHING OF THE CODE

In 1644, soon after the Manchus conquered North China and took over the government, the Regent Dorgon (1612–1650) ordered officials to "analyze the Ming Code" and "refer to the current situation" in preparation for compiling the formal Code and promulgating it to "all under heaven."[21] In May 1645 the compilation of the first edition of the Qing Code (the Shunzhi Code) formally started.[22] It took only about three months for officials to finish the compilation. In August 1645 officials sent the complete draft to the three palace academies (*neiyuan*, the main policy-making agencies in the early Qing) for review.[23] The process of cutting woodblocks for printing the Code began immediately after the Board of Punishments finished compiling the draft. Two officials at the Board of Punishments took charge of assembling the woodblock cutters and preparing the printing. It is possible that the woodblock cutting and printing were done in the Classics Depot (Jingchang), one of the major publishing institutions of the Ming court, which was inherited by the Qing court and served as the official publishing institution in the early Qing.[24] The cutting of the blocks was in progress already even while the Code was still under review in the three palace academies. After revisions were completed, the Board of Punishments assigned an official to collate the woodblocks and correct mistakes.[25] In 1646 the book was sent to the throne for final review. However, Dorgon seemed unsatisfied with the quality of the Code. He decided to send it back to the three palace academies and ordered officials to scrutinize it again in a more careful, character-by-character way. The process of revision and correction was finished a year later. In 1647 the Shunzhi Code was finally published under the name *Statutes of the Great Qing with Collected Commentaries and Appended Substatutes* (Da Qing lü jijie fuli).[26]

The Shunzhi Code may well have been the first imperially authorized book printed and published by the Qing central publishing institution. Although the central government carefully preserved its documents, the original edition of the Shunzhi Code is difficult to find, possibly because of the limited print run. Nowadays, scholars can only conjecture as to the form and content of the Shunzhi Code based on reprinted editions.[27] There were thirty chapters (*juan*) in the Shunzhi Code, including 459 statutes and 449 substatutes. The form and content of the Shunzhi Code borrowed heavily from the Ming Code issued by the first Ming emperor, and it was strongly influenced by various annotated editions of the Code published in the late Ming.[28]

Only a small number of officials had access to printed copies of the Shunzhi Code, including some high officials in the central government and governors-general, governors, and provincial judicial commissioners. Officials in the Shunzhi period complained that the Code was rare and difficult to obtain. For example, in 1655 supervising secretary (*jishizhong*) Wei Yijie (1616–1686) sent a memorial to the throne in which he complained, "Nowadays each government office only has one copy of the Code, locked up tightly and hidden in the inner room. It is impossible for people to see it." He then suggested that the court order provincial governors to print more copies of the Code.[29] However, it seems that the court did not take his suggestion seriously. Throughout the Shunzhi period, copies of the Code, especially the ones printed by official publishing houses, saw limited circulation.

In the Kangxi reign the court engaged in more book printing and cultural production. In 1680 the court established the Wuyingdian Manufacture Department (Wuyingdian Zaobanchu), which soon replaced the Classics Depot and became the main book printing and publishing institution of the court. The Kangxi emperor (r. 1662–1722) enthusiastically printed and published books, especially the Confucian classics, dictionaries, and collections of literary works, viewing it as a method to win the support of Han literati and establish the court's cultural authority. The Kangxi court published at least fifty-six different titles, altogether 5,596 volumes.[30] The court-printed books of this period are famous for their high quality. Jin Zhi (1663–1740), a famous early Qing scholar, highly valued the books printed by the Kangxi court, saying that the beautiful calligraphic style in these books "surpassed all the past and current books" and that the quality of these books was even better than the books printed in the Song period.[31]

Compared with the flourishing enterprise of book printing by the Kangxi court, legislation and publication of the updated Code in the Kangxi reign was a struggling process. The Kangxi emperor seemed less interested in equipping his bureaucracy with the updated Code than in providing the literary world with high-quality editions of classics and literature. He did not intend to make use of the developing printing institutions of the court to print the Code. The legislation process in the Kangxi period was painfully slow. Although in the late years of the Shunzhi reign the emperor felt it necessary to revise the Code and ordered officials to prepare for compiling the updated substatutes and regulations into the Code, this process was not formally finished until 1725, when the Yongzheng Code, the second imperial edition of the Qing Code, was published, about seventy years later.[32] The major legislative work done during the Kangxi period was the compilation of the *Substatutes for the Board of Punishments in Current Use* (Xingbu xianxing zeli)—a collection of new substatutes promulgated in the Kangxi reign. Because the Shunzhi Code was compiled in a hurry, many outdated statutes and substatutes directly adopted from the Ming Code were not deleted or revised. Moreover, many precedents and new regulations that originated in legal and administrative practices postdated the Shunzhi Code and their conflict with the outdated statutes and substatutes had already became an obstacle to the proper functioning of the bureaucracy and legal system.

In 1667 the Kangxi emperor began to pay attention to the newly established precedents and regulations. In 1668 the emperor ordered the Board of Punishments to "compile the current substatutes in current use, sort them out, and send them to the throne for imperial review."[33] Twelve years later, in 1680, the updated substatutes were published under the title *Substatutes of the Board of Punishments in Current Use*.[34] The 1680 edition of the *Substatutes in Current Use* has been lost, probably due to the limited print run. The *Substatutes in Current Use* and the Code were separate books throughout the Kangxi period. Both were published by the Board of Punishments for a small number of high-ranking officials who had responsibility for judicial administration, including top officials of the six boards and the Censorate, Manchu generals in frontier regions, governors-general, governors, and judicial commissioners in the provinces.[35] It seems that the Board of Punishments did not assume responsibility for providing the Code to subprovincial officials, such as prefects and county magistrates, who also had to deal with the laws and legal cases as a part of their routine work. The board formerly suggested that provincial governments reprint the Code for distribution to these subprovincial officials, but extant editions show little evidence that the provincial governments actually did so in the Kangxi period.

Beside the scarcity of the officially printed copies of the Code in the Kangxi bureaucracy, contemporary officials faced another major problem: the separation, and sometimes incompatibility, of the Code and the *Substatutes in Current Use*. Even before the *Substatutes in Current Use* was compiled, some officials began to notice the problems caused by the contradictions between the Code and new laws. In 1664 the Board of Punishments suggested that the current precedents and regulations be incorporated into the Code and that the revised Code be sent to high provincial officials for their reference.[36] The throne approved this suggestion, but no evidence shows that it was applied in practice. Again, in 1671, Zhang Weichi (d. 1676), supervising secretary of the Board of Punishments, memorialized that the separation of the Code and newly established substatutes caused problems, urging the court to compile a "complete book" (*quanshu*) of all the updated statutes and substatutes for all under the heaven to observe. He wrote: "In the early years of the Shunzhi reign, the Board officials compiled the Code. . . . However, in recent years, every time new substatutes were established, it was said that it was not necessary to incorporate them into the Code. Therefore, nowadays, the Code and the new substatutes are separated from and inconsistent with each other."[37]

Then Zhang Weichi narrated two examples of such problems when he reviewed the provincial legal case reports. He identified the cases where different provincial governments issued different punishments for similar crimes based on the Code or new substatutes. He also noticed that although official editions of the Code did not include the new substatutes, several commercial editions did include new substatutes. According to Zhang, this was rather troublesome, because these commercial editions were "not approved by the imperial government" and only contained a portion of the new substatutes. Thus they could easily lead to confusion. Zhang argued that this situation not only harmed the judicial system but also led to corruption among officials and clerks, who could use these inconsistencies in the laws to serve their personal interests.[38] The court should order officials to compile the complete book of the laws and publish it as soon as possible. He wrote:

> I suggest that Your Majesty order the Board to collate the original Code and the new substatutes immediately. As for the new substatutes that have been approved and are appropriate, incorporate them into their proper categories and make them follow their original statutes in the Code according to the method when the Code was compiled. Make sure that they are in proper arrangement. In this way, both the Code and the new substatutes will be incorporated into a single book. As for the officials who take responsibility of hearing cases, each of them should have one such book. They can refer to the book at any time and get everything at one glance, which would save them time and trouble as well as prevent them from giving wrong sentences.[39]

Unfortunately, the emperor ignored Zhang's advice, probably because at that time the court was too preoccupied with other more serious problems, such as consolidating territory and suppressing rebellions.

The troublesome situation caused by the separation of the Code and new substatutes continued. In 1689, when the empire was basically pacified, Sheng Fusheng (1615–1700), investigating censor (*yushi*) of the Censorate, brought up the issue of incorporating the updated substatutes into the Code again. This time the emperor adopted the suggestion and appointed several high officials of the Board of Punishments as chief editors. The process of revising the Code formally started. The major tasks of the revision were to (1) incorporate the *Substatutes in Current Use* into the Code, (2) correct the mistakes in the Manchu translations of the Code, (3) delete repetitive and outdated statutes and substatutes, (4) select and incorporate new administrative regulations into the Code, (5) and select and add explanations and commentaries to the Code in order to clarify the meanings of obscure statutes. The revision process, however, went extremely slowly. Only after nineteen years, in 1707, was the manuscript completed and submitted to the emperor.[40] However, the emperor had lost interest, probably because he was preoccupied with solving his succession disputes among his sons and he was agonizing about the cruelty and punishments of the laws. He never returned or responded to the manuscript. The revision process was then suspended, and the officials' efforts to produce a definitive edition of a complete book of the Qing Code in the Kangxi period failed.

LEGISLATION IN THE YONGZHENG AND QIANLONG PERIODS

When the Kangxi emperor died in 1722, his fourth son, known as the Yongzheng emperor (r. 1723–1735), ascended the throne. Unlike his father, who admired small government and lax regulations, the Yongzheng emperor sought to build an efficient bureaucracy based on solid revenue and effective laws and regulations.[41] He soon found the contradiction between the old substatutes in the Code and newly established substatutes intolerable. Only one month after ascending the throne, he issued an imperial edict to provincial judicial commissioners, criticizing the corruption and malpractice prevalent in the legal system. One of the important reasons for the corruption, the emperor pointed out in this edict, was the lack of clarity of the laws: "Sometimes, two different substatutes [and thus two different penalties] can be applied to the same crime. Then officials can manipulate this situation for personal gain. In this way, how can people get any justice?"[42] Therefore, when an official brought up the issue of integrating the Code and current substatutes as well as publishing a complete book of the laws, the emperor quickly approved. The compilation process formally started in 1723. The revision process was smooth and fast. In 1725 the manuscript was finished.[43]

The Yongzheng Code was a considerable improvement on the Shunzhi Code. For one thing, it incorporated "collected commentaries"—including various private and official annotations and explanations to the statutes and substatutes—into the Code. It also finished the process of integrating the *Substatutes in Current Use* into the Code, realizing the half-century-long dream of Qing legislators. In the Yongzheng Code, the editors reduced the number of statutes from 459 to 436, but they increased the number of substatutes from 449 to 824. They also divided these substatutes into three categories: original substatutes (321 old substatutes in the Shunzhi Code), newly enacted substatutes (299 substatutes established in the Kangxi period), and imperially approved substatutes (204 new substatutes established in the late Kangxi and early Yongzheng periods).[44] The Yongzheng Code, in other words, was a "complete book" for all important up-to-date statutes and substatutes for the Qing legal system, designed to serve as a "definitive edition" of the Qing legal code for all to observe.

In the year of his ascendance to the throne, the Qianlong emperor (r. 1736–1795) decided to revise the Code to incorporate new substatutes, delete outdated ones, and modify some laws he deemed too strict. The emperor organized a new Commission on Statutes (Lüliguan) to undertake the revision.[45] After five years of revision, in 1740, the commission submitted the final manuscript and received the emperor's endorsement. This revision turned out to be an important modification of the Code: it established the basic structure and content of the imperially authorized editions of the Code that did not change again until the late Qing legal reforms in the early twentieth century and included three major revisions. First, the editors systematically removed the "collected commentaries" that had been added to the Yongzheng Code, explaining that these commentaries often originated in commercially published law books and lacked authority and reliability, which would easily lead to complication and confusion. Second, although the number of statutes did not change, the number of substatutes increased from 824 to 1042. The new substatutes were drawn mainly from the new substatutes of the Board of Punishments from 1727 to 1739. Third, the Qianlong Code rearranged the sequence of many substatutes. It abolished the time-based labels that had been added to the substatutes in the Yongzheng Code. All the substatutes in the Qianlong Code were thus organized according to their content.[46]

During the revision process, a new standard for future revisions of the Code was established. Substatutes promulgated after the revision was finished would be revised and compiled every three years. The Commission on Statutes was assigned to do the work, which included examining the imperial edicts and officials' memorials related to the administration of justice, selecting and editing them into substatutes; collating the old and new substatutes and omitting the outdated and redundant ones; listing the substatutes that should be added, changed, moved, and omitted; and compiling them into a manuscript and sending it to the Wuyingdian to print.[47] The books of these new substatutes were named *The Expanded Substatutes of the Great Qing Code* (Da Qing lü xuzuan tiaoli or Da Qing lü zuanxiu tiaoli). The *Expanded Substatutes* later became an important channel whereby officials got access to up-to-date laws. In 1746, after the second compilation of the *Expanded Substatutes*, the Qianlong emperor deemed that every three years was too frequent to revise the substatutes and changed the interval to five years.[48] Henceforth, the substatutes were revised at roughly five-year intervals. From 1743 to 1870, the year of the last imperial revision, the substatutes were revised at least twenty-three times.

TABLE 1.1. Dates of Revisions after 1740

No.	Date	No.	Date	No.	Date
1	1743 (Qianlong 8)	9	1783 (Qianlong 48)	17	**1825 (Daoguang 5)**
2	1746 (Qianlong 11)	**10**	**1790 (Qianlong 55)**	18	1830 (Daoguang 10)
3	1751 (Qianlong 16)	11	1795 (Qianlong 60)	19	1835 (Daoguang 15)
4	1756 (Qianlong 21)	**12**	**1802 (Jiaqing 7)**	20	1840 (Daoguang 20)
5	1761 (Qianlong 26)	13	1805 (Jiaqing 10)	21	1845 (Daoguang 25)
6	**1768 (Qianlong 33)**	14	1810 (Jiaqing 15)	22	1852 (Xianfeng 2)
7	1773 (Qianlong 38)	15	1815 (Jiaqing 20)	**23**	**1870 (Tongzhi 9)**
8	1778 (Qianlong 43)	16	1821 (Daoguang 1)		

Sources: Data from extant imperial editions of the *Great Qing Code* and the *Expanded Substatutes* and indexes of legal books, such as *Zhongguo falü tushu zongmu.*

Note: Boldface indicates major revisions when the complete book of the Code was revised and printed; other years are the ordinary revisions, when only the *Expanded Substatutes* was compiled. Dates generally refer to when the revisions were finished and the manuscripts were sent to the Wuyingdian for printing.

As seen in table 1.1, until 1852 revision of the substatutes was undertaken at fairly regular five-year intervals: eighteen editions of the *Expanded Substatutes* and four editions of the Code were published in this 110-year period. The Qing court suspended and neglected the Code revisions after the Taiping War (1850–64) started, when the court was preoccupied with military concerns. The court formally resumed the revision process in 1863 when it was about to win the war and started trying to reestablish law and order. Seven years later, in 1870, the Commission on Statutes finally submitted the draft of the Code for printing. This turned out to be the last major revision of the Code before the late Qing legal reforms.[49] The product of this revision, the Tongzhi Code of 1870, was the last imperially authorized edition of the Code published in the Qing.

BOOK PUBLISHING ACTIVITIES IN THE WUYINGDIAN

Starting with the Yongzheng Code of 1725, the Wuyingdian Book Editing Department (Wuyingdian Xiushuchu) published all the imperially authorized editions of the Qing Code. As the main publishing institution of the court, the Wuyingdian was quite active in the High Qing period. During the Yongzheng and Qianlong periods, the Wuyingdian published 380 titles, totaling a mind-boggling 26,982 volumes.[50] The books published by the Wuyingdian covered a wide range of genres and subjects, including imperial writings, Confucian classics, almanacs, medical texts, dictionaries, religious texts, dynastic histories, collections of literary works, and various administrative regulations and the laws. As a subsidiary of the Imperial Household Department, the Wuyingdian was part of the government. The book printing and publishing activities in the Wuyingdian were usually under the direct orders of the emperor, to serve, in general, his political purposes. By editing, printing, and publishing various books through the Wuyingdian, the court intended not only to establish its image as a legitimate cultural sponsor but also to ensure its cultural and political authority through the production of standard texts in the field of literature, history, religion, law and regulation.

Like other central institutions, the Wuyingdian operated according to strict and detailed administrative regulations. The number of officials and long-term craftsmen, as well as their ranks and salaries, were fixed.[51] The Imperial Household Department required an annual report on the operation of the Wuyingdian, including the income and expenditures, the number of books printed and sold, the salaries for each official and craftsman, raw materials purchased and consumed, and so on. Even the price and quality of the raw materials to be purchased were preset. For any departure from fixed regulations, officials of the Wuyingdian needed permission from the emperor or the Imperial Household Department.[52] The various detailed regulations on the operation of the Wuyingdian standardized the process and cost of book production but limited the efficiency of book production and reduced the flexibility of the Wuyingdian's response to changes.

Book publishing in the Wuyingdian was a rather time-consuming process because the priority of officials and craftsmen was to guarantee the quality of the books, not the efficiency of publishing. According to the Wuyingdian's administrative regulations, if there was any tiny mistake or discrepancy in editing or printing, the officials and craftsmen who were responsible for it would be punished by a reduced salary or even by demotion. Book production required a series of proofreading procedures, and both manuscripts and printing samples were usually transferred back and forth between the editors and printers for examination.[53] In the Yongzheng and Qianlong periods, because there was no specific schedule for each procedure, it usually took years for the Wuyingdian to publish a book. The situation became even worse after the Qianlong period. Sometimes ten or even twenty years were needed to print a book with multiple volumes. For books like Confucian classics, dictionaries, dynastic histories, and literary and medical works, the Wuyingdian's publishing system worked well, but books like the Qing Code and the *Expanded Substatutes*, whose contents were updated constantly, posed a sizable challenge. Indeed, the Wuyingdian proved unable to provide enough timely updated editions of the Code and the *Expanded Substatutes*.

The books printed in the Wuyingdian circulated through several major channels: (1) submission to the court for the emperor's personal use, (2) presentation as gifts by the emperors to officials and literati, (3) issuance through administrative channels, and (4) sale to individual readers through the Book Circulation Bureau (Tongxing Shuji Chu), an office in charge of sales of Wuyingdian books. Only a small percentage of Wuyingdian books were circulated through the first two channels. Most went through administrative channels, mainly to officials at different levels of the bureaucracy, and students studying in state-sponsored academies.[54]

When the Wuyingdian published new editions of books about laws and regulations, it usually sent copies through administrative channels to officials who needed these books in their daily administration. In Beijing the books were sent directly to top officials of each department; in the provinces, provincial governors usually received all the books from the Wuyingdian and then issued them to the local governments. For example, in 1800, when the revised *Regulations of the Board of Civil Office* was completed, the Wuyingdian sent about sixty copies to each province, and provincial officials issued them to the provincial bureaucracy.[55] Sometimes the Wuyingdian only sent one or two copies of a book as samples to provincial governments, and it was the provincial government's responsibility to cut woodblocks, reprint copies, and distribute them to local governments. Provincial governments also reprinted and distributed edicts, regulations, and new substatutes issued by the central government through the administrative channel to local governments.[56]

On some occasions, the provincial officials could directly request that the Wuyingdian send some books badly needed for local administration. For example, in 1825 the Jilin general stated in a memorial that because of population growth, criminal and civil cases in his jurisdiction had significantly increased. He then complained that his yamen had only one Chinese edition of the *Expanded Substatutes* issued in the Jiaqing period, which was now out of date and was in any case difficult for Manchu officials to read. He then asked the emperor's permission to order the Wuyingdian to provide updated Manchu editions of the *Expanded Substatutes* to his yamen.[57]

The books issued by the Wuyingdian through the administrative channel were the property of governments or schools and were stored in their libraries, often kept in wooden cabinets, under lock and key. Those libraries were built to protect the physical volumes and to inspire the sense of reverence of books, not to ease readers' access to these books. They were not open to the public, and usage of the books was under strict regulations. Even officials and government students had to go through complicated procedures to access the books.[58] Although the regulations were designed to protect books from being damaged or stolen, people complained that libraries in local yamens or schools were "locked up tightly and hidden away" and that readers could seldom see or read the books collected in them.[59]

For individual readers, the most common access to the Wuyingdian books was not through those libraries but through buying reprinted versions or "general circulation" (*tongxing*) versions. The Qing court encouraged local governments, individuals, and sometimes even commercial publishers to reprint the Wuyingdian books. For the books the Wuyingdian printed that could benefit literary circles, such as imperially authorized Confucian classics and dynastic histories, the Qing court usually required provincial administrative commissioners (*buzhengshi*) to recut the woodblocks according to the style and content of the Wuyingdian editions. When the woodblocks were completed, individuals and commercial publishers who wanted to reprint the books could submit a formal written request to the provincial government. When it was approved, they could bring their own paper and ink to the provincial administrative commissioner's yamen and print the books by using the woodblocks. However, few individual and commercial publishers were willing to use woodblocks in provincial offices for reprinting the books, possibly because of the forbidding administrative procedures when applying for permission to print, as well as the extortion of yamen clerks during the printing process.[60]

Officials and commoners also could buy books directly from the Wuyingdian. In the Kangxi and Yongzheng periods, there was no clear regulation of this. Because the number of books printed in the Wuyingdian increased and demand grew with it in the early Qianlong period, Wuyingdian officials started to draft regulations for selling the books. In 1742 the emperor approved new regulations, which stated: (1) All books currently stored in the Wuyingdian may be purchased by officials, who should submit their request and payment through their own departments. As soon as the request and money are received, the Wuyingdian will send the books to the officials. (2) Retired officials and commoners may also buy books from the Wuyingdian. They should submit their request and payment through the Hanlin Academy. (3) Officials who are willing to reprint the books for their personal use are allowed to make use of the woodblocks in the Wuyingdian.[61]

Two years later, in 1744, the Wuyingdian established the Book Circulation Bureau, and bookselling activity was further institutionalized.[62] The bureau was in charge of selling the Wuyingdian books to individual readers. However, although the creation of both the bookselling regulations and the Book Circulation Bureau itself was intended to ensure that individuals had access to the Wuyingdian books, the complexity of the procedures was intimidating to most people. It was difficult for commoners without sufficient social connections to submit their requests and payment through the Hanlin Academy to buy books from the Wuyingdian. Even for officials, buying books from the Wuyingdian was not easy. They had to submit a formal request through their own department and wait for the communication between their department and the Wuyingdian, and the payment was deducted from officials' salaries. This process might take days or even months.[63]

Every book sold by the Wuyingdian through the Book Circulation Bureau was carefully recorded on the department's bookselling registers, including the books' titles and cost and the buyers' names and occupations. Some of these registers from the Tongzhi and Guangxu periods are extant today. Thanks to them, we can learn who the purchasers were and what kinds of books they brought from the Wuyingdian. From 1865 to 1871, the Book Circulation Bureau all together received 70 orders from 46 individuals and sold 766 books. On average it received 10 orders and sold about 109 books per year. Since the publishing activity in the Wuyingdian had been in decline for a long time before the Tongzhi period, the number of books sold by the Wuyingdian in this period was probably less than those sold in the mid-Qing period when the Wuyingdian's publishing was at its height. Because of the absence of sources, the exact statistics on book sales in the mid-Qing period are not clear. According to a financial report submitted by the Wuyingdian's officials in 1792, the Book Circulation Bureau sold 187 books in that year.[64] Since the Wuyingdian's printing and publishing businesses were most active and the printed books most abundant in stock in the mid- and late Qianlong period, it can be roughly estimated that the Wuyingdian sold around two hundred books per year in the late Qianlong period. The number probably gradually declined thereafter until the Tongzhi period, when, as we have seen, the bureau sold about one hundred books per year. Thus the number of books sold through the Book Circulation Bureau was limited.

According to the bookselling registers from 1865 to 1871, purchasers of the Wuyingdian books were from various social backgrounds, including Manchu princes (20 percent of the books sold by the Wuyingdian), officials and clerks in the central government (43 percent), craftsmen of the Wuyingdian (13 percent), and commoners (22 percent). Most purchasers of the Wuyingdian books, however, were people with close connections to the Qing central bureaucracy, especially with the Imperial Household Department and the Wuyingdian itself. For example, the vice director of the Wuyingdian, whose abbreviated name was Chun on the registers, placed 7 orders and bought 89 books in total. One Wuyingdian craftsman named Zhao Junying placed 7 orders and bought 96 books, including many duplicates.[65] Some of these purchasers bought the Wuyingdian books for their own use, but some probably bought for their friends or even for sale on the book market. Although a broader audience might get access to the Wuyingdian books through their friends working in the Wuyingdian or through bookstores in Beijing, considering the small number of books sold by the Wuyingdian (only 766 books in 7 years), the audience was probably not large. The audience for books sold by the Book Circulation Bureau was thus small and restricted to certain social groups.

Generally speaking, the books sold by the Wuyingdian were not expensive. Because the Wuyingdian was not a profit-oriented publishing institution, pricing was based on the cost of materials and labor as well as some overhead charges. According to the "Catalog of the Wuyingdian Books for Circulation" (Wuyingdian tongxing shuji mulu qingce), a document probably compiled in the Qianlong period, 154 titles were on sale in the Book Circulation Bureau. The price ranged from 0.007 taels to 14.6 taels, based on how many volumes the book contained and on the kind of paper used. Most of the books cost less than five taels. Some were even cheaper than similar books sold by bookstores. For example, while the price of the Code, a forty-volume book, was only about 1.1 taels (table 1.2), similar editions printed by commercial publishing houses and sold in bookstores ranged from 2.4 to 7 taels.[66]

The books sold by the Book Circulation Bureau covered a wide range of categories. According to the Department's bookselling registers from 1865 to 1871, histories were the most popular genre of the books sold by the Wuyingdian. In seven years, the Wuyingdian sold 239 history books, about one-third of all copies it sold in this period. The works of the Qing emperors (191 copies, 25 percent of all copies sold by the Wuyingdian), Confucian classics (135 copies, 18 percent), and dictionaries (105 copies, 14 percent) were also in demand. Books about laws and regulations, however, were not popular among readers. From 1865 to 1871, the Wuyingdian altogether sold only one copy of books related to law and regulations—*The Substatutes for Arresting Escapees* (Dubu zeli). It did not sell a single copy of the Code or the *Expanded Substatutes* between 1865 and 1871. According to the "Catalog of the Wuyingdian Books for Circulation," there were twenty books on Qing laws and regulations for sale by the Book Circulation Bureau (table 1.2), which was about 14 percent of the 154 books.[67] However, from 1867 to 1871, such books only comprised 0.1 percent of all books sold by the Wuyingdian. The reason for this is unclear based on the Wuyingdian's documents. It is possible that these books were out of stock in the Book Circulation Bureau. A more plausible explanation is that readers were not interested in purchasing such books from the Wuyingdian, as commercially published editions of the Qing Code and some other books about Qing laws and regulations were better quality and easier to buy from various bookstores.

THE CODE PUBLISHED BY THE WUYINGDIAN

Throughout the Qing period altogether the Wuyingdian appears to have published seven imperially authorized editions of the Qing Code, in 1725, 1740, 1768, 1790, 1802, 1825, and 1870, at an average interval of twenty years. The Wuyingdian also published at least eighteen editions of the *Expanded Substatutes*, at an average interval of five years (see table 1.1). Because the laws usually went into effect immediately after they were promulgated and Wuyingdian editions were the only authorized editions acknowledged by the Qing court, it was necessary for the Wuyingdian to provide the Qing bureaucracy with the updated Code and the *Expanded Substatutes* in a timely fashion. In fact, however, because the reviewing and printing process in the Wuyingdian was rather slow, it usually took several years to finish printing a multivolume book like the Code.

TABLE 1.2. Prices of Wuyingdian Books Relating to Laws and Regulations

Book Title	Volumes (*ben*)	Price (taels)
The Great Qing Code (Chinese)	40	1.10
The Great Qing Code (Manchu)	40	2.50
The Expanded Substatutes (Manchu)	2	0.10
The Expanded Substatutes (Chinese)	2	0.05
The Expanded Substatutes, 1743–1745 (Manchu)	3	0.15
The Expanded Substatutes, 1743–1745 (Chinese)	3	0.11
The Expanded Substatutes, 1746–1750 (Manchu)	2	0.12
The Expanded Substatutes, 1746–1750 (Chinese)	2	0.08
Administrative Regulations of the Eight Banners (Baqi zeli; Chinese)	4	0.67
Administrative Regulations of the Eight Banners (Manchu)	4	0.40
Treatises on the Management of Military Affairs (Zhongshu zhengkao) (Chinese)	18	1.68
Treatises on the Management of Military Affairs (Manchu)	18	2.94
Regulations of Sacrifice (Jisi tiaoli) (Manchu)	6	1.15
The Collected Statutes of the Great Qing with Administrative Regulations (Da Qing huidian bing zeli)	120	12.46
Regulations of Civil Service Examinations (Kechang tiaoli)	5	0.29
The Chart for the Three Exiles (Sanliu daoli biao)	4	0.21
Substatutes for Arresting Escapees (Dubu zeli) (Chinese)	2	0.27
Substatutes for Arresting Escapees (Manchu)	2	0.33
Administrative Regulations of the Board of Civil Office (Libu zeli) (Chinese)	28	2.77
Administrative Regulations of the Board of Civil Office (Manchu)	22	5.69

Source: Weng, *Qing neifu keshu*, 738–51.

The proofreading and printing process for the Code, for example, generally involved the following procedures:

1. After the draft of the updated edition of the Qing Code was compiled by the Commission on Statutes, it was sent to the Wuyingdian for proofreading. Upon receiving the draft, Wuyingdian scribes copied the whole

draft into a prototype (*yangben*) in the style and format in which it would be printed.

2. When the prototype was ready, it was sent back to the commission, where the officials collated it with the original draft to correct mistakes. When finished, the prototype was sent back to the Wuyingdian again.

3. When Wuyingdian officials received the revised prototype, they ordered scribes to rewrite the pages on which mistakes had been found. Then the revised prototype went back to the commission, where the officials examined it again. The revised sample would go back and forth between the Wuyingdian and the commission until officials of both institutions found no more mistakes.

4. When the two sets of officials had agreed upon the final version, craftsmen started to cut woodblocks. When all the woodblocks were completed, craftsmen printed several sample copies and sent them to the commission for proofreading again.

5. Commission officials marked any mistakes in the sample copies, and craftsmen in the Wuyingdian rewrote the pages with mistakes, pasted them on the woodblocks, and recut the erroneous woodblocks accordingly. When the revised woodblocks had been cut, the formal printing process finally started.[68]

The proofreading process was thus time-consuming, and it usually took years for the Wuyingdian to get the books printed and published. Sometimes when there were major changes in the Code and the Qing officials wanted to promulgate the laws as soon as possible, they had no choice but to use temporary measures to circulate the new laws. For example, many statutes and substatutes were significantly changed in the 1740 revision. After the Qianlong emperor approved the draft of the revised Code, officials in the Board of Punishments felt it urgently necessary to implement the new laws, especially the revised substatutes that reduced the harshness of the original penalties. These officials argued that the revised substatutes should come into force as soon as possible in order to save people's lives and show the emperor's benevolence. Zhang Zhao (1691–1745), vice minister of the Board of Punishments, submitted a memorial to the emperor, in which he wrote: "The compilation of statutes and substatutes has been finished, but it will still take a long time for the Code to be printed and published. I ask Your Majesty's permission to send one draft copy of the Code to our Board so that we can follow the revised laws."[69]

The emperor approved the suggestion. About half a year later, he approved a request that reflected the same policy from another official, Wu Yuan'an, who supervised the district courts in Beijing. Wu wrote that it was taking too long for district judges in Beijing to get the printed Code issued by the Wuyingdian and asked that such judges be permitted to send clerks to the Board of Punishments to hand-copy the new substatutes. Although some officials could ask the emperor's permission to obtain the updated laws through other means, it was difficult for officials and commoners in the Qing empire to get access to the updated laws in a timely fashion. For example, about three years after the promulgation of the 1740 Code, the Jiangsu judicial commissioner finally received a copy. The delay became much longer after the high Qing period, when the efficiency of the Wuyingdian significantly declined because of budget cuts and poor management. In the Jiaqing and Daoguang periods, it generally took the Wuyingdian ten or even twenty years to print a multivolume book.[70]

The print run of the imperially authorized editions of the Code was small. For example, after three years of proofreading and printing the 1740 imperial edition, the Wuyingdian produced 150 copies of the Manchu version of the Code and 350 copies of the Chinese version, which were sent only to offices of high-ranking officials. The chief editor provided a comprehensive list of recipients in a memorial: in the capital, copies were sent to all the main administrative agencies of the imperial court and the central government, including the Court of the Imperial Clan (Zongrenfu), the Imperial Household Department, the Grand Secretariat, the six boards, the Censorate, the Court of Judicial Review, and so on. In provinces, copies were sent to provincial-level civil and military officials, including generals, provincial military commanders (*tidu*), governors-general, governors, salt controllers (*yanzheng*), administrative commissioners, judicial commissioners, education commissioners, and so on. The chief editor explained the reason for not sending copies to subprovincial government offices: "There are such a large number of circuits [*dao*], prefectures, and counties. If they all need copies sent from the capital, we cannot withstand the burden!"[71] He suggested that the Wuyingdian send two extra copies to the administrative commissioner in each province and let them arrange for recutting woodblocks based on the Wuyingdian edition and distributing reprinted copies in local governments. Commercial publishers were also allowed to print from these recut woodblocks. The only evidence for such reprinting, however, is the Guizhou governor-general's memorial in 1743, in which he briefly mentioned that he had finished reprinting the Code based on the Wuying-dian edition.[72] Such reprinted editions are not in evidence, so it seems that such reprintings were not prevalent.

The imperial editions of the Code symbolized imperial judicial authority. The cover page of imperial editions was printed in vermillion ink with a unique decoration that no other editions were allowed to use: the title of the Code was printed in a square frame surrounded by flying dragons. When receiving an imperial edition, an official had to treat it with the utmost reverence required for other imperial gifts. For example, after receiving an imperial edition of the Code in 1743, the Guangxi governor recorded the ritual he performed: "Upon hearing that the imperial edition of the Code would arrive, I went outside the city gate, where I knelt and waited. I respectfully brought the Code to my office. I set up an incense table, kowtowed towards the direction of the imperial palace, and expressed my gratitude for this imperial grace."[73] Then he submitted a memorial to formally extend his gratitude to the emperor. The Code would probably be enshrined in the government's library. Imperial editions of the Code were the emperor's gift and the government's property—a book to revere, not to consume. Extant imperial editions of the Code show few, if any, traces of use: there are few marks, notes, or worn pages. If people actually read these editions, they must have done so with extreme care.

The quality of the Code published by the Wuyingdian was high in the Yongzheng and early Qianlong periods, but as printing quality declined in general in the Wuyingdian after the mid-Qianlong period, the quality of the Code also dropped.[74] The physical size of each edition of the Code did not shrink, and there were no significant differences in the quality of paper used in each edition. However, the quality of the woodblocks, ink, and printing decreased dramatically, especially for the editions printed after the Jiaqing period. For example, in the 1725, 1825, and 1870 editions of the Code, the cover page (with the title and the flying dragon imprint) was the most elegant page of the whole book, which represented the highest quality of woodblock cutting and printing of the Code that the Wuyingdian published. The vermillion ink used to print the cover page of the 1725 edition was purer, brighter, and longer lasting than that of the 1825 and 1870 editions. Compared with the cover page of the 1725 edition, the vermillion ink on the 1825 edition's first page has faded almost beyond recognition, though it was printed a century later. The 1870 edition is even worse: instead of a rich vermillion color, the ink used in the 1870 edition appears garish pink, and the dragons surrounding the title were cut much more coarsely than the ones in the 1725 edition.[75]

Beside the cover page, the printing quality of other pages in each of the three editions also declined. In the 1725 edition, the characters throughout the text were neatly cut, tidy, and easy to read. Although the woodblocks were cut by different craftsmen, the style of the characters was uniform. The woodblocks were also apparently newly cut, and the edges of each stroke were sharp and clear. Compared with the 1725 edition, the quality of the printing in the 1825 edition was obviously inferior. The woodblocks were worn, and sometimes it is even difficult to identify the characters (figure 1.1). The situation was worse still in the 1870 edition. Many characters are blurry and difficult to read. The woodblocks are significantly worn, the printing was done carelessly, and the style of the

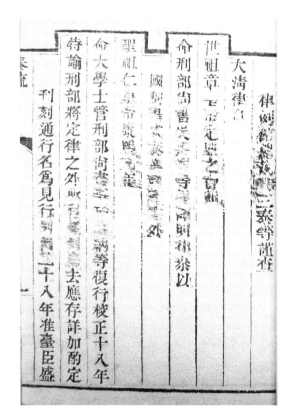

FIG. 1.1. Blurred characters in the 1825 imperial edition of the Code, caused by careless printing and a worn woodblock. *Da Qing lüli*, "Santai zoushu," 1a, printed in 1825 by the Wuyingdian. Courtesy of the Library of Congress.

characters is not unified. Characters on some pages are dramatically different from those on other pages. Generally speaking, the 1725 edition was exquisite by any standard and could be viewed as a work of art, the 1825 edition was of lower printing quality but was still readable, and the printing quality of the 1870 Code was nearly unacceptable—the text was not only unpleasant to read but sometimes even illegible.

An important reason for the decline in printing quality was that the Wuyingdian used the same woodblocks for many years. The maximum printing capacity of woodblocks ranged from several thousand to more than twenty thousand copies based on the quality of wood and the care devoted to block preparation.[76] Because of the relatively dry climate in Beijing, the Wuyingdian's woodblocks were prone to crack after years in storage. Therefore, if the Wuyingdian intended to maintain high printing quality, it needed to repair or recut the woodblocks regularly. However, in printing the Code, it seems that the Wuyingdian usually used the same woodblocks to print several editions. There were no significant changes of the structure or content of the Code after 1740. For each Code revision process, the Qing legislators added some new substatutes and deleted some outdated ones. Most of the content was not changed. Therefore, the Wuyingdian usually did not need to recut all of the woodblocks. In most cases, it just took out the woodblocks in which the content had been changed, replaced them with new ones containing the revised substatutes, and printed them together with the old, unchanged woodblocks. Even in the Qianlong period, when the printing activities in the Wuyingdian were most active and financially secure, they did not recut the woodblocks for printing the Code for more about fifty years after 1740. In 1789, when the officials of the Commission on Statutes intended to print the revised Code, they found that many characters on the old woodblocks were blurred and suggested that all of the woodblocks be recut. This was approved by the emperor.[77] Readers of the later editions of the Code printed by the Wuyingdian were not so lucky. Judging from the later editions, many blurred or even cracked woodblocks were still in use. For example, there was an obvious crack on the page of Foge's memorial in the preface of the 1825 edition, which showed that the woodblock for printing this page had been used or stored for many years. Then, on the same page of the 1870 edition, the crack was still there, and the characters were even more blurry (figure 1.2). It is clear that the cracked woodblock had been kept in use. Although it was cheaper to reuse the old woodblocks to produce new editions of the Code, it significantly lowered the

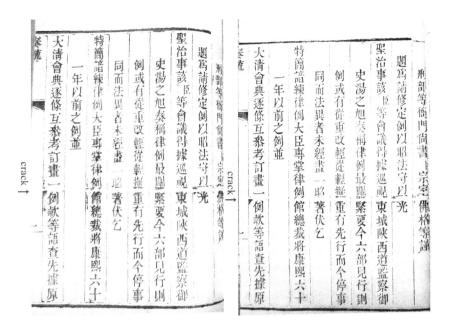

FIG. 1.2. The same page ("Foge zoushu," 1a), from the 1825 imperial edition of the Code (*right*) and the 1870 imperial edition (*left*). The same crack appears just below the middle of both pages, indicating that the same cracked and worn woodblocks were used to print both editions. Courtesy of the Library of Congress.

printing quality, which made it difficult for the Wuyingdian's editions to compete with commercially published ones.

PUBLICATION AND CIRCULATION OF THE EXPANDED SUBSTATUTES

Compared with a multivolume book like the Code, the *Expanded Substatutes* was much smaller and contained only the revised substatutes and thus took less time and money to print. The 1740 edition of the Code, for example, was a forty-seven *juan* book. The *Expanded Substatutes* printed in 1746 had only two *juan*. The cost of printing the *Expanded Substatutes* was also far lower. According to the "Catalog of the Wuyingdian Books for Circulation," the price for the Code was about 1.1 taels, and the price for the *Expanded Statutes* was only 0.05 taels (see table 1.2). From 1746 to 1870, Qing laws were formally revised twenty-two times, but only five imperial editions of the Code were published (see table 1.1). In other words, in most instances of Code revisions, only the *Expanded Substatutes* was formally published and distributed, not the entire Code. The *Expanded Substatutes*, therefore, was one of the main official carriers of the updated laws circulating in the Qing bureaucracy.

Each edition of the *Expanded Substatutes* consisted of newly revised substatutes, which were usually sorted into five categories: expanded, revised, revised and merged (*xiubing*), revised and moved (*yigai*), and removed substatutes.[78] Substatutes in the *Expanded Substatutes* were compiled according to the sequence of statutes in the Code. In other words, each substatute appeared under a specific category of the laws based on the original category of statutes in the Code. This arrangement made it easier for the readers of the *Expanded Substatutes* to correlate the statutes and substatutes in the Code with the updated substatutes. The printing style of the *Expanded Substatutes* closely followed that of the Code. Both usually used the same size and quality of paper, and the characters were usually cut in the same size and style. In fact, each page of *Expanded Substatutes* was designed so that users could bind it into the Code, and the Code was also designed in a way that the new substatutes could be easily inserted. In the "General Editorial Principles" of the first edition of the *Expanded Substatutes*, the editors explained this arrangement in detail:

> The Code is divided into six sections [*bu*], and each section has general categories [*zongmen*]. Under each general category, there are the categories of statutes [*lümu*], and the substatutes follow the statutes. Now we have examined the Code and found that each category of statutes does not follow the previous category on the same page, but starts on a new page. It was originally designed to leave some spaces [for inserting new substatutes] and make it easier for the readers to look for. Therefore, we make the new substatutes follow the statutes, and put each of them under the related categories of statutes that are used as titles for the substatutes in the book. Each category also starts on a new page, and the font and size of the characters are printed in the same style as those of the Code. In this way, the *Expanded Substatutes* can be read as a single book, and its pages can also be easily combined with the Code.[79]

Because all editions of the Code published by the Wuyingdian used the traditional thread-binding style, it was not difficult to unbind the original pages, insert some new ones, and sew them back again into a book.[80] Moreover, since each category of statutes in both the Code and the *Expanded Substatutes* started on a new page, the original text would not be interrupted when the new pages were bound into the Code.

When each edition of the *Expanded Substatutes* was completed, it was issued mainly through administrative channels. Although some editions of the *Expanded Substatutes* are listed for sale in the "Catalog of the Wuyingdian Books for Circulation" to individual readers, few copies were sold.[81] Government offices above the county level were the main recipients of the Wuyingdian's editions of the *Expanded Substatutes*. In memorials reporting on the Code revision process, officials mentioned that they would distribute the *Expanded Substatutes* to "the yamens inside and outside the capital that had judicial responsibilities (*neiwai wenxing yamen*)." In one memorial submitted in 1789, officials offered a more detailed list of the recipients of the book, including governors-general, governors, generals in the frontier regions, and prefects.[82] County magistrates, who assumed the most important responsibility for local judicial administration, were not in the list of recipients of the Wuyingdian's *Expanded Substatutes*. Since the publishing process in the Wuyingdian was slow, the Board of Punishments regularly published compilation of new or revised substatutes before the Wuyingdian published the formal editions of the *Expanded Substatutes*. The board often printed "draft editions" (*caoben*) of the *Expanded Substatutes* and circulated them in the bureaucracy when the revisions were finished. Provincial governments often reprinted new substatutes issued by the board through the administrative channel and issued them to local governments.[83]

In addition to Wuyingdian editions of the *Expanded Substatutes*, information about updated substatutes was circulated in several other channels. The *Beijing Gazette* (Jingbao or Dichao) was probably the most timely and efficient way for Qing people in and out of the bureaucracy to access updated laws. Published regularly every few days, the *Beijing Gazette* contained communications from the capital, such as edicts, rescripts, and memorials, many of which led to the establishment or revision of the laws. Writings of Qing officials and commercial publishers indicated that they frequently relied on the *Beijing Gazette* for updated legal and administrative information.[84] However, the *Beijing Gazette* was much less authoritative than the Code or the *Expanded Substatutes* as a source of updated laws. In most cases, the *Beijing Gazette* did not explicitly include updated substatutes or regulations issued by the central government. Instead, it contained imperial edicts and memorials that would eventually lead to the change of the laws. Therefore, its legal information often had not gone through the compiling and editing process in the Commission on Statutes, and its form and content were often different from the final version of updated substatutes issued in the *Expanded Substatutes*. Moreover, Qing legislators were selective when establishing new substatutes, and thus a large percentage of legal information contained in the *Beijing Gazette* would not become formal laws, and judicial officials could not cite it when sentencing legal cases.

The Qing government was administrated on the cheap.[85] The concern of cost and efficiency was probably the main reason the Qing central government chose to circulate only updated substatutes rather than the whole updated editions of the Code. From the perspective of readers, however, using these updated substatutes issued separately from the Code was not convenient. Judicial officials had to read updated substatutes and the Code together extremely carefully to fully understand the changes to the laws and to cite the right substatutes when sentencing cases. The situation became even worse when several editions of the *Expanded Substatutes* had been published but the Code itself had not yet been updated. It was quite easy for readers to confuse the outdated substatutes from the old editions of the Code with the updated ones in the *Expanded Substatutes* if they were not reading with sufficient care. Officials complained about this situation. Wang Ding (1768–1842), executive minister of the Board of Punishments, pointed out in 1830: "The substatutes accumulated quickly. . . . They have been compiled every five years. Although the compilations were done in a rather careful way, nowadays the *Expanded Substatutes* issued by the Board has accumulated to a large number of volumes. Because these new substatutes have not been sorted out, we cannot avoid feeling perplexed and confused." An acting provincial judicial commissioner in the Daoguang period also complained that "with the gradual accumulation of the new substatutes, the old editions of the Code are difficult to read."[86] Accumulation of updated substatutes and their separation from the Code led to confusion among judicial officials. Many of them thus turned to commercial editions of the Code, which were updated more frequently than the imperially authorized ones.

CONCLUSION

In his classic study of the laws and administrative regulations of the Qing bureaucracy, Thomas Metzger argues that Qing law books were "written in a straightforward style full of fairly loose but still clear expressions." He also points out that a weakness of these law books was that compilers usually failed to categorize the contents and to pull together "all information having practical bearing on a topic." As for the compilation and distribution of the Qing law books, he distinguished the penal law (the Code and the *Expanded Substatutes*) from the administrative laws, arguing that regular revisions and publications of the Code were efficient and facilitated judicial procedure, in contrast with irregular revisions of various administrative regulations, which to some extent impeded administration. He also pointed out that "there was bound to be a huge gap between publication and the bureaucracy's output of cases as a whole," but he admitted that "to what extent the amount of compilation kept up with the need is not clear."[87]

Metzger based his research mainly on books of administrative regulations. Careful examination of the publication and distribution of the imperial editions of Code and the *Expanded Substatutes* sheds new light on the topic. First, it is difficult to discuss the Qing period as a whole in terms of the publication and distribution of law books. The mid-Qing central government efficiently published and distributed high-quality editions of the Code and the *Expanded Substatutes*, but the work was slow and quality low in the early and late Qing period. Second, the Code and the *Expanded Substatutes* were indeed clear in their contents. Editors made efforts to compile precise legal information in these books and organize it in an easy-to-understand way so that officials could understand what had changed in the laws when they received and read an updated edition of the *Expanded Substatutes*. But the accumulation of updated substatutes and their separation from the Code created confusion, which could result in disorder in judicial administration. Further, readers must have suffered from the significant decline of printing quality after the Qianlong period, which sometimes made the texts in the Code and the *Expanded Substatutes* rather difficult to read. Third, careful examination of the distribution of the imperially authorized editions of the Code and the *Expanded Substatutes* indicates that there was a gap between the official publication of the Code and the *Expanded Substatutes* and demand for these books among officials. Subprovincial government officials, including circuit intendants, prefects, and county magistrates, who usually needed to deal with legal cases on daily bases, could not receive imperial editions of the Code. Officials complained that it was difficult for them to get access to these books; people outside the bureaucracy had a much harder time getting them.

The last imperially authorized edition of the Code was published by the Wuyingdian in 1870. Because of the persistent financial crisis in the late Qing, the court found it could spare no funds to maintain such a lavish publishing institution as the Wuyingdian. At the same time, the state publishing sector was gradually taken over by the newly rising provincial publishing bureaus, established by high provincial officials as a means of cultural restoration after the Taiping rebellion. As a final blow, in 1869 a huge fire broke out in the Wuyingdian, destroying many old woodblocks and printing presses. Soon after that, the publishing activities in the Wuyingdian were formally ended.

2 COMMERCIAL PUBLICATIONS OF THE CODE

COMMERCIALLY COMPILED AND PRINTED EDITIONS OF THE CODE far outnumber the imperial editions. I have found about 120 different commercial editions, and the actual number was probably much higher. Most commercial editions did not simply reproduce the imperial editions. In most cases, they did not even adhere to the same format, instead enriching their offerings with commentaries, administrative regulations, and case precedents. Commercial editors and publishers saw such additions as potentially marketable tools to help readers better understand the Code. Updated substatutes were usually included in commercial editions even before they were formally incorporated into imperial editions.

DIVERSITY AND CHANGES: COMMERCIAL EDITIONS OF THE CODE IN THE EARLY QING, 1644–1722

Although a large number of books in various genres were commercially published in the late Ming period, the rise of commercial publications of the dynastic code was largely a Qing phenomenon. Historian Wu Yanhong's research on over thirty commentaries on *The Great Ming Code* sheds new light on that code's publication history in the late Ming. Many of these commentaries can be viewed as predecessors of commercial editions of the Qing Code. According to her study, several features of the publications of these commentaries and texts of the Code during the late Ming publishing boom are noteworthy. First, most authors, editors, and compilers were judicial officials working in the central government. Second, publishers of these books were often local governments. Although some commercial publishing houses participated in producing legal texts, official publishers still played a major role in printing and publishing the commentaries and texts of the Code.[1] Therefore, judicial officials by and large monopolized the production of commentaries and texts of the Ming Code.

This situation changed dramatically in the Qing period. Exploration of both official and commercial editions of the Code shows that, compared with the Ming period, non-official editors and commercial publishers played a far more important role than official publishers in producing commentaries and reproducing the texts of the Code. Commercial editions of the Code were prevalent, with more produced in both the early and late Qing than in the High Qing period (table 2.1). Five commercial editions of the Code date to the Shunzhi period. These early Qing editions did not include information about editors or publishers, annotations or commentaries, administrative regulations, or case precedents. Moreover, they resemble each other in terms of structure and layout, though judging from their printing styles it is obvious that they were printed by different publishing houses.[2] It seems that they followed a standard: probably the imperially authorized edition of the Code published in 1647.

TABLE 2.1. Editions of the Code Printed in the Qing

Reign Period	Number of Imperial Editions	Number of Commercial Editions
Shunzhi (1644–1661)	1	5
Kangxi (1662–1722)	0	11
Yongzheng (1723–1735)	1	0
Qianlong (1736–1795)	3	11
Jiaqing (1796–1820)	1	17
Daoguang (1821–1850)	1	17
Xianfeng (1851–1861)	0	4
Tongzhi (1862–1874)	1	14
Guangxu (1875–1908)	0	38
Xuantong (1909–1911)	0	1
Date Unknown	0	2
Total	8	120

Note: Historian Shimada Masao views the 1670 edition of the Code as an official edition published by the Board of Punishments. See Shimada, "Qinglü zhi chengli," 482–83. I read the edition in the Library of Congress and found no decisive evidence indicating that this Code is indeed an official edition.

Commercial editions from the Kangxi period were more diverse and reflect a livelier publishing milieu than the Shunzhi editions. Although five of the Kangxi commercial editions still adhered to the format and content of the imperial edition, six departed from this format: *The Great Qing Code with Annotations and Explanations* (Da Qing lü jianshi, 1689), *The Combined Copy of the Great Qing Code with Annotations and Explanations* (Da Qing lü jianshi hechao, 1705), *The Complete Book of the Statutes of the Great Qing with the Extensive Collection of Vermillion Annotations* (Da Qing lü zhuzhu guanghui quanshu, published between 1662 and 1722), *The Complete Book of the Great Qing Code with the Extensive Collection of Vermillion Annotations* (Da Qing lüli zhuzhu guanghui quanshu, 1706), *The Great Qing Code with Collective Annotations* (Da Qing lü jizhu, 1715), and *The Great Qing Code with Substatutes and Annotations* (Da Qing lü fuli zhujie, 1717). Their most important feature is that besides the original statutes and substatutes from the imperial editions of the Code, they also included a large number of individual or collective commentaries and annotations. In the late Ming, officials had engaged in annotating the statutes and substatutes of the Code and had published some influential works of commentary. Because the early Qing change the statutes in the Ming Code only minimally, editors of commercial editions incorporated some late Ming commentaries into their publications. For example, *The Combined Copy of the Great Qing Code with Annotations and Explanations* adopted Wang Kentang's (1549–1613) *Annotations and Explanations of the Statutes and Substatutes* (Lüli jianshi), a famous late Ming commentary published in 1612. Each page of the *Combined Copy* was divided into two horizontal registers (*lan*): the original statutes and substatutes were printed in larger characters in the lower registers; Wang's commentaries were printed in smaller characters in the upper registers, usually in accord with the sequence of the statutes and substatutes in the lower registers (figure 2.1). This arrangement made it convenient for readers to locate the statutes and related commentaries.

Some Kangxi-era scholars made their own contributions to statutory commentaries. The most influential was Shen Zhiqi, who composed *The Great Qing Code with Collective Annotations* and published it in 1715. Unlike earlier standalone commentaries, Shen's book included the original text of the Code, following the same two-register-per-page arrangement as the *Combined Copy*. Shen's book counts as a commercial edition of the Code. The title of Shen's book as printed at the end of each chapter is not *Da Qing*

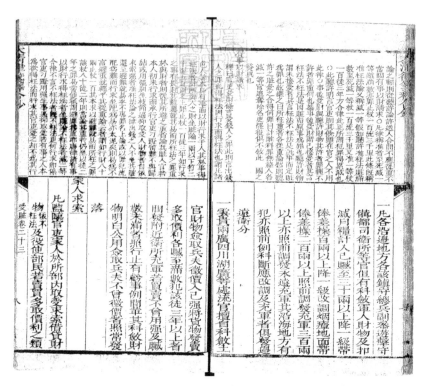

FIG. 2.1. Two registers in *The Combined Copy of the Great Qing Code with Annotations and Explanations* (Da Qing lü jianshi hechao; 1705 ed., *juan* 23, 7b–8a). The upper register includes Wang Kentang's commentaries; the lower register includes the statutes and substatutes of the Code. Courtesy of the Institute for Advanced Studies on Asia, University of Tokyo.

lü jizhu but *Da Qing lü jijie fuli*—the original title of the imperial edition of the Code.

Not all of the commercial editions published in the Kangxi period used this two-register format. For example, *The Great Qing Code with Annotations and Explanations* (1689) used the traditional single-register format, in which commentaries were printed in small characters after each group of statutes and substatutes. The *Complete Book of the Great Qing Code with the Extensive Collection of Vermillion Annotations* (1706) combined upper-register commentaries and interlinear commentaries in one book. In this large, elegantly printed book, the original statutes and substatutes of the Code were printed in black ink in larger characters. All of the commentaries were printed in smaller red characters (figure 2.2). While some

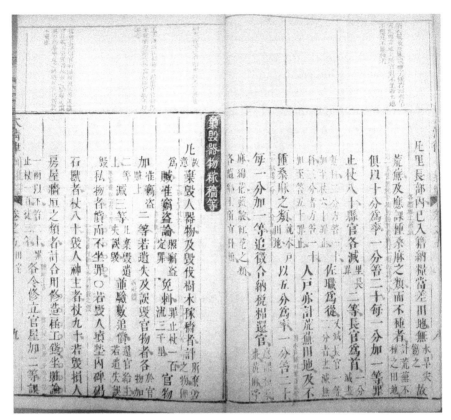

FIG. 2.2. A color-printed page of *The Complete Book of the Great Qing Code with the Extensive Collection of Vermillion Annotations* (Da Qing lüli zhuzhu guanghui quanshu; 1706 ed., *juan* 5, 8b–9a), with both upper-register commentaries and interlinear commentaries. Larger characters (statutes and substatutes) were printed in black ink, and smaller characters (commentaries) in red ink. Courtesy of the Library of Congress.

commentaries that explain or clarify the meanings of a certain statute were put in the upper registers, other commentaries were printed alongside the word or phrase they annotate.

The combination of the Code and commentaries seems to be a selling point of these diverse Kangxi commercial editions. Commercial publishers added eye-catching words like "combined copy with annotations and explanations" (*jianshi hechao*) and "extensive collection of vermillion annotations" (*zhuzhu guanghui*) to the title of the edition. They also printed short phrases indicating that the books included commentaries prominently on the cover page, which was usually the first place inside a book that Qing readers looked at. For example, on the cover page of *The Complete Book of the Great Qing Code with the Extensive Collection of Vermillion Annotations*, the publisher printed "Various annotations and explanations are included in their entirety and printed in vermillion ink" in red ink to the left of the book's title.[3] It is clear that the publisher intended to notify potential purchasers that the book included a large collection of commentaries.

Another popular Kangxi-era style responded directly to delays in court printing, which further diversified the market for legal books. Because the Kangxi court updated the imperially authorized editions of the Code slowly, new substatutes and administrative regulations, which were periodically published separately from the Code, began to play an increasingly important role in the judicial system. In response to this change, a new genre of commercial legal publications—the "combined compilation" books—became popular in the late Kangxi period, represented by the *Combined Printing of Substatutes and Case Precedents* (*Dingli cheng'an hejuan*) and the *Complete Collection of Substatutes* (*Dingli quanbian*). These combined compilation books often left out the original statutes and substatutes of the Code but incorporated new substatutes, administrative regulations, case precedents, and a variety of other legal information. They even included many new substatutes and regulations that the central government had not formally announced. This sort of inside and updated legal information attracted readers. Comprehensiveness was another appealing feature of these combined compilation books. For example, on the cover page of the *Combined Printing of Substatutes and Cases Precedents*, to the right of the book title, was stamped in red ink: "All of [the information] included in the original and updated editions of this book is from *mufu*."[4] On the left side, the publishers advertised what they had included in the book:

> One collection: Imperially authorized administrative sanctions of the six boards;
> One collection: Newly established administrative regulations of the six boards;
> One collection: Current substatutes of the Board of Punishments in use;
> One collection: Treatises on the management of military affairs;
> One collection: Imperially authorized substatutes for arresting escapees;
> One collection: Substatutes for arresting escapees of the Board of War;
> One collection: Various internal (*neibu*) substatutes that have not been promulgated or issued;

One collection: Internal documents that have been issued to or that have
   replied to high provincial officials;

One collection: Internal case precedents that have been agreed upon by
   the boards;

One collection: Various case precedents that were cited or corrected
   by the three high courts.[5]

Therefore, through commercial publications like the *Combined Printing of
Substatutes and Cases Precedents*, internal legal information became open,
accessible to the public outside the bureaucracy.

The editors of combined compilation books also showed flexibility in
terms of what legal information they should compile into the books and how
they should arrange it. Some books, such as the *Combined Printing of Substatutes and Cases Precedents*, sorted the substatutes, administrative regulations, and case precedents according to the category and sequence of the
statutes in the Code. Others, such as the *Complete Collection of Substatutes*,
were compiled according to the structure of the *Collected Statutes of the
Great Qing* (Da Qing huidian). Commercial editors did not simply copy the
entire contents of the imperial editions. Based on readers' needs and interests, commercial editors sometimes made their own selections of substatutes and regulations in the compilation process. For example, in the
Complete Collection of Substatutes, the editor deleted many substatutes and
regulations about the Imperial Household Department, the Court of Colo-
nial Affairs (Lifanyuan), the Office of Imperial Garden (Shanglinyuan), and
several other offices in the central government, which were of little use for
the majority of potential readers of the book. These substatutes and regulations were originally contained in the Code and the *Huidian*. The editor
explained in the "General Editorial Principles": "They are not related to civil
affairs [*minshi*], and thus it is not necessary to redundantly record them."[6]

Editors of commercial editions of the Code and the combined compilation books were from various levels of society. Some of them were scholar-
officials. For example, Li Nan, the editor of *The Great Qing Code with
Annotations and Explanations*, was censor-in-chief (*duyushi*) of the Censorate, and the proofreader, Cai Fangbing, was a famous scholar who gained
his *jinshi* degree in 1679. One editor was a book merchant. Li Zhen, the
owner of the Rongjintang bookstore on Liulichang Street in Beijing, compiled and published the *Complete Collection of Substatutes* in 1715.[7] The
majority of the editors who can be identified, however, were private legal

advisors (*muyou*). All of these men were from the Jiangnan region, and many of them were Suzhou natives. Legal advisors were the true legal experts of the Qing period. They not only went through years of legal training but also accumulated experience in dealing with real cases.[8] Many editors of commercial editions of the Code announced that the compilation was a product of their longtime accumulation of knowledge and experience. For example, the editor of the *Complete Collection of Substatutes and Cases* (*Li'an quanji*), Zhang Guangyue, a legal advisor of Jiangsu administrative commissioner, described his experience in compiling the book in the preface:

> Since I was mediocre and accomplished nothing [in the civil service examinations], I traveled far away from home and made a living as a legal advisor. Now, it has been thirty years. I poured my effort into studying the laws, exploring all the details. Besides all sorts of published books, I hand-copied all [the laws and regulations] that could be cited as substatutes but have not been officially compiled [into the Code]. I classified them according to categories and carefully arranged them. It accumulated in the long course of time, and finally I had a completed book.[9]

Commercial editions of the Code and the combined compilation books published in the early Qing frequently updated their content by adding new substatutes and regulations into the books and by deleting the old ones. Commercial publishers believed that only books containing updated legal information would be reliable and attractive to readers. Many publishers promised on the cover page of their books that they would continue to update as the substatutes changed over time. For example, on the cover page of the *Combined Printing of Substatutes and Cases Precedents*, the publisher pointed out that all of the substatutes and case precedents included in the book were from "before the summer of the fifty-eighth year of the Kangxi reign [1719]," and "if there are new substatutes and case precedents in the future, we will continue to print them quarterly [*anji xuke*]."[10] Commercial publishers usually did not recut all of the woodblocks for updates. They only cut new woodblocks for new or updated substatutes and regulations and removed the outdated ones. Then they printed the books by combining the old and new woodblocks. This method provided a timely and economically efficient way to make updates.

Updated legal information in commercial editions came from two main sources. The first one was the legal information issued by the central government and circulated through the administrative channel, such as updated substatutes, regulations, and case precedents. Although the Qing government did not provide its bureaucracy with updated editions of the Code, it did disseminate updated laws to officials as separate books or documents from the Code. Many editors of commercial editions were legal advisors working for officials in the government. Although not officials themselves, legal advisors had access to up-to-date information distributed through administrative channels when dealing with legal and administrative paperwork. When receiving updated substatutes issued by the central government, officials often sent them to their legal advisors for their reference.[11] Legal advisors played an important role in transmitting updated legal information from the government to commercial publishers and then to the public. Another important source of updated legal information was the *Beijing Gazette*. Often printed by commercial publishers, the periodical was available not only to officials but also to ordinary readers who could afford to buy it.[12] Some commercial publishers acknowledged they relied on it for updated substatutes and administrative regulations. Li Zhen, for example, the book merchant who compiled the *Complete Collection of Substatutes*, collected, edited, and compiled imperial edicts and memorials that contained updated legal information in the *Beijing Gazette* into his book. Liang Maoxiu, a legal advisor and the editor of the *Expanded Collection of Regulations and Substatutes* (Dingli xubian), also wrote in the preface that he used the *Beijing Gazette* as his source of updated laws.[13]

Only four commercial editions in the Kangxi period contain information about the publisher. These include the *Complete Book of the Great Qing Code with the Extensive Collection of Vermillion Annotations*, sold by the Tingsonglou bookstore in Nanjing, the *Combined Printing of Substatutes and Case Precedents* by the Lejingtang in Suzhou, the *Complete Collection of Substatutes* by the Rongjintang in Beijing, and the *Complete Collection of Substatutes and Cases* by the Sijingtang in Nanjing. Nanjing, Beijing, and Suzhou were all important publishing centers in the early Qing period. Not a single extant edition from the Kangxi period appears to have been published in Hangzhou, which became the center of commercial publications of the Code in later periods. It is difficult to say that there was a publishing center or a standard pattern for commercial editions of the Code in the

Kangxi period. Editions printed by different commercial publishing houses are usually distinct. Editors from different social backgrounds and printing houses in various cities engaged in publishing books about the dynastic laws and regulations.

DECLINE AND STANDARDIZATION: COMMERCIAL PUBLICATIONS OF THE CODE IN THE MID-QING PERIOD, 1723–1788

In the Yongzheng and early Qianlong periods, the number of commercial editions of the Code suddenly dropped. I have found no commercial edition of the Code published in the Yongzheng reign and only eleven commercial editions from the sixty-year-long Qianlong reign (table 2.1), mostly from after 1789. Booming official publishing activities contributed to the decline of commercial publication. The central government in this period made more efforts in compiling, printing, and distributing updated editions of the Code. It was probably easier for officials, legal advisors, and other literati to get access to official editions than it had been previously or would become later. Thus the demand for commercial editions dwindled.

Further, while the Shunzhi and Kangxi government did not regulate commercial legal publications, the Yongzheng and Qianlong court exercised much tighter control over these law books. In 1725 the Yongzheng emperor ordered that all new substatutes and administrative regulations be promulgated and printed under imperial authorization. He also banned unauthorized printing and selling of books related to board regulations, for example, the *Regulations of the Six Boards* sold by commercial publishing houses. In 1742 the Qianlong emperor launched an empire-wide campaign to eliminate the printing and sale of "secret handbooks for litigation masters" and other books that would "incite litigation" (*gousong*).[14] Although they were not the target of this campaign, commercial publications of the Code suffered too. Tighter regulation and the censorship, as well as the relative abundance of official editions, reduced commercial editions of the Code in the mid-Qing.

Only two works printed in this period are worth mentioning. First, *The Great Qing Code with Collective Annotations* was originally compiled by Shen Zhiqi in 1715 but was revised and republished by Hong Hongxu in 1745 and 1755. Hong was a Hangzhou native and probably a legal advisor. Major revisions of the Code in the Yongzheng and early Qianlong periods had rendered Shen Zhiqi's original work outdated. Hong's revision retained Shen's commentaries in the upper registers but revised the statutes and substatutes in the lower registers according to the Code officially published in 1740. Second, Wan Weihan's *The Great Qing Code with Comprehensive Annotations (Da Qing lüli jizhu)* was originally published in 1769 and then revised at least twice, by Hu Qian and Wang Youhuai in 1784 and 1786. Wan Weihan kept Shen Zhiqi's two-register printing format and his commentaries borrowed heavily from Shen's. In the "General Editorial Principles," Wan admitted that half of the commentaries in his book were from Shen's book.[15]

Mid-Qing commercial editions of the Code demonstrate several new features. First, the structure and printing format of these commercial editions became increasingly standardized. Few of the combined compilation books that were popular in the late Kangxi period were published in the Yongzheng and Qianlong periods, probably because of the Yongzheng ban, or perhaps because the Qing Code, with its major revisions in 1725 and 1740, finally achieved a position of authority in the Qing legal system. The update compilations of the early Qing were no longer necessary. Another sign of gradual standardization among commercial editions of the Code was that most commercial editions from this period adopted the two-register-per-page printing format. Furthermore, commercial editions of the Code printed in this period closely followed the updates in the *Expanded Substatutes* that was issued by the Board of Punishments. In the Kangxi period, many commercial editions indicated that their updated substatutes and Board regulations were obtained through less authoritative channels, such as the *Beijing Gazette*. In the Qianlong period, with the establishment of routine revisions of the substatutes by the Committee on Statutes, the Qing central government began to issue updated editions of the *Expanded Substatutes* every five years. These updates became the most authoritative channel for the dissemination of updated laws in the Qing bureaucracy. Commercial publishers in the Qianlong period and afterwards began to mainly rely on the board-issued *Expanded Substatutes* for updated laws.

Commercial editions usually compiled new substatutes into the Code before the imperial editions of the Code did. For example, in *The Great Qing Code with Comprehensive Annotations*, the editors wrote: "The 'complete book of the statutes and substatutes' [*lüli quanshu*] was issued in the fourth year of the Qianlong reign. . . . Although new substatutes are established, they have not been incorporated into the 'complete book.' Therefore we collect new substatutes issued by the Board in the twenty-eighth year, the thirty-third year, the thirty-eighth year, the forty-third year, and the

TABLE 2.2. Editorial Boards of Commercial Editions of the Code, 1789–1805

Date	Title (Publisher/Publishing Place)	Chief Editor(s)	Editorial Board
1789 and 1792	*Da Qing lüli huizuan* 大清律例彙纂 (Amalgamated Compilation of the Great Qing Code; Hangzhou)	Shen Shucheng 沈書成	**Editors (9):** Wu Fen 吳棻, Wang Xin 王新, Wu Tang 吳棠, Wang Youhuai 王又槐, Wu Zhangzhu 吳章珠, Min Lian 閔濂, Yu Cai 俞采, Wu Tao 吳燾, Zhu Guangbao 朱光葆 **Proofreaders (2):** Shen Xingyao 沈星曜, Shen Xinglang 沈星朗
1793	*Da Qing lüli huizuan* 大清律例彙纂 (Amalgamated Compilation of the Great Qing Code; Hangzhou)	Shen Shucheng 沈書成 Wang Youhuai 王又槐	**Editors (11):** Luo Yunsui 羅允綏, Feng Bing 馮柄, Wang Yongsui 王承綏, Yin Tengda 尹騰達, Sun Guanglie 孫光烈, Lu Ji 陸基, Miao Zhu 繆蠸, Yan Shaozhen 顏紹震, Cheng Jifei 程際飛, Wang Youwu 王又梧, An Bingren 安秉仁 **Proofreader (1):** Lu Tianchi 陸天墀
1796	*Da Qing lüli quanzuan* 大清律例全纂 (Complete Compilation of the Great Qing Code; Hangzhou: Mingxintang 銘新堂)	Yao Guan 姚觀	**Editors (15):** Cheng Ying 程英, Wan Shilin 萬士霖, Tang Baoming 湯寶銘, Yu Shilu 余世祿, Xu Lichun 徐立純, Huang Benxian 黃本賢, Feng Bing 馮柄, Lou Yanxi 婁延僖, Wu Zongpi 吳宗丕, Yu Shiling 余世苓, Wang Dexiu 王德秀, Zhu Daqi 朱大頎, Chen Shi 陳㮮林, Yu Yufang 余毓芳, Zhu Haishan 朱海山 **Proofreader (1):** Wang Youhuai 王又槐
1799	*Da Qing lüli quanzuan jicheng* 大清律例全纂集成 (Comprehensive Complete Collection of the Great Qing Code; Hangzhou)	Li Guanlan 李觀瀾 Wang Youhuai 王又槐 Sun Guanglie 孫光烈	**Editors (7):** Wei Zhaofan 魏兆蕃, Yao Ying 姚瑩, Zhao Zuowen 趙佐文, Liu Rui 劉濬, Qiu Boji 邱伯驥, Chen Dezhen 陳惪愼, Pan Ningzu 潘寧祖 **Proofreaders (5):** Kang Ning 康寧, Lin Baozeng 林報曾, Zhu Buzhou 朱步洲, Guo Shiqi 郭世竒, Yang Shiji 楊士績
1805	*Da Qing lüli tongzuan* 大清律例通纂 (General Compilation of the Great Qing Code)	Hu Zhaokai 胡肇楷 Zhou Menglin 周孟鄰	**Editors (11):** Min Nianzu 閔念祖, Li Jihui 李繼會, Gao Yousong 高友松, Wang Fen 王汾, Wu Zaikuan 吳再寬, Lai Jun 來均, Zhu Wenyao 朱文堯, Ni Yuan 倪垣, Kong Jilie 孔繼列, Wang Youhuai 王又槐, Lin Shikai 林士楷

Sources: Da Qing lüli huizuan (1792), "Canding tongren xingshi," 1a–b; *Da Qing lüli huizuan* (1793), "Canding tongren xingshi," 1a–b; *Da Qing lüli quanzuan* (1796), "Bianji tongren xingshi," 26a–b; *Da Qing lüli quanzuan jicheng* (1799), "Bianzuan tongren xingshi," 19a–20a; *Da Qing lüli chongding tongzuan jicheng* (1813), "Canding tongren xingshi," 40a–b.

forty-eighth year of the Qianlong reign, sort them according to categories, and compile them behind the original statutes, in order to make them easier to find and read."[16] This indicates that the editors incorporated the newly established substatutes according to the board-issued *Expanded Substatutes* into their book when the imperially authorized editions had not. In fact, no new imperially authorized edition of the whole Code was published between 1768 and 1790 (table 1.1). When this commercial edition of the Code was published in 1784, several new editions of the *Expanded Substatutes* had been published but had not yet been officially edited into the Code by the Committee on Statutes.

COLLECTIVE COMPILATION AND THE RISE OF HANGZHOU EDITIONS, 1789–1805

After the late Qianlong period, the policy on commercial legal publications eased, and official publishing houses began to decline. Private and commercial editing, printing, and publishing of the Code rebounded. The late Qianlong and early Jiaqing period was an important transition for commercial publications of the Code. There were at least five major commercial editions of the Code, which laid the foundation for all of the later editions published in this period.

Unlike earlier commercial editions, which were usually compiled by one or two scholars, all of the five major commercial editions of the Code printed between 1789 and 1805 were products of collective editing and proofreading (table 2.2). For the commercial editions listed in the table, both the *Amalgamated Compilation of the Great Qing Code* (Da Qing lüli huizuan, 1792 edition) and *Comprehensive Complete Collection of the Great Qing Code* (Da Qing lüli quanzuan jicheng) had ten editors, the smallest editorial boards among these editions. The *Complete Compilation of the Great Qing Code* (Da Qing lüli quanzuan) had the largest editorial board, including sixteen editors and one proofreader. On average, each editorial board had about twelve editors. There were no official titles, examination degrees, or occupations attached to the editors. These editions listed only their names, style names (*zi*), and native places. The sequence in which the editors' names appear seems to follow no particular logic, with only one exception—in the *Complete Compilation*, the book specifically indicates that the editors were listed according to their ages.[17] Proofreaders were usually listed after editors. It seems that proofreading work was assigned to junior members of the editing community. For example, both proofreaders of the *Amalgamated Compila-tion* (1792)—Shen Xingyao and Shen Xinglang—were the chief editor Shen Shucheng's sons. Lu Tianchi, the proofreader of the *Amalgamated Compi-lation* (1793), was the chief editor Wang Youhuai's student. That the proof reading work was assigned to junior members of the community shows that proofreading was probably viewed by Qing legal experts as a less sophisti-cated job that needed less experience and knowledge than editing work.

Due to the lack of records, it is hard to know the exact occupations of all of these editors and proofreaders. Several of them, however, can be identi-fied through various prefaces written by the editors or their friends. Unsur-prisingly, all of the editors who can be identified were private legal advisors. Some of them had achieved quite prominent positions as legal advisors for high provincial officials. For example, Huang Benxian worked as a legal advisor for Zhejiang judicial commissioner Qin Ying (1743–1821) when he participated in editing the *Complete Compilation*. Shen Shucheng, the chief editor of the *Amalgamated Compilation* (1792), worked as legal advisor in various provinces.[18] Editors such as Li Guanlan, Wang Youhuai, Xu Lichun, Wu Zongpi, Feng Bing, Zhu Daqi, Sun Guanglie, Hu Zhaokai, and Zhou Menglin were also private legal advisors, so the other editors likely were too. Therefore, legal advisors dominated editor positions of commercial editions of the Code published in this period.

Editors were usually men from core urban centers in the Jiangnan area, especially the Hangzhou-Shaoxing region. This is not surprising because this area was famous for producing a large number of legal advisors in the Qing period. According to an official survey of the Qianlong period, most legal advisors in the mid-Qing were from Zhejiang. Hangzhou and Shaox-ing were among the most productive incubators of legal advisors. To some extent, people from the region monopolized this occupation through care-fully knitted family and social networks.[19] The commercial editions printed between 1793 and 1823 identify 81 editors (table 2.3). Thirty were from Hangzhou prefecture, and 26 were from Shaoxing prefecture. Of these 81 editors and proofreaders, 79 were from Zhejiang and Jiangsu, with only two exceptions—one editor of the *Amalgamated Compilation* (1792), named Zhu Guangbao, was from Changsha in Hunan, and one editor of the *General Compilation of the Great Qing Code* (Da Qing lüli tongzuan), named Wu Zaikuan, was from Wanping County in Zhili.[20]

Many of these editors and proofreaders gathered in Hangzhou. As the capital of Zhejiang, many important government offices were located in

TABLE 2.3. Editors' and Proofreaders' Native Places, 1789–1823

Province	Prefecture	Number of Editors	County (Number of Editors)		
Jiangsu	Suzhou	5	Wuxian (2)	Changshu (1)	Unknown (2)
	Changzhou	4	Wuxi (2)	Jinkui (1)	Unknown (1)
	Songjiang	3	Yunjian (1)	Huating (1)	Louxian (1)
	Yangzhou	2	Yizheng (1)	Jiangdu (1)	
Zhejiang	Hangzhou	30	Qiantang (15)	Renhe (5)	Haining (2)
			Unknown (8)		
	Shaoxing	26	Shanyin (11)	Xiaoshan (5)	Kuaiji (5)
			Zhuji (3)	Shangyu (2)	
	Huzhou	4	Wucheng (2)	Gui'an (1)	Unknown (1)
	Jiaxing	2	Tongxiang (1)	Unknown (1)	
	Ningbo	2	Jinxian (2)		
	Quzhou	1	Unknown (1)		
Hunan	Changsha	1	Unknown (1)		
Zhili	Shuntian	1	Wanping (1)		
Total		81			

Sources: Data are based on *Da Qing lüli huizuan* (1792); *Da Qing lüli huizuan* (1793); *Da Qing lüli quanzuan* (1796); *Da Qing lüli quanzuan jicheng* (1799); *Da Qing lüli tongzuan* (1805); *Da Qing lüli chongding tongzuan jicheng* (1813, 1815, 1823).

Hangzhou city, including the yamens of the Zhejiang governor, provincial administrative commissioner, provincial judicial commissioner, and Hangzhou prefect. Legal advisors working for the provincial government, especially for the judicial commissioner, enjoyed prestige because of their important role in provincial judicial administration. Some of the chief editors of these commercial editions were legal advisors working for high provincial officials in Hangzhou. They enjoyed reputation, influence, and connections that enabled them to gather editorial teams for commercial editions. For example, Shen Shucheng, the chief editor of the *Amalgamated Compilation* (1792) was a Hangzhou native from a prominent family of legal advisors. His father served as legal advisor for Zhejiang judicial commissioner for many years. In his early twenties, Shen Shucheng began to receive legal training from his father and accompanied him in Hangzhou for years.

Shen Shucheng successfully worked for various officials in Jiangsu, Henan, and Fujian for a long time. When he returned home in 1786, he gathered nine old friends to edit the draft of the *Amalgamated Compilation* and published it in 1789.[21] Beside Shen, five other editors of the *Amalgamated Compilation* were Hangzhou natives too. Thus native place connections contributed to Shen's ability to put together a publishing team. So did his and his father's professional connections in the judicial commissioner's yamen, which Shen emphasized in his preface.

Since legal advisors working in higher administrative levels enjoyed more authority and privilege, legal advisors working for local governments were willing to participate in activities organized by their counterparts at higher administrative levels. With sixteen editors, the *Complete Compilation* had an exceptionally large editorial board. Huang Benxian, one of the editors of the book, was a prominent legal advisor employed by Zhejiang judicial commissioner Qin Ying. When Huang and several of his friends who shared the same professional interests (*tongzhi zhuyou*) finished compiling the book in 1796, Qin Ying wrote a preface at Huang's request. Qin highly praised the efforts of Huang and his friends and wrote that this edition of the Code was "a truly excellent edition." Several other editors of the book were also legal advisors working for Zhejiang officials. Both Xu Lichun and Wu Zongpi were working for magistrate Zhang Yutian of Haining, a county in Hangzhou prefecture. Feng Bing and Zhu Daqi also probably worked for Zhang Yutian. Cheng Ying appeared to have worked for Zhang Yingji (b. 1742), a Zhejiang grain tax circuit intendant (*liangchudao*) whose office was also located in Hangzhou city.[22] The *Complete Compilation*, therefore, resulted from the cooperation of a number of legal advisors working in and near Hangzhou.

For legal advisors who did not achieve prominent positions, being a member of an editorial board would enhance their reputation and increase their opportunity to get a better job. Being a legal advisor was one of the few well-paying jobs available to the Qing educated elite. From the mid-Qing period, the job market for legal advisors had become highly competitive. A legal advisor working in the latter half of the Qianlong reign estimated that only one-tenth of the men who finished their years of legal training could actually get hired as a legal advisor.[23] One needed connections or a reputation. The flourishing book market provided excellent opportunities for legal advisors to become known as learned legal experts. By being listed with more prominent and successful legal advisors on the editorial boards of a popular commercial edition of the Code, an otherwise unknown legal advisor might hope to convince readers that he was truly familiar with laws and that other legal experts accepted his abilities. Since the main audience for these books was officials, being on an editorial board was an efficient way for these legal advisors to get recognized by potential employers. This was probably an important reason that some chief editors in these commercial editions included their relatives and students in the editorial board.

Commercial editions appear to have been motivated by competition as well. Although all five of the mid-Qing editions were published in or near Hangzhou in the late Qianlong and early Jiaqing period, they seem to have been published by different publishing houses. The editorial boards were also rather different. Among the eighty-one named editors, only Wang Youhuai, Cheng Ying, and Sun Guanglie appeared on more than one editorial board (table 2.2). In other words, each of these commercial editions was compiled by a different group of private legal advisors, though almost all of them were living in several core urban centers in the Jiangnan area in the same period. It is thus probable that several groups of legal advisors in and around Hangzhou were competing with each other for reputation and limited job opportunities for their members. To some extent, the five different editions of the Code published between 1789 and 1805 were the product of this competition.

Editors in this period boasted that their work was superior to the others. For example, on the cover page of the *Complete Compilation*, the editors declared: "We respectfully collect administrative regulations issued by various Boards, administrative sanctions for civil and military officials, general circulars [*tongxing*], and case precedents. All of the valid rules and regulations are recorded in details in the book. Our book is more complete than the *Amalgamated Compilation* [Huizuan] and the *Amalgamated Collection* [Huibian]." In the "General Editorial Principles," the editors of the *Complete Compilation* continued to attack other editions: "The *Amalgamated Compilation* and other editions published in recent years do not closely follow the pattern [*shiyang*] of the Code issued by the Board. Even chapters and page numbers are different from the Code."[24] Then the editors noted that the text of the Code that was printed in lower registers of their book precisely accorded with the newest edition of the Code issued by the Board of Punishments. Their book was definitely superior to other commercial editions.

In the *Comprehensive Collection* (1799), published only three years after the *Complete Compilation*, chief editor Wang Youhuai also openly criticized other contemporary popular commercial editions. In his preface, he declared:

> In recent years, editors [*bianji zhijia*] rise one after another. Works like the *Amalgamated Compilation* and the *Complete Compilation* collect a large number of administrative sanctions and case precedents. Although they are great accomplishments, they still have shortcomings. Sometimes the content of those editions is too simple and abridged, and sometimes it is too complicated and redundant. Sometimes it is wrong or repetitive, and sometimes important things are omitted. Sometimes new substatutes have been changed, but the old ones are not deleted. Sometimes special regulations have been issued, but the old text is still there. They only dazzle our eyes and puzzle our hearts.[25]

Here Wang Youhuai mentioned the problems and shortcomings of his book's major rivals—the *Amalgamated Compilation* and the *Complete Compilation*. The shortcomings and mistakes of these editions, Wang Youhuai implied, justified his decision to gather a group of learned legal experts to compile and publish the *Comprehensive Collection*. The cover page of the book bears an inscription stating, "Our book is more complete and has more details than the *Amalgamated Compilation*, the *Amalgamated Collection*, and the *Complete Compilation*." In the preface, Wang Youhuai boasted that his book was "a complete compilation of all the valid laws of our dynasty" (*ji chaoting chengxian zhicheng*).[26]

Earlier commercial editions were based on the extended accumulation of individual experience and knowledge, and thus the compilation process usually took years. Collective editors of mid-Qing editions compiled and proofread more efficiently and cooperatively, and they usually finished their project within a year. For instance, Hu Zhaokai, Zhou Menglin, and other editors only spent seven months to finish compiling and proofreading the *General Compilation*.[27] During the compilation process, editorial teams systematically collected useful information from various books, classified it according to the chapters and categories in the Code, and proofread it together. For example, Zhang Yutian, a county magistrate and a friend of several editors of the *Complete Compilation*, described the compiling and proofreading of the book in his preface: "The editors broadly collected all the books and documents they could find, and compiled statutory annotations and commentaries, case precedents, administrative sanctions of the Board, and memorials. They sorted them into categories, made selections, and added notes and tags. Then they examined and questioned each other's work as they proofread over and over again."[28]

Editors often boasted that their works had comprehensive and updated information as well as few mistakes, thanks to the careful compiling and proofreading by a group of legal experts. As Wang Youhuai enthusiastically wrote in his preface of the *Comprehensive Collection*: "We have corrected all the mistakes and added things that were omitted by previous works, hoping that there is not a single unnecessary character or mistake."[29] Wang might have exaggerated his team's achievements. Generally speaking, however, the editions under collective compilation had high quality in editing and proofreading and were comprehensive and consistent, which contributed to their popularity among readers.

In spite of fierce competition, these commercial editions were quite similar in terms of content and printing format. All commercial editions published in this period have three registers per page for the main body of content (figure 2.3), instead of the two-register format popular earlier. A cross-index was printed in the upper register. For each statute or substatute, editors reminded readers via the cross-index of similar statutes or substatutes to cite the exact right one when making a sentence. Shen Shucheng's *Amalgamated Compilation* (1789) is the earliest edition I have seen with a cross-index. Evidently, readers appreciated this feature. Almost all of the commercial editions of the Code published after 1789 adopted similar cross-index listings in their upper registers.

The whole text from the imperially authorized Code was printed in the bottom register, so the bottom register of all commercial editions of the Code from this period looks more or less similar. All of them follow the content, layout, and printing style of the imperially authorized editions. They all have nine lines per register, and each line has seventeen characters, the same as the imperial editions. The chapter division of the bottom register also follows the imperial editions. This arrangement made it easier for readers to find a particular statute or substatute in the book. Commercial editors also added some interlinear individual or collective commentaries, printed in the same size and style as the imperially authorized small commentaries (*xiaozhu*) in the Code. It was usually difficult for readers to distinguish unofficial commentaries from official commentaries. Therefore, commercial

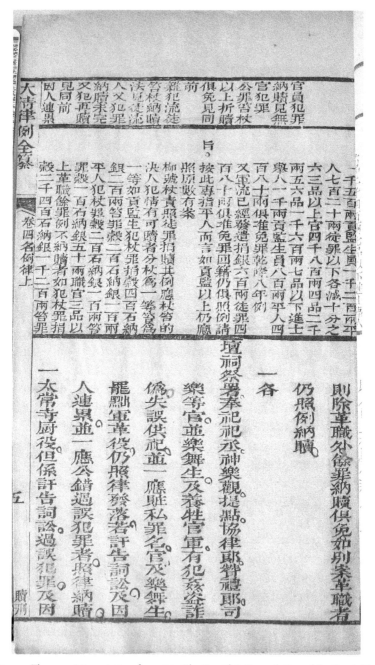

FIG. 2.3. Three-register printing format in *The Complete Compilation of the Great Qing Code* (Da Qing lüli quanzhuan; 1796 ed., *juan* 4, 5a). Courtesy of the Institute for Advanced Studies on Asia, University of Tokyo.

editions greatly enhanced the authority and potentially increased the usage of unofficial commentaries in judicial practice.

The major differences among the commercial editions usually can be found in the middle register, bearing statutory commentaries, administrative regulations and sanctions, case precedents, and other valid rules and regulations commercial editors selected according to their own judgment and market considerations. Editors could choose from a large number of statutory commentaries available in this period, such as Wang Kentang's *Annotations and Explanations of the Statutes and Substatutes*, Wang Mingde's *Reference for Reading the Code* (Dulü Peixi), Shen Zhiqi's *The Great Qing Code with Collective Annotations*, and Wan Weihan's *Great Qing Code with Comprehensive Annotations*. For example, the editors of the *Amalgamated Compilation* (1792) announced in the "General Editorial Principles" that their statutory commentaries were based on Shen Zhiqi's and Wan Weihan's commentaries. In the *Complete Compilation*, editors pointed out that they not only referred to Shen Zhiqi's and Wan Weihan's books when selecting statutory commentaries but also relied on five other commentaries. The editors of the *General Compilation* (1805) obviously preferred Shen Zhiqi's commentaries over others.[30]

Case precedents, which were printed after statutory commentaries, occupied the largest portion of the space in the middle register. Commercial editors usually chose cases that defined specific circumstances and corresponding sentences that statutes and substatutes did not clearly explain. The number of case precedents following each statute ranged from several cases to dozens. Most case precedents included in commercial editions of the Code were penal cases that were decided at the central level, with a significant number decided by the Board of Punishments. A small percent of these case precedents belonged to the "general circular" category—that is, the case precedents formally issued by the Board of Punishments to the entire judicial bureaucracy, which had the binding force in judicial sentences and would be revised into substatutes in the future. Most case precedents included in commercial editions, however, were not general circulars and thus were not formally published by the Board of Punishments. It seems that commercial editors collected these cases from work or from published collections of case precedents.

Besides commentaries and case precedents, the middle registers also included administrative regulations, imperial edicts, memorials, and other legal information, following Shen Shucheng's lead in the *Amalgamated*

Compilation (1789). Shen's preface explained that he frequently traveled for work and found various laws books in his bookcases too voluminous and heavy to carry. He thus selected legal information from those books and noted it above the relevant statutes in his copy of the Code. He found that this format was convenient and useful in that it allowed him to grasp the exact meaning of the laws by reading them together with supplementary materials. When he compiled the *Amalgamated Compilation*, he used the same arrangement.[31] That all the competing editorial groups in this period followed a similar practice in compiling and editing the text of the Code, therefore, represented a consensus in the community of legal advisors and perhaps also among the magistrates, prefects, and provincial officials they worked for.

That commercial editors adopted the three-register printing format and included a large number of private commentaries and case precedents was inseparable from Qing legal culture and judicial practice. The imperial government achieved its control over the judicial bureaucracy mainly through the centralized and rigid automatic judicial review process, which focused on scrutinizing judicial officials' performance and application of the laws in dealing with criminal cases. In contrast to strict regulations on the application of the laws, the Qing state took a rather lax attitude toward the interpretations of the laws. Unlike the Ming Code, the imperial edition of the Qing Code published in the Shunzhi period also printed small commentaries between the lines of statutes and substatutes. A large percentage of these small commentaries came from private commentaries published in the late Ming.[32] Although the legislation was quite active, and many new laws were promulgated after the Shunzhi Code, Qing legislators did not incorporate updated commentaries into the Code. The only exception of the short-lived general commentaries (*zongzhu*), which were added to the 1725 Yongzheng Code but were quickly abolished in the 1740 Qianlong Code. In addition, Qing legislators did not impose any rules regarding statutory interpretation. In this context, private commentaries flourished. It is estimated that more than 150 private commentaries were produced in the Qing.[33] Some influential ones, such as Shen Zhiqi's *Collective Annotations* and Wan Weihan's *Comprehensive Annotations*, considerably influenced the Qing legislation and judicial sentences and in many cases functioned as a "source of law" in judicial practice even though their authority was not formally acknowledged by the state. Qing officials frequently referred to and sometimes even cited private commentaries when sentencing legal cases.[34]

Similarly, case precedents played an increasingly important role in Qing judicial practice. Reference to case precedents (especially cases decided at the Board of Punishments and other central judicial agencies) was essential to legal reasoning in the Qing judicial system. Before 1738, there was no specific regulations regarding using case precedents in judicial sentences, and officials often cited or referred to case precedents when they found that existing statutes and substatutes could not perfectly match the circumstance of a certain crime. As one Qing scholar pointed out: "When making judicial decisions based on the laws, if the statutes cannot satisfy the condition, we will refer to the substatutes. If the substatutes cannot satisfy the condition, we will refer to case precedents."[35] When there was a conflict between case precedents and the statutes and substatutes, some judicial officials even abandoned the statutes and substatutes and referred to case precedents to sentence cases. Because the Board of Punishments did not openly circulate or publish official collection of case precedents, judicial officials often relied on unauthorized commercial editions to get access to case precedents.[36] The situation aroused Qing rulers' concern, and in 1738 the central government prohibited officials from citing case precedents that were not issued by the Board of Punishments as general circulars in judicial sentences. The prohibition, however, was partially revoked in 1743 and was not effectively enforced afterward. Based on extant case reports, modern scholars find that it was still common for Qing judicial officials to make use of case precedents in legal reasoning and judicial sentences after the 1738 ban.[37]

The structure and content of commercial editions of the Code not only reflected the legal culture but also played a crucial part in shaping the legal culture and judicial practice in the Qing. As chapter 3 shows, the three-register format commercial editions of the Code transformed readers' reading experience, changed the relationship between imperially promulgated laws and non-official legal information, and redefined and reinterpreted the laws in judicial practice. Compared with earlier editions, commercial editions of the Code in the mid- and late Qing included more supplementary information. A large percentage of this supplementary information was not formally authorized and openly circulated by the state. The space for original text of the imperially authorized editions of the Code (i.e., statutes and substatutes) was greatly reduced. The late Qianlong and early Jiaqing period was a transitional period in the publishing history of the Code, which established principles on what legal information should be incorporated alongside the Code and how should it be arranged. After this period, almost all commercial editions of the Code followed these principles, and Hangzhou editions of the Code continued to dominate the market until the final years of the Qing.

THE RISE AND DOMINANCE OF *COMPREHENSIVE INTEGRATION* EDITIONS, 1805–1911

In 1805 a legal advisor named Zhou Menglin intended to compile a new edition of the Code. He invited Hu Zhaokai, also a legal advisor, and eleven other friends to be coeditors. As with other commercial editions of the Code published in the mid-Jiaqing period, Zhou and Hu's book—*General Compilation of the Great Qing Code (Da Qing lüli tongzuan)*—followed the three-register format. The content and format of the book borrowed heavily from another popular commercial edition, the *Complete Compilation* (1796). However, beside updated substatutes, case precedents, and some other legal information issued after 1796, the two books have one other major difference: While the commentaries included in the middle register of the *Complete Compilation* were selected from various individual or collective commentaries, editors of the *General Compilation* basically adopted one individual commentary—that is, Shen Zhiqi's commentaries in *The Great Qing Code with Collective Annotations*. In the preface, Hu Zhaokai and Zhou Menglin praised Shen's book as having the most accurate commentary. They criticized other commercial editions of the Code for adopting random and miscellaneous private commentaries, which made it difficult for readers to understand the true meanings of the laws. Their effort to compile this new edition of the Code, as Hu and Zhou pointed out, was to restore the commentaries from Shen Zhiqi's work.[38] Judging from the texts, it seems that Hu and Zhou kept their word—they faithfully preserved Shen's commentaries in their book. They also added their own commentaries to elaborate some points that Shen had neglected and provided explanations to a number of substatutes established after Shen's death. Hu and Zhou's book won some prominent officials' support. Qin Ying, Guangdong judicial commissioner, wrote a preface to the book. In the preface, Qin recalled his experience of writing a preface to the *Complete Compilation* when he was serving as acting Zhejiang judicial commissioner in Hangzhou in 1796. He said that compared with the *Complete Compilation*, Hu and Zhou's work was more precise and comprehensive. In his preface, he praised the book as the "guidebook for judicial administration" (*yanyu zhi zhinan*).[39]

In 1811 Hu Zhaokai and Zhou Menglin updated the book and republished it under a new name—*Comprehensive Integration of the Great Qing Code* (Da Qing lüli tongzuan jicheng). Chen Ruolin (1759–1832), Guangdong judicial commissioner and a renowned legal expert, wrote a preface to this revised edition. He worked in the Board of Punishments for many years after earning the *jinshi* degree in 1787. He participated in revising the 1811 imperial edition of the Code and gained his reputation through solving many complicated legal cases. Chen's preface was full of praise for the book. He said that the book was truly helpful for both officials and legal advisors trying to learn the laws and assign the right sentences to legal cases. It had up-to-date legal information and contained no mistakes.[40] By inviting established officials like Qin Ying and Chen Ruolin to write prefaces, the editors wanted to assure readers that not only was their book of reliable quality but also that high-ranking judicial officials had recognized its authority.

In 1823, with the accumulation of new substatutes and case precedents, the old editions of *Comprehensive Integration* were out of date. A prominent legal advisor named Yao Run, a Shaoxing native, decided to update it. When he revised *Comprehensive Integration*, he had been working as a successful advisor in Hangzhou for years. Other than adding new substatutes and case precedents and deleting old ones, Yao did almost nothing to change the content. The structure of the book, the layout of pages, and even the printing style were left unchanged. Yao added a new preface written by Wu Tingchen (1773–1844). Wu was an influential scholar-official and was serving as Yunnan judicial commissioner when he wrote the preface for Yao. In it, Wu wrote that Yao had served as his legal advisor during his tenure as Hangzhou prefect. He admired Yao's legal learning and personality. Wu also wrote that he had known of *Comprehensive Integration* for years and was happy to see that Yao had updated the book. He praised the book as a comprehensive compilation of the laws, including not only the Code itself but also supplemental texts useful in legal practice.[41]

In 1826 Yao Run again updated *Comprehensive Integration*. By this time, he had achieved a more prominent position as a legal advisor working for Zhejiang judicial commissioner, Qi Gong (1777–1844). Qi was already an established judicial official with long experience working in the Board of Punishments. Like Chen Ruolin, who had written an earlier preface for *Comprehensive Integration*, Qi Gong later became the minister of the Board of Punishments. Yao's new revision received Qi's generous support. In the preface, Qi wrote that Yao had extensive learning of laws and thoroughly understood administrative affairs. He and Yao always discussed legal cases together. Yao had given Qi a copy of the 1823 edition of *Comprehensive Integration* as a gift. Qi carefully read the book and admired its clarity and usefulness. In 1825 the Committee on Statutes finished a major revision of the Code and issued the updated edition of the *Expanded Substatutes* to officials. As soon as Qi received the copy, he gave it to Yao and asked him to revise *Comprehensive Integration* accordingly. When Yao finished revising the book, Qi wrote a preface and praised it as a standard (*guinie*) for judicial administration.[42]

After 1826 Yao Run continued to revise and update *Comprehensive Integration*. Every time he finished a revision, he invited an influential official to write a new preface. He asked Changde, former acting Zhejiang judicial commissioner and Yao's current employer, to write a preface for the 1829 revision. In 1836 Wang Ding, the assistant grand secretary (*xieban daxueshi*) who was in charge of the Board of Punishments at the time, wrote a preface for *Comprehensive Integration*. In the preface, Wang Ding wrote that with the accumulation of new substatutes, old editions of the Code were rather difficult to read, and that was why "Mr. Yao publishes and prints *Comprehensive Integration*." Then he commended the quality of the book and encouraged people to read it: "This book collects all of [the laws] with no omissions, and sorts them into categories, in order to make it easy for people to read and understand. It is precisely 'the secret book for legal experts' [*fajia zhi miji*]. . . . When I received this book and read it, I found that everything in it was carefully selected and clearly categorized, and all of the details are listed. It is indeed 'an excellent edition of the Code' [*lüli shanben*], which will contribute to our Sacred Dynasty's benevolent judicial administration. That is why I am willing to write this preface and introduce the book to 'all readers in the realm who read the Code' [*tianxia dulüzhe*]."[43]

Both Wang Ding and Yao Run were silent on how Yao had been able to invite Wang to write a preface for his book. Wang Ding was not a Jiangnan man and he spent most of his official career working in the central government. His life had little intersection with Yao Run, a legal advisor from Shaoxing, who worked mainly in Hangzhou. We are even not sure whether or not these two men actually met each other in person. Judging from Wang's preface, it sounds as though the quality of Yao's book, rather than a personal connection, persuaded Wang to write his preface. From any perspective, Wang's preface was impressive. It was a powerful message that confirmed the authority and reliability of *Comprehensive Integration* in the eyes of the top official of the Qing judicial system. Qin Ying, Chen Ruolin, and Qi Gong, three of the five preface writers of *Comprehensive Integration* before 1836, also achieved top positions in the Board of Punishments. Supported by these leading officials in the Qing judicial system, the authority of *Comprehensive Integration* became unchallengeable.

After Yao Run, several other legal advisors updated *Comprehensive Integration*. One of the major updates was done by Hu Zhang, another legal advisor from Shaoxing. In 1838 Hu Zhang accompanied his employer— newly appointed Hangzhou prefect Wen Zhu (1784–1846)—to Hangzhou. At that time, Yao Run's editions of *Comprehensive Integration* dominated Hangzhou book market. Presumably because printing and selling *Comprehensive Integration* was profitable, publishers and bookstore owners in Hangzhou began to invite legal advisors to update the book. When Hu Zhang arrived at Hangzhou, a book merchant came to visit him, asking him to update *Comprehensive Integration*, and Hu agreed.[44] Hu's major contribution was to add a number of case precedents from a recent compilation, *The Conspectus of Legal Cases* (Xing'an huilan). When he finished the revision, Hu Zhang asked his employer, Hangzhou prefect Wen Zhu, for a preface.[45] By updating case precedents according to *The Conspectus of Legal Cases*, Hu Zhang combined the advantages of the two books and made *Comprehensive Integration* a more up-to-date and reliable source of legal information.

The compilation and publication of commercial editions of the Code was interrupted by the Taiping War (1850–1864). This massive civil war devastated many cities in the Jiangnan area, including the most important center of the commercial compilation and publication of the Code—Hangzhou. During the war, both books and printing blocks were seriously damaged or ruined.[46] In the early Tongzhi period, Wu Xu (1809–1872), a Hangzhou native, obtained an original edition (*yuanban*) of Yao Run's *Comprehensive Integration* during his tenure as Jiangsu Administrative Commissioner. When Wu retired the war had ended, and the demand for *Comprehensive Integration* resurged. Wu then decided to republish the book. He hired one of his old friends, Ren Pengnian, a Shaoxing native and legal advisor working in Hangzhou for Zhejiang judicial commissioner Wang Kaitai (1823–1875), to proofread and update the content. After Ren finished his revision, Wu Xu hired craftsmen to cut the woodblocks. He then printed and sold the book in the market in 1868. When a major official revision of the Code was finished and the last imperial edition of the Code was published in 1870, Wu Xu promptly updated *Comprehensive Integration* accordingly and republished it in 1871.[47]

Another influential revision of *Comprehensive Integration* was completed in 1878. In 1877 Mr. Qiu, the owner of the Juwentang publishing house in Hangzhou, asked Tao Jun and Tao Nianlin to update *Comprehensive Integration*. Tao Jun and Tao Nianlin were from Shaoxing and probably working in Hangzhou at the time. They declined the invitation at first, saying that they did not have enough talent and experience to do the job. But after the bookstore owner invited two other legal advisors who were also working in Hangzhou to help them update the book, Tao Jun and Tao Nianlin finally accepted the invitation and spent about half a year on updating the book. Then Qiu, the publisher, used his personal connections to ask Ying Baoshi (1825–1890), former Jiangsu judicial commissioner, to write a preface for the book.[48]

Preface writers for *Comprehensive Integration* in the Tongzhi and Guangxu period were also high-ranking provincial officials. Both Wang Kaitai (preface writer for the 1867 edition) and Ying Baoshi (preface writer for the 1878 edition) were judicial commissioners, and Wu Xu had been acting administrative commissioner in Jiangsu. As earlier preface writers had, they used their prefaces to express their approval of the quality of the book, describing it as an authoritative and comprehensive compilation of the laws at the time. In Wang Kaitai's 1867 preface, he pointed out that officials received *Comprehensive Integration* as a standard edition (*guinie*). After Ren Pengnian's revision, the book became even more complete and reliable, and it would make a real contribution to the world. Ying Baoshi also wrote in his 1878 preface that *Comprehensive Integration* was a standard edition for officials to assign sentences to legal cases, and it was an essential guide (*zhinan zhiche*) for people who were studying the law.[49]

Interactions among private legal advisors, high provincial judicial officials, and book merchants contributed to the compilation, revision, and publication of *Comprehensive Integration* in the late Qing period. Private legal advisors, especially those from Shaoxing and working in Hangzhou, to a large extent monopolized these projects. The editors of various major editions of *Comprehensive Integration*, such as Yao Run, Hu Zhang, Ren Pengnian, and Tao Jun and Tao Nianlin, were all from Shaoxing and working as legal advisors in Hangzhou. Their diligent work revising and updating *Comprehensive Integration* kept the book up-to-date and popular among readers for more than one hundred years. Officials, especially provincial judicial commissioners, also played an important role. They were the top legal officials and judges in provinces, and their influence on provincial judicial administration was profound. They were usually the employers for editors of *Comprehensive Integration* and provided support for these projects. Their effusive prefaces helped *Comprehensive Integration* attract readers and establish its authority as a "standard edition" and an "essential guide" for people who needed to know the laws. Book merchants played an increasingly important role in publishing *Comprehensive Integration*. Publishing *Comprehensive Integration* was a profit-oriented commercial activity. Because printing and selling *Comprehensive Integration* were profitable, book merchants invited or hired established legal advisors to update the book. Some powerful bookshop owners were even able to invite high-ranking provincial officials to write prefaces.

Based on the number of extant editions, commercial publication of the Code flourished from the Jiaqing to the Guangxu period, though there was a modest decline in the Xianfeng and Tongzhi periods because of the Taiping War (table 2.1). Altogether I have found ninety-one commercial editions printed in this period, a much larger quantity than I have found from the first century and a half of Qing rule. These late Qing editions also far outnumber the imperially authorized editions, only three of which were published after the Qianlong reign. Various publishing houses in Hangzhou, Beijing, and Shanghai accepted and adopted the content, structure, and even the printing style of *Comprehensive Integration*. In other words, almost all of the commercial editions of the Code printed in the late Qing closely followed the design and editing principles of *Comprehensive Integration*. The design of imperially authorized editions lost favor among commercial publishers. Even provincial publishing bureaus (*guanshuju*) established by provincial officials after the Taiping War discarded the design of the imperially authorized editions of the Code and adopted the content and format of *Comprehensive Integration*.[50] Therefore, after *Comprehensive Integration* was first published in 1805, its content and design replaced that of the imperially authorized editions and other commercial editions. Thanks to the efforts of legal advisors and the support of provincial judicial officials, *Comprehensive Integration* editions became the dominant form of the Code in circulation.

BENEFITING THE WORLD: THE IDEA OF PUBLISHING THE CODE

Commercial editors and publishers increasingly felt justified in editing and publishing the Code. Most embraced the idea that printing and disseminating the Code would contribute to "the way of governance" and popular well-being. In the early Qing, some editors and publishers still doubted whether they were allowed to publish the Code. When they decided to print it, they adhered strictly to the format of the official editions and were reluctant to make any modification, as we saw for the Shunzhi period. Many Ming and early Qing collections of commentaries on the statutes did not include the statutes and substatutes of the Code because the editors and publishers thought it was inappropriate to do so. Gu Ding, who revised and republished Wang Kentang's *Annotations and Explanations of the Statutes and Substatutes* in 1691, explained why he did not print the statutes and substatutes along with Wang's commentaries:

> The statutes and substatutes are the foundations of the government and institutions of our Great Dynasty. They are also the great laws for ruling the people. . . . I do not print the entire text of these statutes and substatutes, not because I do not want to print them and make it convenient for people to read both [the commentaries and the laws]. It is because without official authorization, I dare not to print it arbitrarily. I am merely a commoner with no official title, and thus I am not able to do so no matter how much I want to.[51]

Because of his concern that it might not be appropriate for a commoner to print the entire text of the Code without official authorization, Gu printed Wang's commentaries without the statutes and substatutes of the Code.

After the mid-Kangxi period, however, editors and publishers were increasingly confident that it was morally good and politically appropriate to print the Code. The majority of commercial editions of the Code and the combined compilation books printed after the mid-Kangxi period include the names of their editors or publishing houses, which indicates that editors and publishers were no longer afraid to reveal their identities. Moreover, increasing numbers of editors and publishers of the Code in the Qing period not only thought it appropriate for them to publish the Code but also considered it justified for them to add extra texts, such as statutory commentaries and updated substatutes. For example, in 1705 Qian Zhiqing and Lu

Fenglai published *The Combined Copy of the Great Qing Code with Annotations and Explanations*, based on Wang Kentang's commentaries as revised and republished by Gu Ding in 1691. While Gu Ding had been reluctant to print the text of the Code together with Wang Kentang's commentaries because he thought he lacked the authority to print the Code, Qian and Lu published Wang's commentaries (printed in the upper registers) together with the text of the Code (in the lower registers). The editors combined the two books into one for readers' convenience.[52] This arrangement of printing the Code along with private commentaries was quite common since the late Kangxi period. It is difficult to find any commercial edition of the Code printed after the Kangxi period without these extra texts. As time went on, more and more supplementary texts, such as a cross-index, case precedents, administrative regulations, and other legal information, were incorporated into the commercial editions of the Code. The amount of space taken up by the imperially promulgated statutes and substatutes greatly shrank in commercial editions from the early Qing to the late Qing.

Some Qing editors and commercial publishers even considered it acceptable to delete or rearrange the text of the Code. The combined compilation books popular in the late Kangxi period are an example of this. The editors and publishers of those books did not hesitate to rearrange or delete the original text of the Code. Liang Maoxiu, the editor of the *Expanded Collection of Regulations and Substatutes*, explained this in the "General Editorial Principles": "Various books about the statutes and substatutes . . . are edited by high officials in the court. Originally, it is considered inappropriate for commoners [*caomao*] to delete anything without authorization. However, for the part of the original text that is not important, or for the words and sentences that are redundant, we also dare not to include them into the book to distract our readers' eyes. Therefore, we delete the redundant ones, retain the important ones, and split the complicated ones, in order to make everything perfect and exact."[53] In Liang Maoxiu's opinion, the reader's need for convenience outweighed the potential offense of violating official authority in editing the Code, so he boldly omitted some parts of the Code that he thought were unimportant or redundant for his audience.

In the mid- and late Qing period, most editors and publishers proclaimed that their works made a great contribution to the government and society. Mentions of *gong* (contribution; benefit; merit) and *gongchen* (contributor; lit., meritorious official) frequently appear in the prefaces of commercial editions. Editors and publishers explained that the great contribution of these editions of the Code was to make the laws easily available to scholars, officials, and commoners. They usually pointed out that imperial editions of the Code and other law books were difficult for people to obtain. Also, because these imperial editions were not always updated quickly, it was difficult for readers both within and beyond the Qing bureaucracy to learn updated legal information. Official publications could not meet the huge demand for new editions of law books.

Commercial editors and publishers thought their books could help fill this gap. As Li Guanlan, the editor of a commercial edition of the Code, pointed out: "*The Great Qing Code* is issued by the decree of our Great Emperors to all of the people of the realm. . . . The *Expanded Substatutes* is compiled and issued every five years. . . . I am concerned that people living in small towns and remote areas could not get the 'complete book' [*quanshu*] of the Code. Thus I respectfully compiled the expanded substatutes as well as various regulations issued by the Boards in recent years into my book, in order to make it a "complete edition" [*quanben*]."[54] Li Guanlan also emphasized that his book not only included updated substatutes and administrative regulations, but also contained a large collection of statutory commentaries. His book would thus greatly ease readers' access to the updated and comprehensive information about the laws. Li Zhen, the editor of *Complete Collection of Substatutes* (1715), also mentioned that he compiled the book only because "the statutes, substatutes and regulations are vast and numerous" and "gentlemen who have not obtained official appointments yet [*weishi junzi*] have no means to read them." Therefore, he compiled the book for "gentlemen who are interested in explaining and reading the statutes and substatutes" and hoped that his book would benefit "the way of government" (*zhidao*).[55]

Editors and preface writers also emphasized that commercial editions of the Code and other law books made the laws easier for readers to understand. By combining the original text of the Code with statutory commentaries, case precedents, and other legal information, they could help readers understand the statutes and substatutes. In their prefaces, they used the language usually reserved for classical commentary to describe their achievement. They viewed the original texts of the Code (i.e., the statutes and substatutes) as *jing*, comparing them to the original text of Confucian classics, and they considered the statutory commentaries as *zhushu*, classical commentaries and annotations used to help readers to understand the classics.[56] These editors pointed out that just as scholars could not fully understand the Confucian classics without commentaries and annotations, people could not understand the exact meanings of the statutes and sub-statutes without the help of statutory commentaries. Authors of these statutory commentaries as well as editors who collected these commentaries and printed them were thus compared to ancient scholars such as Zuo Qiuming and Zheng Xuan, who commented on Confucian classics. For example, Guan Heng, the preface writer of *The Great Qing Code with Comprehensive Annotations* (1784), wrote that the editor of the book, Wan Wei-han, "resembled the meritorious minister Mr. Zuo [Qiuming]."[57]

Although editors and publishers of commercial editions were certainly interested in profiting financially from their books, they generally believed that the publication and circulation of their books would contribute to the well-being of the state and society. In their opinion, the state should educate commoners about the statutes and substatutes from the Code because when commoners knew the laws and punishments, they would not dare to commit crimes. Knowing the laws would also reduce the chance of committing crimes due to ignorance.[58] Officials should carefully study the laws in the Code. It would help them apply the right sentences to legal cases and not violate administrative regulations. In this way, not only would they secure their official careers, but they would also reduce the number of wronged people. Students who were preparing for the civil service examinations should also read the Code to prepare for their future official careers. Therefore, printing and publishing the Code, as a preface writer pointed out, would help "officials closely follow the laws, scholars easily read the laws, and the common people obey the laws," and thus, "it is a great accomplishment!"[59]

THE MARKET FOR COMMERCIAL EDITIONS OF THE CODE

Commercial editions of the Code had a broader range of target readers than the imperial editions. Many editors and preface writers emphasized the importance of the Code and encouraged people to buy and own it. They claimed that not only should each official and legal advisor who had to deal with legal cases have one such book, but scholars and students who intended to be officials in the future should also own and read the Code. For example, one preface writer of the *Amalgamated Compilation* (1792) pointed out: "*The Great Qing Code* is issued by the emperors to all of the people of the realm. Not only should every official working in various yamens that have judicial responsibilities have it, but also all of the students who study in schools and the gentry who pay attention to the way of government should own it in order to prepare for being officials and governing people in the future."[60] Jiang Chenxi (1653–1721), the Shandong governor who wrote a preface for *The Great Qing Code with Collective Annotations*, also pointed out that officials should not put aside this book even for one day, and every scholar and gentleman should have a copy at hand in order to culti-vate his morality and establish himself in life (*liming*).[61] Besides officials and scholars, legal advisors were also apparently major target readers. Referred to as "legal experts" (*shen han jia*), "people who learn the laws" (*xi fajiayan zhe*), and "guests who handle the legal cases" (*bing'an zhi ke*), legal advisors were frequently mentioned as target readers in commercial editions.[62]

Commercial editions of the Code were not cheap, but for officials and legal advisors, they were affordable. In the early Qing period, the price was relatively low. *The Complete Book of the Great Qing Code with the Extensive Collection of Vermillion Annotations* (1706), a beautiful ten-volume book printed in black and red ink, cost only 2.4 taels. Prices of the Code increased in the mid- and late Qing period due to inflation as well as expansion of contents in these commercial editions. On average, the number of volumes increased from about ten in the early Qing to about twenty-four in the late Qing period, which cost more to compile and print. A *Comprehensive Inte-gration* edition printed in 1823 by the Wubentang bookstore in Hangzhou was sold at 3.2 taels. In the late Qing period, the price of commercially pub-lished editions of the Code increased to around 6 taels. An 1859 edition of the Code was sold by the Sanshantang bookstore in Hangzhou at 6.4 taels. The 1878 and 1907 edition published by the Juwentang in Hangzhou were also priced at 6.4 taels. The Qinglaitang edition of *Comprehensive Integra-tion*, published in 1894 in Hangzhou, was a little more expensive at 7 taels. The price of editions published in Beijing also ranged from 6 to 6.4 taels.[63] Commercial editions cost much more than imperially authorized editions, which were fixed at only about 1.1 taels (table 1.2). However, because these commercial editions were frequently updated, had more comprehensive contents, and were much easier to buy than the imperial editions, they were still popular among readers. Although it might have been difficult for lower literati (e.g., poor or moderately prosperous students and schoolteachers) or ordinary people to afford them, these books only cost a small fraction of the annual incomes of the main target readers—officials and legal advisors, who usually earned from several hundred to several thousand taels per year.[64]

Commercial editions of the Code were sold in several major book markets in the Qing empire. Jiangsu was an important printing center and book market for the Code in the early Qing. Among the 120 commercial editions, 10 came from Jiangsu: 7 were printed in Suzhou, 2 in Nanjing, and 1 in Changzhou (table 2.4). Several Jiangsu editions were quite influential in the early and mid-Qing, including *The Complete Book of the Great Qing Code with the Extensive Collection of Vermillion Annotations*, sold by the Tingsonglou in Nanjing, and Wan Weihan's *The Great Qing Code with Comprehensive Annotations*, published by the Yunhuitang in Suzhou in 1769.[65] Before the Jiaqing period, only two commercial editions of the Code were printed in Hangzhou. Suzhou seems to have produced more commercial editions of the Code than Hangzhou in the early and mid-Qing. However, with compiling and publishing activities flourishing in Hangzhou since the late Qianlong period, Hangzhou editions quickly dominated the market for the Code. Thus commercial activities of compiling and publishing the Code in Suzhou declined. Only two more editions were published after the Qianlong reign in and around the Suzhou area, and both of them seem to be reprinted copies of Hangzhou editions. In the same period, publishing houses in Hangzhou produced at least thirty-three editions.

TABLE 2.4. Publishing Places of Commercial Editions of the Qing Code, 1644–1911

Place	Editions
Hangzhou	33
Beijing	16
Shanghai	9
Suzhou	7
Nanjing	2
Ningbo	1
Changzhou	1
Xiugu	1
Quzhou	1
Unknown	49
Total	120

The largest book market for these commercial editions of the Code was in Hangzhou, where many influential commercial editions were produced and sold, especially after the mid-Qianlong period. Among the 120 commercial editions, 71 had specific information on the place where they were published or sold. Of these 71 commercial editions, 33 were compiled and published in Hangzhou (table 2.4), including almost all important and influential commercial editions of the Code after the mid-Qianlong period, such as Shen Shucheng's *Amalgamated Compilation*, Yao Guan's *Complete Compilation*, Wang Youhuai's *Comprehensive Collection*, and various editions of *Comprehensive Integration*. Commercial publishing houses in Hangzhou that were active in printing and selling the Code included the Mingxintang, Youyizhai, Wubentang, Sanshantang, Tongwentang, Qinglaitang, and Juwentang. These bookstores not only published law books but also printed and sold other genres of books, including history books, Confucian classics, and literature works. Editions produced in Hangzhou were famous for their high compilation and printing quality. This contributed to their reputation as the best editions of the Code in the mid- and late Qing period. As a Shanghai publisher of a commercial edition of the Code in 1891 wrote in praise of various editions of the Code published in Hangzhou, "These editions have become a fashion in the empire, and people view them . . . as excellent editions [*shanben*]."[66] Bookstores in other cities also sold Hangzhou editions. For example, Yao Guan's *Complete Compilation*, now held by Tokyo University, was compiled and printed in Hangzhou. In the left column of its cover page, the following lines appear in black ink: "The woodblocks are stored in the Yang family's Mingxintang, located on Yangshi Street, inside Qingtai Gate in Hangzhou, Zhejiang." Below it, stamped in red ink, are the words "Retailed by the Tuosuzhai paper store located on West Street, in front of the yamen of the Jiangxi administrative commissioner."[67] This demonstrates that the book was printed in the Mingxintang in Hangzhou but was sold at the Tuosuzhai in Nanchang, Jiangxi.

As the Southern Song capital city, Hangzhou was a prominent publishing center in the Song period and the Ming period, but its leading role in the book printing and publishing industry began to decline in the late Ming and early Qing period. Historian Zhang Xiumin does not list Hangzhou as an important publishing center in the Qing period in his magisterial study of Chinese print history.[68] Generally speaking, although Hangzhou still produced many books in the Qing period, in terms of quantity and quality it could not be compared to other important printing centers like Beijing,

Suzhou, and Guangzhou. However, in terms of the publishing history of commercial editions of the Qing Code, Hangzhou's leading role could not be challenged. The high concentration of legal experts in the city contributed to a flourishing production and booming market for the Code. Legal advisors resident in Hangzhou not only played an important role in compiling and editing the Code; they were also potential consumers of the Code. Legal advisors from nearby prefectures like Shaoxing and Jiaxing also frequently traveled to Hangzhou and could potentially buy the Code there. Moreover, as the administrative center of Zhejiang and the southern terminus of the Grand Canal, Hangzhou attracted a large number of officials, examination candidates, students, tourists, and travelers who were also potential buyers of commercial editions.

Bookstores that retailed commercial editions of the Code in Hangzhou were usually in prosperous commercial areas near government offices and schools. Qinghefang was the most prosperous commercial area in the center of Hangzhou city. Near famous scenic spots like Wu Mountain and West Lake, Qinghefang attracted tens of thousands of visitors every year. Qinghefang was also close to several government offices, such as those of the Zhejiang administrative commissioner, Hangzhou prefect, Renhe county magistrate, and Qiantang county magistrate. The Hangzhou Prefectural School also was in this district. Therefore, beside visitors, many officials, legal advisors, clerks, and government students gathered in this area. Many bookstores thus were in Qinghefang. The locations of six Hangzhou bookstores that participated in printing, publishing, and selling the Code can be identified, and three of them were in Qinghefang. The other three bookstores were also in relatively prosperous and convenient-to-reach districts. For example, the Wubentang bookstore was inside the Wangjiang Gate, near the Zhejiang governor's yamen. The Mingxintang bookstore was on the Yangshi Street—a flourishing market near the office of the Zhejiang Salt Inspector and the Qiantang county government school.

Another publishing center for commercial editions of the Code was Beijing. At least sixteen editions were printed or sold in Beijing (table 2.4). Most of the bookstores that participated in publishing the Code and other law books, such as the Rongjintang, the Shanchengtang, and the Hongdaotang, were on the famous Liulichang Street, the largest book market in North China. Bookstores that published the Code usually belonged to the category of official directory shops (*jinshenpu*), which focused on printing and selling official directories (*jinshenlu*), law books, official handbooks, examination aids, and various books for officials' and scholars' practical use. The main customers who frequented the Beijing bookstores were officials and scholars working or sojourning in Beijing. These men spent their spare time in Liulichang, socializing with friends as well as reading and purchasing books.[69] Before leaving Beijing, they might buy books at Liulichang that they could not easily obtain in local book markets outside the capital.

Compared with book buyers in Hangzhou, customers in Beijing's bookstores generally had higher social status. Since many legal advisors were living in and around Hangzhou, the main social group who bought the Code there was probably legal advisors. In Beijing, however, the majority of customers of the Code were officials. Thus specialized bookstores like official directory shops that targeted mainly an official clientele could flourish in Liulichang. Officials were required to have a certain level of legal knowledge, but they were amateurs compared with legal advisors who made a living as legal professionals. Moreover, Beijing lacked the atmosphere of legal expertise Hangzhou experienced because of the large number of legal advisors living in and around Hangzhou. Qualified editors and revisers were also less numerous in Beijing. Even officials and clerks working in the Board of Punishments who might have been able to edit or update commercial editions of the Code seem not to have been interested in doing so. Therefore, although Beijing bookstores produced at least sixteen commercial editions of the Qing Code, generally speaking, these lack originality—most of the Beijing editions simply copied Hangzhou editions. The names of editors or compilers were often omitted from Beijing editions, and the prefaces written by various officials under the invitation of editors in the original Hangzhou editions were sometimes deleted, probably to avoid potential disputes over proprietary content.

When Western lithographic printing technology was introduced to China in the late nineteenth century, Shanghai quickly rose as a major publishing center.[70] Shanghai publishing houses printed at least nine editions of the Code in the late Qing period (table 2.4). Several famous publishing houses in Shanghai, such as the Wenyuan Shanfang and the Saoye Shanfang, engaged in printing and selling the Code. The earliest Shanghai edition of the Code I have found was printed by the Saoye Shanfang in 1887. All Shanghai editions can be viewed as reprinted editions of *Comprehensive Integration*. Lithographic printing technology was widely used in printing the commercial editions of the Code in Shanghai, so Shanghai editions were smaller but clearer than the traditional woodblock printing used to print commercial editions of the Code by all publishing houses outside Shanghai. The Wenyuan Shanfang publishing house alone printed at least five editions of *Comprehensive Integration*, in 1896, 1899, 1904, 1906, and 1908, which indicated that commercial editions of the Code were still in great demand in the last years of the Qing dynasty and that publishing such editions was probably still profitable.

The market for commercial editions of the Code was competitive, especially in the late Qing period. Many bookstores in cities like Hangzhou and Beijing were selling similar editions at similar prices in the same period. Fierce competition among different editions and publishing houses were reflected on their cover page, where publishers usually announced that their edition was newly updated, more comprehensive, and more precise than other editions. They also criticized other publishing houses for pirating their books, saying that those pirated editions were low in quality and full of mistakes. For example, on the cover page of an 1826 edition of *Comprehensive Integration*, printed by the Lüsutang and sold by the Sanyutang bookstore in Hangzhou, the publisher printed the following statement in red ink: "The book is closely associated with judicial administration and punishments, and thus we proofread and printed it with extreme carefulness. Recently, there are unauthorized reprinted editions that are full of errors. Some bandits even forged the stamp of our publishing house and pirated our book to pursue profit. I hope gentlemen who know well about the book can distinguish [it from those pirated ones]." The Juwentang bookstore in Hangzhou made the similar statement in its editions of *Comprehensive Integration*. The publisher announced in the book: "Our Zhejiang has been famous for producing the best editions of the Code for a long time. Our editions are popular throughout the empire. . . . In recent years some old editions with outdated substatutes printed in other provinces have been sold. All of them are blurry in printing and full of errors. . . . The worst ones are from Jiangxi, which are clumsily printed on bad paper. Not a single new substatute is included!"[71] Then the publisher claimed that his edition not only contained new substatutes and updated case precedents but also was carefully proofread and printed; scholars and merchants who want to purchase the book should recognize the Juwentang stamp. Besides the Lüsutang and the Juwentang, many other publishers made similar statements in their books. Expressions such as "The woodblocks are stored in our publishing house" (*benya cangban*) and "Unauthorized reprinting will definitely be investigated" (*fanke bijiu*) frequently appeared on the cover page of Hangzhou editions from the mid- and late Qing period.

Qing laws did not specifically protect copyright, and unauthorized reprinting was not illegal, but there was a concept of intellectual property. Publishers in late imperial China had several methods to protect their publications, including using their connections with local governments, sometimes by bringing lawsuits to local court, to ban unauthorized reprinting; distinguishing their publication from pirated editions by using special marks; and establishing guild regulations (if a guild existed) to prohibit unauthorized reprinting.[72] No evidence indicates that commercial publishers of the Code had a guild or that they turned to court to solve the unauthorized reprinting problem. Thus expressions such as "Unauthorized reprinting will definitely be investigated" were probably merely warnings on paper, and likely publishers seldom took real action on investigating piracy. Most commonly, renowned Hangzhou publishers of the Code tried to protect their publications by distinguishing their editions from others' editions, as we have seen in the Lüsutang and the Juwentang's cases. They usually stamped remarks asserting the superior quality of their editions relative to other editions on their cover page, indicated the location of the bookstores, and encouraged readers to distinguish "good editions" from "bad editions."

In spite of these efforts, unauthorized reprinting of these editions was rampant, partly because of the lack of copyright law. A more important reason was that printing and selling these books were so lucrative that various publishing houses and bookstores competed to pursue profit. Reprinting also contributed to the distribution of the Code and other legal texts outside the major printing centers. Of the 120 commercial editions of the Code, forty-nine editions do not have information about their publishers or editors, and most of them obviously are reprinted from popular Hangzhou editions. Many of these unauthorized reprints were produced in less prominent printing centers, such as those in Jiangxi (as mentioned in the Juwentang's statement) and Fujian. For example, the Zaizitang in Sibao, a rural printing center of Western Fujian, printed a commercial edition of the Code in the early nineteenth century. Some large printing houses in major printing centers established extensive bookselling networks. For example, the Shanchengtang bookstore in Liulichang, which published the 1888 edition of the Code, had branch shops in Hankou, Chendu, Chongqing, Jinan, Xuwanzhen (Jiangxi), Dongchang (Shandong), and Botouzhen (Zhili).

Itinerant book merchants and branch shops of these bookselling networks could have brought the Code and other legal texts to readers outsides the coastal urban centers and the capital.[73]

There is a surge of the number of extant commercial editions from near the end of the Qing dynasty. The Tongzhi and Guangxu periods produced at least fifty-two commercial editions of the Code, which accounted for more than 43 percent of all commercial editions published in the Qing (table 2.1). One possible reason for the high percentage of late Qing editions is that books published later have higher survival rates. Another possible reason is that the Code was in high demand in the late Qing, so commercial publishers produced more editions than they had in previous periods. The changing legal and international context might have contributed to scholar-officials' rising interests in law and legal education in the late Qing. Prevalent case backlogs and high litigation rates in local society aroused the state's concern about officials' legal knowledge and their ability to solve legal cases. In 1866 the government established by far the strictest regulations in late imperial history on new officials' legal training and examination. Moreover, legal imperialism and extraterritoriality, which became a major threat on China's sovereignty after the First Opium War (1839–1842), aroused new public interests in law and legal studies. Law schools (*fazheng xuetang*) sprang up in Beijing and provincial capitals in the late Qing, and *The Great Qing Code* was often used as a textbook or a major reference book.[74] Therefore, there might have been a rising demand for the Code among readers that contributed to the flourishing commercial publishing activities in the late Qing.

CONCLUSION

From the Ming to the late Qing period, commercialization and commodification of printing and publishing the Code increased. Market forces gradually took the place of the government in disseminating up-to-date legal knowledge. In the Ming period, officials and the government played a significant role in compiling and publishing the Code. In the Qing, however, editors, compilers, and proofreaders were overwhelmingly private legal advisors who worked for officials but were not a formal part of the bureaucracy. Legal advisors could access the latest legal information circulating through the bureaucracy because of their work, and they took advantage of this when compiling, editing, and updating the Code. Although officials still participated in publishing commercial editions of the Qing Code, usually by writing prefaces for the books, they no longer directly engaged in editing, compiling, and publishing tasks. Compared with their Ming predecessors, their importance in the publication of the Code was diminishing. Moreover, in the Qing period, most editions of the Code were published by profit-oriented commercial publishing houses and sold by bookstores in Hangzhou, Beijing, Suzhou, Shanghai, and other urban centers. Few provincial or local governments participated in editing and publishing the Code.

That legal advisors played the dominant role in editing and publishing commercial editions of the Code and many other law books epitomized the rise of a new legal professional community that was beyond the control of the Qing government. The rise of legal professionalism in the last hundred years of the Ming dynasty constituted an important part of the sprout of early modernity of Chinese legal culture, with most legal experts working in the central government as judicial officials. The situation, however, significantly changed in several ways in the Qing. First, private legal advisors rather than judicial officials constituted the core of professional legal community in the Qing, with some three thousand legal advisors working in Chinese courts in any given year from roughly 1711 to 1911.[75] Personally hired by officials, legal advisors were not bound by various administrative regulations that the state designed to control officials. Although the central government tried to regulate legal advisors, especially in the high Qing period, evidence indicates that most of these efforts failed—and legal advisors were by and large beyond the control of the state throughout the dynasty. Second, legal advisors developed their professional identity and independence, represented by the emergence of a new discourse of "the way of muyou" (*mudao*), defined by historian Li Chen as "a shared understanding of the standards and principles of legal advisors' professional training, competence, practice, ethics, and responsibilities."[76] Exemplified by the rise and dominance of the three-register commercial editions of the Code, the professional community of legal advisors formed a common learning of the law since the late Qianlong period, which was rather different from imperial standards on how the Code should be edited and printed. Through editing and publishing the Code, legal advisors not only gained authority and cultural capital for themselves but in many ways redefined and reinterpreted the laws in judicial practice. If the development of the professional legal community independent from the state is a key factor of legal modernity, the Qing legal system obviously had some early modern features.

Commercial editions differed in compilation, publication, and circulation from imperially authorized editions of the Qing Code. Commercial editions were produced in much larger quantities and were more frequently updated than were imperial editions. Commercial editions were much easier to obtain—they were sold in bookstores in several major book markets and were available to anyone who could afford to buy them. Besides statutes and substatutes originally in the Code, commercial editions provided detailed statutory commentaries and annotations, updated substatutes and case precedents, board regulations, cross-index, and other useful legal knowledge to their readers. Their target audience included officials, legal advisors, students, and other literati—a much broader social spectrum than for imperial editions. Commercial editions were much more widely circulated and used by people inside and outside the bureaucracy. The proper functioning of the judicial administration depended upon timely dissemination and circulation of up-to-date legal information. Commercial publications, to a large extent, provided this information to people working in the Qing legal system, especially officials in lower levels of the bureaucracy and private legal advisors. The impact of commercial editions on the judicial system, however, went beyond providing officials with updated editions. Commercial editions, with their three-register format and additional legal information, significantly influenced legal reasoning and judicial sentencing in Qing courts.

3   READING THE CODE

ON A SUMMER DAY IN 1835, ZHANG JIXIN (1800–1878), FIRST-degree compiler (*bianxiu*) of the Hanlin Academy, came to the palace for an individual imperial audience with the Daoguang emperor, who had decided to interview junior members of the Hanlin Academy for official positions in the provinces. After asking Zhang several questions about his experience, the emperor told him to read useful books (*youyong zhi shu*) and to not spend too much time reading and writing useless poems and essays: "Try to think about it. How can prose and verse contribute to the rule of the state?" At the end of the interview, the emperor emphasized reading useful books once again: "When at home, it would be best to read books about statecraft [*jingshi zhi shu*]. Attending drinking and poetry parties are the bad habits of Hanlin academicians. Don't waste your time on that!"[1]

The emperor clearly considered "useful books" to be those about statecraft. The Jiaqing and Daoguang periods witnessed a revival of statecraft thinking and practical learning (*shixue*). In this time of crisis, more and more officials and scholars paid attention to the learning and techniques that would contribute to a functioning economy, performance of administration and the legal system, the welfare of society, and so on. Useful books—including the Code, the *Huidian*, various official handbooks, collections of works of established officials, and the *Compendium of Writings on Statecraft from the Present Dynasty* (Huangchao jingshi wenbian)—were often contrasted with useless books, particularly mediocre poetry and essays, outdated annotations to Confucian classics, examination aids, unimportant memoirs and literary collections, and poorly written gazetteers.[2]

In the Daoguang period, the Qing empire faced many challenges, including bureaucratic decline, local rebellions, and impending foreign invasion. From the emperor's perspective, choosing and appointing capable field administrators was an essential solution to the empire's problems. The conversation during Zhang Jixin's audience indicates that the emperor believed that reading useful books about statecraft would prepare his classically educated Hanlin officials for future positions in field administration. Most Qing officials, including Zhang Jixin, had passed the metropolitan civil service examinations, which mainly tested candidates' literary talents, not their administrative and legal knowledge. When they prepared for these highly competitive examinations, few candidates had the spare time or energy to read books about law and administration. In his autobiography, Zhang Jixin himself did not mention that he had read any such books before receiving his *jinshi* degree. Born to a literati family of modest means in Yizheng, Jiangsu, Zhang studied Confucian classics with various teachers in his hometown. After he passed the provincial-level examinations in his early twenties, he moved to Beijing, working as a tutor in an official household while preparing for the examinations. At the age of twenty-nine, he passed the *jinshi* examinations and began to work at the Hanlin Academy. By 1835 he had worked in the academy for seven years. When the emperor interviewed him, Zhang was a young, promising official with no experience whatsoever in field administration, the career path to which he aspired. So the emperor told him twice during the audience to read useful books and prepare himself well for his future job.

A year later, in 1836, Zhang Jixin was appointed as Shuoping prefect in Shanxi, the start of a thirty-year-long career as a local and provincial official. Between 1836 and 1865, he served in such positions as prefect, circuit intendant, provincial judicial commissioner, provincial administrative commissioner, and acting governor in several provinces. In the nineteenth century, local governments usually were backlogged with unsolved legal cases (*ji'an*), sometimes numbering in the thousands. Clearing up backlogs affected the reputation and promotion of officials. Though a Confucian-educated literatus, Zhang Jixin showed an amazing familiarity with laws and legal procedures. He did not brag about his legal and administrative knowledge in his autobiography, but his skill and confidence in solving legal cases was evident, even at the beginning of his career as a prefect in Shanxi. Zhang had probably acquired knowledge of the law and administrative techniques by reading books when he waited in Beijing for his appointment. When he was acting Taiyuan prefect, within only half a year, he resolved more than two hundred backlogged legal cases. In his autobiography, he expressed distrust of private legal advisors, insisting that officials should have robust legal knowledge and be able to make sentences on legal cases themselves to avoid being deceived or misled by self-serving advisors. When he was in Shanxi, he wrote his own responses to the plaints filed with his court and decided whether to accept them instead of relying on advisors. During his years as circuit intendant in Fujian, he himself reviewed all of the legal case records submitted by local governments and let the legal advisor deal only with routine paperwork.[3]

In his career working in local and provincial governments, Zhang Jixin paid close attention to acquiring legal knowledge and techniques of judicial practice. He and his legal advisors often debated the proper sentences in complicated cases. He also emphasized the need for legal training for inexperienced officials. When he was acting Taiyuan prefect, he sent twenty new county magistrates to the Provincial Auxiliary Court (Fashenju), which dealt with capital appeals and automatic judicial reviews, where they could gain useful legal experience. He also ordered these new magistrates to read the Code after work and discuss the laws during the day. He set up an attendance roster for them at the court to supervise their legal training. Through this training, Zhang believed that new magistrates would be better prepare for their jobs. He wrote, "Someday in the future when they assume their own offices, they will be confident in dealing with legal cases, so other people [i.e., legal advisors and clerks] cannot easily manipulate them."[4]

Zhang's experience indicates that an official without formal legal training could know a great deal about the laws. After all, judicial administration was a crucial part of Qing field administration, and local officials often had to deal with legal cases on daily basis. It is hard to believe that an official without any working legal knowledge could fulfill his task, even with the help of legal advisors. Reading the Code, legal treatises, and official handbooks was probably the most important method for officials like Zhang Jixin to get access to legal knowledge and prepare themselves for judicial work. These books were widely printed and disseminated in the Qing period at affordable prices for officials.

REGULATIONS AND POLICIES REGARDING OFFICIALS' LEGAL KNOWLEDGE

The Qing Code required that officials and clerks know the laws; otherwise they would be punished. The statute of "Explaining and Reading the Laws and Regulations" read, "The officials and clerks must read the laws so that they are familiar with them and are able to explain clearly the meaning of the laws in order to analyze and decide matters. At the end of every year, both in the capital and outside, each of them will be examined and checked by his superior. If he cannot explain the law, and does not understand its meaning, then, if he is an official, he will be fined one month's pay. The clerks will receive 40 strokes of the light bamboo."[5] Beside the Code, imperial edicts and administrative regulations also emphasized examinations on officials' legal knowledge. For example, in 1725 the Board of Punishments announced that all lower-ranking officials in the board had to take an examination at the end of each year, in which they were asked to recite a statute selected from the Code. The test results would affect promotions.[6]

From the mid-Qing period, the judicial system faced increasing pressure from accumulated unsolved legal cases. In official discourse, local officials were supposed to clear up case backlogs as soon as possible because these backlogs not only prolonged the suffering of people involved in legal cases but also could lead to social instability. The situation faced by late Qing officials was more challenging than that of their early and mid-Qing predecessors: they had to deal with more legal cases and resolve them more efficiently. Officials made many suggestions to enhance the judicial system's efficiency to solve the backlog problem, including legal training for new officials. In 1860 the Board of Punishments established a regulation that required all new officials in the board to study law and judicial practice with current board officials for two years. Only after finishing this training could they be in charge of reviewing legal cases on their own.[7]

In the following years, some officials tried to persuade the court to extend such legal training to the whole bureaucracy and to establish a new form of legal examination for all newly appointed officials.[8] In response to these recommendations, the Qing court issued an edict in 1866 establishing by far the strictest regulations in late imperial history on new officials' legal training and examination. The edict noted that "statutes and substatutes are related to governance. All officials should always pay particular attention to them, study them thoroughly, and think about them carefully." The edict ordered first that in the capital, ministers of each board would test new officials' knowledge of the board regulations. If new officials were not familiar with the board regulations, they would be sent back to the Board of Civil Office to wait for official openings again (this was intimidating because the waiting process was usually several years or longer in the late Qing), or they could stay in the board for three more years studying laws and administrative regulations. Second, in provinces, governors-general and governors would hold an examination on the Code for officials who were waiting for appointment. Officials' test results would determine whether and when they would get a good position. In this way, the emperor hoped, officials would pay more attention to studying law.[9] Evidence indicates that the policy was carried out, at least in some provinces. The *Beijing Gazette* recorded some test reports from the Shanxi governor in the Guangxu period. In these reports, the governor restated the imperial edict and said that he tested new officials in his province according to the edict, indicating that the policy was in effect until at least the early Guangxu period.[10]

Besides taking legal tests, in the late Qing period many new officials had to go through one-year legal training in the Provincial Auxiliary Court (Fashenju). The Provincial Auxiliary Court first developed in several provinces in the Jiaqing period. At the beginning, it was a temporary institution, usually established in provincial capital cities and designed to assist provincial officials to clear up case backlogs and to investigate capital appeals.[11] Beginning in the Daoguang period, the Provincial Auxiliary Court had gradually been institutionalized and became permanent in most provinces. The Provincial Auxiliary Court had a pivotal role in the provincial judicial system: its responsibilities included dealing with cases of capital appeals, cases submitted by subordinate courts for provincial review, and cases that were overruled by the Board of Punishments and sent back for retrial.[12] The majority of the staff were expectant officials (*houbu*) who held official titles but were still waiting for actual openings. Many provinces also sent new county magistrates to the Provincial Auxiliary Court for legal training, as Zhang Jixin did in Shanxi. For example, in 1897 the Jiangsu governor sent two new county magistrates to the court. In his memorial to the emperor, he explained the reason: "People in those two counties are cunning and deceitful and legal cases are numerous. It is difficult for officials who are not clever and experienced to fulfill the job. . . . These two officials are just entering the official world. They do not have any experience. . . . Therefore I sent them to the Provincial Auxiliary Court and let them assist in hearing trials and drafting sentences in legal cases, through which they can gain useful experience." Similarly, based on the palace memorials that I have read from 1872 to 1910, at least 108 new county magistrates in Shandong, Sichuan, Henan, Shanxi, Guangxi, Zhili, Guangdong, Ningxia, Gansu, Anhui, Jiangsu, Hunan, and Jiangxi stayed in the Provincial Auxiliary Court for about one year to study law and assist in trying legal cases.[13] In the late Qing period, therefore, although there was no written regulation, governors in many provinces embraced the strategy of sending inexperienced new magistrates to the Provincial Auxiliary Court, where they could learn laws and gain judicial experience.

The Provincial Auxiliary Court was a perfect place for inexperienced officials to get practical legal training. Legal cases sent to the court were usually complicated and had been unresolved for years. Dealing with such cases required care and familiarity with the laws. Officials usually were trained to examine case reports, attend trials, and suggest sentences on their own, not depending on private legal advisors. Officials' performance in the Provincial Auxiliary Court was carefully evaluated, and the evaluation would influence their future appointment or promotion. For example, the Shanxi Provincial Auxiliary Court established a regulation in 1836: officials who solved more than thirty cases submitted by subordinate courts for provincial review or more than eight cases of capital appeal within one year could get an early appointment. Bad performance led to administrative fines or prevented future appointments.[14] Beside dealing with real cases, supervisors of the Provincial Auxiliary Court often asked new officials to read and explain statutes and substatutes from the Code. After one-year training of dealing with real cases and studying the Code, new officials could gain valuable legal experience as well as robust legal knowledge.

Qing rulers and officials clearly were concerned about legal knowledge and judicial performance. However, the state systematically removed legal tests from the civil service examinations. The early Qing provincial examination and metropolitan examination required examinees to write five *pan* (hypothetical judicial decisions), the structure and content of which were inherited from the Ming dynasty. In 1756, however, the Qianlong emperor ordered the abolition of all such tests, claiming that the *pan* tests "always follow stale models, make it easy for candidates to guess the answers, and have nothing to do with their real learning."[15] After that, the civil service examinations no longer required legal tests.

Some previous research views the abolition of the *pan* tests as evidence that Qing rulers ignored official candidates' legal training and were unwilling to promote legal education in society.[16] However, abolition of the *pan* tests indicated the Qing rulers' strategy to raise the bar for formal legal education in response to contemporary social demographic changes, rather than a signal of their "ignorance" or "reluctance" regarding officials' legal education. Compared with previous dynasties, the Qing civil service examinations were, because of population growth, far more competitive. Most candidates could not pass the provincial examination and had no hope of becoming officials. The Qing rulers feared that if they emphasized legal tests in the provincial examination, candidates might become "too familiar" with the laws. Failed candidates could easily turn into so-called litigation masters who would "incite litigation" and "disrupt social harmony."[17] For example, Yi Jingqing (b. 1791), investigating censor in the Censorate, submitted a memorial to the throne in 1835. This memorial emphasized that officials should have sufficient legal knowledge and suggested restoring the legal tests in the metropolitan examination. But he insisted that legal tests in the provincial examination were harmful. He wrote in the memorial: "If we require legal tests in the provincial examination, I am afraid that there may be many disadvantages. Not all the candidates taking the provincial examination have good moral qualities. Some tricky students and bad licentiates [*diaosheng liejian*] who know some laws may instigate lawsuits and take advantage of officials."[18] He went on to explain that candidates who passed the provincial examination usually had real learning and good moral qualities, and thus encouraging them to study law and testing their legal knowledge in the metropolitan examination would not create similar problems. Therefore, by emphasizing legal tests and training for entry-level officials and canceling the *pan* tests in the civil service examinations, Qing rulers intended to equip their new officials with legal knowledge just before they assumed office and simultaneously to reduce the chance for those who failed the civil service examinations to abuse the laws and manipulate the legal system.

READING THE CODE IN SCHOLAR-OFFICIALS' DISCOURSE

Providing justice to the people was an important signal of a benevolent government, and the capacity to deal with legal cases promptly and properly was an essential attribute of a magistrate. Most Qing official handbooks stressed the importance of the laws and of officials' skills in dealing with cases. Xu Dong (1792–1865), a magistrate and the author of an influential official handbook, wrote, "Nowadays, talking about administration, the most important things are the laws and punishments [*xingming*] because they not only determine the rewards or punishments of officials but also involve people's life and death."[19]

Official handbooks published in the Qing period encouraged officials, especially newly appointed county magistrates, to carefully read the Code and familiarize themselves with the laws and judicial procedures.[20] For example, Tian Wenjing (1662–1732) and Li Wei (1687–1738), two famous

governors-general in the Yongzheng period, emphasized in their imperially authorized official handbook that new county magistrates should especially pay attention to reading the Code: "*The Great Qing Code* is our
dynasty's constant canon, which establishes laws for ten thousand years. . . .
All officials, scholars, and common people should read the Code carefully
and be able to explain the laws clearly. Especially for county magistrates who
receive an appointment for the first time, they should not put down the book
even for a moment."[21] They also pointed out that statutes and substatutes
from the Code were great guidelines (*dagang*) for an official who needed to
rule the people. New officials should read and discuss law instead of wasting their time on prose and verse. Only through carefully legal study could
officials fulfill their responsibilities.

In additional to this general emphasis on the importance of laws in
administration and governance, officials and scholars pointed out specific
reasons why officials should be familiar with the laws and how legal knowledge facilitated their work. First, many authors stressed that sufficient legal
knowledge enabled officials to try legal cases more efficiently and to avoid
embarrassment in the courtroom. They pointed out that although legal
advisors could help officials prepare most of the paperwork for a legal case,
they could not assist officials to try the case, because Qing regulations did
not allow advisors to appear in court. For example, Fang Dashi (1821–1886),
an experienced local official, wrote in his official handbook: "You can rely
on legal advisors to deal with the paperwork of a case, but you are totally
on your own when trying a case. This is not something that advisors can
do for you. . . . You should remember as many statutes and substatutes as
possible, and during a trial you will know what to do."[22] Similarly, Chu Ying,
a magistrate in the Guangxu period, pointed out in his handbook that legal
advisors "can only help officials handle paperwork but cannot help officials
manage various situations during a trial." Officials thus should always read
legal books carefully and equip themselves with legal knowledge that they
could draw upon when making a decision during a trial. In this way, officials could use the proper language and get useful confessions in the court.
If officials made mistakes out of their ignorance of the laws in the courtroom, Chu Ying wrote, they might become a target of local gossip, and even
a laughingstock (*xiaobing*).[23]

Second, many authors warned new officials that if they were not familiar with the laws, legal advisors and clerks could easily manipulate legal
cases for their own benefit, leading to corruption and injustice in the legal

system. It would not only disturb local administration and increase the number of wronged people but also ruin the officials' career if this corruption and injustice were someday discovered.[24] Litigation masters could also take advantage of officials' ignorance of the laws. Many officials and legal advisors wrote that if officials knew the law well and showed confidence in their legal knowledge during trials, they would scare litigation masters away from the court and thus reduce the number of false accusations and protect local people's wealth and livelihood. Liu Heng (1776–1841) wrote in *Questions and Answers for Fellow Officials in Sichuan* (Shuliao wenda): "How can we prohibit pettifoggers from filing false accusations and harassing our courts? The only method is that we officials read *The Great Qing Code* carefully over and over again." Wang Huizu (1730–1807) also pointed out in his famous handbook *Superfluous Sayings about Learning to Administer* (Xuezhi shuozhui) that officials should thoroughly study the laws. During a trial, officials could not conveniently consult with their legal advisors. If officials showed any hesitation when making a decision, litigation masters would immediately know that the officials did not know the laws well and would take advantage of this in the future. On the other hand, if officials were familiar with the laws and could make proper decisions promptly in the court, litigation masters would submit out of awe and the number of false complaints would naturally decrease. It would reduce the local judicial burden and greatly benefit officials.[25]

Qing officials universally blamed legal advisors, clerks, and pettifoggers for many administrative and social problems, such as corruption, case backlogs, false accusations, and high litigation rates. Although many officials' accusations against legal advisors, clerks, and pettifoggers were false or unfair, their fear of them was real.[26] Officials often implied that a magistrate or prefect faced a rather challenging situation in the late imperial period: they were trying to govern a yamen and local society where the people themselves were familiar with the laws. In an age of abundant and high-quality commercial printing, law and legal knowledge, which had been the secret and privileged information of officials and the government, became more widely disseminated in print and more affordable as well. Reading the Code and studying legal knowledge, therefore, were necessary for officials to survive in this legally sophisticated bureaucracy and society.

Third, some Qing scholars pointed out that reading the Code was a method of self-examination (*zixing*). By carefully studying the laws from reading the Code, one could become a better gentleman and a more competent official in the future. For example, Bao Shichen (1775–1855), an influential thinker and a private advisor in the early nineteenth century, expressed this idea specifically in an article titled "An Explanation for Reading the Code" (Dulü shuo):

> I always encourage my friends and students who are devoted to learning to read the Code. Some think that it is because they will be officials in the future and studying the laws will prevent them from being deceived by private legal advisors. But my true reason is not that. I see many talented people . . . indulge themselves and easily engage in evil and heterodox things. . . . How can they be corrected and saved from these evil things? The only way is to let them read the Code and examine their deeds according to the laws. When they are aware of the punishments for these deeds, they must feel shamed and scared. Therefore, reading the Code is an essential way of self-examination.[27]

Bao Shichen continued that one would try hard to atone for his wrong deeds if he felt scared and ashamed. Such a person would be willing to help people, uphold education for local society, and do good deeds to benefit the world. When becoming an official in the future, he could turn out to be a careful and considerate official who would devote himself to benefiting local society. Reading the Code and studying legal knowledge, therefore, not only would benefit judicial administration and local society but also would lead scholar-officials to self-examination and self-cultivation and would allow them to "complete themselves as gentlemen" (chengren).[28]

Bao Shichen was not alone in viewing law as more than a pure (amoral) instrument for regulating the society, useful only where Confucian moral education failed, but rather as essential part of moral self-cultivation. Knowing the laws would generate fear and restraint. When writing about reading the Code and studying the laws, Qing scholar-officials frequently invoked expressions such as "regulating oneself" (lüji), "cultivating oneself" (xiushen), "establishing oneself in life" (liming), and "completing oneself as a man" (chengren), which were usually associated with Confucian self-moral cultivation. As a Qing official wrote about reading the Code: "Every scholar and gentleman should have this book on his desk. It will assist him in self-cultivation (xiushen) and establish him in life (liming). . . . Through reading the Code, he will be cautious not to commit crimes. This will greatly benefit people." Reading the Code not only contributed to scholar-officials' self-cultivation, but also would benefit people and the world in the long run. As Zhang Sichang, Guangdong judicial commissioner, wrote in his preface to *The Great Qing Code with Collective Annotations* (Da Qing lü jizhu) in 1745: "This book can help the reader establish himself [*shushen*] in the short run, and can benefit the world [*shanshi*] in the long run. The book will contribute to governance when we distribute it and perform according to it. Can we say that it is not a 'useful book' [*youyong zhi shu*]?"[29]

Emphasis on officials reading the Code also was in accord with a changing attitude toward learning and a new sense of the ideal role of officials in the late imperial period. As noted at the beginning of the chapter, the late Qing period witnessed a revival of substantive learning (*shixue*) and statecraft thought. Scholars associated with substantive learning upheld the idea that learning should be of use (*youyong*)—that is, useful for cultivating oneself and regulating the world. Facing the quite complicated and sophisticated late imperial society, many scholars and officials who embraced statecraft thought that guiding the people through moral correctness and personal example (the ideal Confucian style of administration) was not enough. Officials should be versed in various practical techniques and skills in areas such as hydraulic engineering, relief management, judicial administration, and so on.[30] The importance of techniques and knowledge to rule was emphasized, and legal knowledge was an important part of the skill set that officials must have. Wasting time in "empty" literary production, such as writing poems about clouds and wind and memorizing examination-oriented essays, was strongly opposed. Instead, scholar-officials should spend their time in reading useful books to learn practical skills that would order the world and benefit the people.

USEFUL BOOKS AND QING OFFICIALS' PERSONAL LAW LIBRARIES

The flourishing book market in the Qing eased officials' access to the Code and other legal and administrative books. Many officials and legal advisors owned one or several commercial editions of the Code. They kept the book on top of their desks for ready reference. As a governor in the Daoguang period observed: "Regarding books like *The Great Qing Code* and *Washing Away of Wrongs* [Xiyuanlu], every official certainly has them on his desk."[31] The ownership of the Code transformed how officials read the book and gained access to the laws. The Code and a number of other commercially printed books formed a core bibliography and a foundation of legal and administrative knowledge on which many Qing officials reached a consensus. Among more than seventy official handbooks I have read, three include detailed reading lists for officials. Using these lists as a foundation, this section explores what books officials bought and what books they thought they should read.

The first reading list is from Fang Dashi's *Ordinary Sayings* (Pingping yan), an official handbook published in 1878. Fang was a Hunan native with a clear statecraft orientation. He was a well-acknowledged competent official, and achieved most of his accomplishments between 1855 and 1878 when working as county magistrate and then prefect in Hubei.[32] During his years as an official, Fang compiled an instructive manuscript on how to be a good official, intending to pass it down as family instructions (*jiaxun*) to his sons and grandsons who were studying for the civil service examinations.[33] The content of *Ordinary Sayings* was full of practical instructions (altogether 284 tips) on being an official in the troublesome late Qing period. Fang wrote in a direct, plain, and easy-to-understand way, just like a father teaching his sons. He sounded sincere and honest, with little embellishment or self-promotion. Fang's 284 tips cover a variety of aspects of the official world at the time.

One instruction Fang provided in the book was that "expectant officials should read books" (*houbu yi dushu*). He pointed out that the years of being an expectant official were the perfect time to read useful books and become prepared for future official work. Fang then provided a list of thirty-eight books that expectant officials should read. Almost all related to practical aspects of administration and the functioning of local government, which covered the areas of law, agriculture, famine relief, hydraulic engineering, and military strategy. Fang excluded genres popular among Qing literati, such as the Confucian classics, dynastic histories, and belles lettres, explaining, "When you become an official, you should no longer act as a student staying at home and reading such books all day." Officials must read useful books that concerned practical administrative skills and legal knowledge. "Our dynasty establishes officials originally for the sake of the common people," Fang argued, so officials should not waste their time on reading books and learning useless skills that "were not related to the common people's difficulties and sufferings."[34]

Fang prescribed not only dynastic laws and regulations, such as the must-read Code and *Administrative Sanctions* (Chufen zeli), but also various

TABLE 3.1. Books Relating to Laws in the Three Reading Lists

	Liu Heng	Fang Dashi	Yanchang
Dynastic laws	*Da Qing lüli* 大清律例	*Da Qing lüli* *Da Qing huidian* 大清會典	*Da Qing lüli* *Da Qing huidian*
Administrative regulations	*Chufen zeli* 處分則例	*Chufen zeli* *Xuezheng quanshu* 學政全書	*Liubu chufen zeli* 六部處分則例 *Gebu gesi zeli* 各部各司則例 *Libu xinding baoju zhangcheng* 吏部新定保舉章程
Collections of case precedents	*Bo'an xinbian* 駁案新編 *Luzhou gong'an* 鹿州公案	*Bo'an xinbian xubian* 駁案新編續編 *Luzhou gong'an* *Xing'an huilan* 刑案匯覽 *Zheyu guijian* 折獄龜鑒	*Bo'an xinbian xubian* *Qiushen shihuan bijiao* 秋審實緩比較
Official handbooks	*Fuhui quanshu* 福惠全書 *Zuozhi yaoyan* 佐治藥言 *Xuezhi yishuo* 學治臆說 *Shizheng pian* 實政篇	*Fuhui quanshu* *Zuozhi yaoyan* *Xuezhi yishuo* *Shizheng lu* 實政錄 *Menghenlu jiechao* 夢痕錄節鈔 *Yongli yongyan* 庸吏庸言 *Shuliao wenda* 蜀僚問答	*Fuhui quanshu* *Juguan rixing lu* 居官日省錄
Forensic handbooks		*Xiyuanlu* 洗冤錄	*Xiyuanlu xiangjie* 洗冤錄詳節
Legal handbooks			*Junwei daoli biao* 軍衛道里表 *Lüli bianlan* 律例便覽 *Mingfa zhizhang* 名法指掌 *Lübiao* 律表
Treaties		*Geguo tongshang tiaoyue* 各國通商條約	

Sources: Fang Dashi, *Pingping yan*, juan 1, 3a–7a; Liu Heng, *Shuliao wenda*, 15b–16a; Yanchang, *Shiyi xuzhi*, juan 1, 9a–11a.

books that would help officials comprehend the laws and apply them in practice (see table 3.1). He wrote: "Officials should deem laws and regulations their teachers [*yi faling weishi*]." He recommended that expectant officials read legal case collections including the *Conspectus of Legal Cases* and *New and Expanded Compilations of Legal Cases Overruled by the Board* (Bo'an xinbian xubian). Reading collections of case reports would help officials understand real meanings of the laws and apply them accurately when sentencing a case. "Case precedents usually have complicated plots," he wrote next to his recommended case collections, "and many of them explain the detailed applications of the laws that the Code does not specifically indicate." Beside case collections, he also recommended several popular official handbooks that contained chapters explaining the laws and legal procedures based on local officials' own experiences, such as the *Complete Book concerning Happiness and Benevolence* (Fuhui quanshu) and *Admonitions on Assisting with Governance* (Zuozhi yaoyan). According to Fang, books about the laws were obviously useful books, and reading them would not only contribute to administration and society but would also benefit the officials' own career.

Fang Dashi was not alone among Qing scholar-officials who included the Code, case collections, and official handbooks in their recommended reading list. Liu Heng, an established local official and the author of several influential official handbooks in the late Qing, wrote in *Questions and Answers for Fellow Officials in Sichuan* (Shuliao wenda): "Some people ask me whether there are other books besides the Code that contribute to governance." Liu Heng then answered with a short list of famous official handbooks and collections of legal cases (see table 3.1). In Liu's opinion the Code was obviously the most important book for officials to read, but official handbooks and collections of legal cases were also "essential books to good governance."[35] Almost all of the books in Liu Heng's reading list also appeared in Fang Dashi's list. The two men, and probably many other contemporary scholar-officials, believed that officials must carefully read this core bibliography of useful books.

The third book list comes from Yanchang, a Manchu official of the late Qing period. In his official handbook *Essential Knowledge for Administrative Affairs* (Shiyi xuzhi), Yanchang listed more than fifty-one books that he took with him when he left Beijing for his appointment as prefect in Xunzhou, Guangxi.[36] Yanchang's books can be grouped into seven categories: books about laws and regulations, imperial edicts, official handbooks, books relevant to ritual performance, books about history and geography, literature, and medical books. Yanchang's list is longer and more diverse than Fang Dashi's. While Fang excluded imperial edicts, historical and geographic works (except model officials' biographies), literature, and medical books, Yanchang listed many of these works—he even brought popular novels like *Strange Tales from the Liao Studio* (Liaozhai zhiyi) and *Dream of the Red Chamber* (Hongloumeng). The two lists differ in that Fang Dashi's was composed of books officials were supposed to read, but Yanchang's consisted of the books he actually took with him, including those he might want to read in his spare time. Obviously, Yanchang was not only concerned with how to be a competent official and how to deal with administrative and legal challenges in local government; he also considered his health, entertainment, and future promotion.

Although Yanchang did not have so obvious a connection with the substantive learning and statecraft movements as Fang Dashi did, and he did not include as many statecraft books, he and Fang shared the same interest in law books and official handbooks. Yanchang brought at least eleven books about laws and regulations (table 3.1). Yanchang listed more books about laws and regulations than books in any other category. He thought that he would need these legal books as a prefect in Guangxi. Judging from the legal books he chose, his main concern was his own official career, which he closely related to his performance in dealing with legal cases in his jurisdiction. He included several books about the regulations of officials' promotions and punishments. He brought at least two books of tables of laws (*Guide for Clarifying the Laws* and *Chart for Statutes*), a popular genre of Qing legal handbook that reorganized simplified statutes and substatutes into tables so that officials could easily locate and cite them.[37] Like Fang Dashi and Liu Heng, Yanchang also included several collections of legal case reports and official handbooks in his list. Therefore, Yanchang's personal law library could provide him with a whole range of legal knowledge that he might use in office, from the statutes, substatutes, administrative regulations, and case precedents to various books for simplifying, clarifying, reorganizing, and explaining these laws and regulations.

If the authors of these three lists are representative, Qing officials, especially magistrates and prefects in the late Qing period, included many legal books in their reading list and personal library. Fang Dashi, Liu Heng, and Yanchang were all magistrates or prefects working in local government for many years. Their experience told them that legal books were important for their job, and thus they all recommended that their fellow officials buy and read these legal books. They also agreed that besides the most important legal book—the Code—officials also needed to read and possess other books about laws and regulations, including administrative regulations, legal treatises, and official handbooks. The three reading lists overlap with each other in terms of the titles and genres of the legal books that the authors recommended reading. This indicates that officials, at least in the late Qing period, probably agreed on a core bibliography for officials to build their legal and administrative knowledge. Most of these books were published by commercial publishing houses and circulated in the public book market.

READING THE CODE

Many Qing officials agreed that reading the Code was important, and they also owned the book and included it in their reading lists. But possessing the Code was one thing, and reading it, especially reading and understanding it efficiently and effectively, was another. The Code was notorious for its complexity and length. Although its compilers had a clear principle of classification in their mind—they put these statutes and substatutes into six categories based on the division of labor of the six boards in the central government—in fact many statutes and substatutes dealing with similar crimes were spread across various chapters. Another barrier to understanding were the numerous minutely different punishments for slightly different crimes. The Code compilers tried to assign exact punishments for every crime in every circumstance. If readers of the Code did not read with extreme care, they would soon be lost in the seas of circumstances that seemed similar but led to different punishments. Although most officials were advanced readers with years of classical training, they usually found reading the Code and thoroughly understanding the laws difficult. As one Qing official commented, "The contents of the Code are complex, lengthy, redundant . . . and tedious; it is quite easy to fall asleep when you read it."[38]

To help officials overcome these difficulties, authors of many official handbooks summarized the theories and methods of reading the Code, usually based on their own reading experience. Most authors admitted that it was impractical for an official to read and remember every single statute and substatute in the Code. They suggested officials focus on the chapters that were most useful for them. As Wang Mingde, a renowned legal expert of the early Qing, pointed out, the first principle of reading the Code was to "grasp the important points." He noted that reading the Code was quite different from reading Confucian classics: "If you intend to read the entire Code from beginning to end and make notes on everything, just as an old Confucian scholar or a young student reads the classics, you will soon get tired, lost in the complexity of the content, and even reluctant to open the book again." Wang went on to point out that the situation would become even worse when officials were reading under pressure: "When there are major legal cases unresolved and deadlines impending, you will find that your mind goes blank, your heart beats fast, and your eyes become dizzy." Under such circumstances, in Wang's opinion, it was almost impossible for officials to effectively read and understand the Code. Wang Mingde's solution was to select the most important chapters—"General Public Disorder and Theft," "Homicide," and "Affrays and Blows"—to read first and most carefully. Wang pointed out that these chapters included only about seventy statutes and 130 substatutes. He also emphasized that officials should pay special attention to the first two chapters of "Terminology of the Statutes and Substatutes," which explained the general principles of punishments and specific terms used in the Code. As for the method of reading these important chapters, Wang Mingde suggested that officials not try to read the whole text at one time, but try to read several statutes every day, making notes and considering the exact meanings of each paragraph, each section, each sentence, and even each character. By frequently reviewing what they had read, officials could grasp the exact meanings of these statutes and substatutes within several months.[39]

Another renowned legal expert, Wang Huizu, also had a method for reading the Code. Because he had worked as a legal advisor for years before he became a county magistrate, he understood the differences between the two jobs and pointed out that because legal advisors made a living based on their legal expertise, they needed to remember all of the statutes and substatutes. Officials, on the other hand, had little spare time, and thus they should study the chapters that were most relevant to the cases they heard, such as "Terminology of the Statutes and Substatutes," "Fields and Houses," "Marriage," "General Public Disorder and Theft," "Homicide," "Affrays and Blows," "Judicial Procedure and Litigation," "Forgeries and Counterfeiting," "Fornication," "Miscellaneous Offenses," and "Judicial Judgments and Prisoners." For the chapters in the Code that had little relation with local criminal and civil cases, such as chapters relating to administration, rites, military, and public works, Wang Huizu implied that officials could leave them to their advisors.[40]

Besides focusing on important chapters, many Qing officials indicated that discussions with legal advisors would help them read the Code more efficiently. Liu Heng wrote that before hearing a case, officials should review the statutes and substatutes relating to the case. They should read them carefully and discuss them with their private legal advisors. Case by case, officials could accumulate some legal knowledge, and in the long run, they could grasp the meanings and applications of the laws in the Code.[41] Muhan (1804–1863), a Manchu magistrate, also pointed out that officials should spend time discussing the laws and legal cases with their legal advisors. He said that every advisor would be willing to discuss the laws if officials requested help modestly and showed true eagerness to learn. Officials could also carefully read cases that had been concluded, learning how to apply the law in practice. In this way, officials could at least have a general idea about the statutes and substatutes of the Code, even if they could not remember all of them, enabling them to deal with cases by themselves when their legal advisors were on leave.[42]

As suggested by the book lists, many officials pointed out that the Code should be read in conjunction with other books and legal documents, especially official handbooks, case reports, and administrative regulations. Only through closely reading the Code along with these books could officials gain comprehensive legal knowledge that enabled them to deal with actual legal cases in practice. For example, Liu Heng wrote in *Questions and Answers for Fellow Officials in Sichuan* that after officials became familiar with the statutes and substatutes of the Code, they must read the *New Compilation of Legal Cases Overruled by the Board* (Bo'an xinbian) and *Administrative Sanctions* (Chufen zeli). When closely reading the legal cases reports, Liu wrote, officials could clarify the subtle differences among various similar substatutes and think about how the laws were applied in practice, and when reading the administrative sanctions, officials could be alert to various administrative violations in judicial procedures, and if they knew the boundaries, they could become more confident when dealing with cases.[43] Thus, in Liu Heng's opinion, officials should read these three books (the Code, the case report collections, and the administrative sanctions) together.

By following these methods, reading the Code and studying the laws seemed less intimidating for officials. While legal advisors probably had to spend several years to go through legal training, many officials mentioned that several months were enough for them to read the Code and familiarize themselves with the laws that they would use in their work. For example, Wang Huizu said that following his method, officials could learn enough legal knowledge for their work within only a few months. Liu Heng recalled his experience of reading the Code and said that it only took him eight months to thoroughly understand the laws.[44]

Qing officials thus built up their legal knowledge mainly through three channels: reading the Code itself, together with official handbooks, collections of case reports, and administrative regulations, all of which they could easily obtain from the book market; consultation with their legal advisors about law and judicial practice; and judicial practice with real cases in local governments. Among them, carefully reading the Code was the most important channel, and Qing officials advised that the reading should be conducted selectively but intensively, accumulating legal knowledge bit by bit every day.

THE CODE AS TEXT

In *A History of Reading in the West*, Guglielmo Cavallo and Roger Chartier point out that "any history of the practice of reading is . . . necessarily a history of both written objects and the testimonies left by their readers."[45] The previous section discusses what readers wrote about their methods of reading the Code and accumulating legal knowledge. This section will focus on the physical aspects of the Code, exploring how the printing format and the organization of the text of the Code, especially those of three-register-per-page commercial editions, influenced Qing readers' reading experiences and their interpretation and application of the laws.

In the three-register printing format, commercial editors kept the original text from the imperial editions of the Code in the bottom register and added a cross-index in the upper register. In the middle register, they included private commentaries, case precedents, and administrative regulations. In commercial editions, the proportion of additional legal information was usually far larger than that of the original statutes and substatutes from imperial editions. For example, in the imperial edition of the Code published in 1870, the "Fornication" (Fanjian) article has only one statute and fourteen substatutes. In a commercial edition published in 1873, the editors attached to the article at least twenty-eight case precedents, eight paragraphs of commentaries, two administrative regulations, and a cross-index.[46]

The three-register printing format was a product of the evolution of commercial printing culture since the late Ming. The multiple-register printing format first became popular in the Wanli period (1573–1620).[47] Late Ming commercial publishers widely adopted the multiregister printing format in several popular genres, such as drama miscellanies and everyday encyclopedias (*riyong leishu*). In most cases, the texts that were printed in different registers on the same page are unrelated to each other. In terms of late Ming drama miscellanies, literary scholar Shang Wei argues, the multiregister printing format has at least two implications. On the one hand, "it served as a means for ordering otherwise disorganized text"; on the other, it "presented readers with choices, allowing them to select what to read as they turned from page to page." Historian Yuming He also points out that the multiregister layout constantly interrupted the linear temporality of the reading process. Through providing choices, readers of multiple-register imprints could take a more active role in selecting texts, shaping the connections, and negotiating the meanings of the texts. The multiregister format also transformed the relationship of the texts printed in different registers, fostering competition among the texts. That editors utilized a multiregister printing format and presented different texts in different registers on the same page "dramatizes not merely choice but the competition to be chosen."[48]

Qing publishers adopted this multiregister printing format in commercial editions of the Code. While late Ming publishers often printed unrelated and heterogeneous texts on the same page, Qing editors of the Code organized texts in the middle and upper register following the content of imperially promulgated statutes and substatutes in the bottom register. Statutes and substatutes in the bottom register played the leading role in relation to the texts in the other two registers. Commentaries and case precedents usually supplemented the statutes and substatutes below and defined various subtle circumstances of crimes and suggested suitable punishments that the statutes and substatutes did not specify. The editors of *Amalgamated Compilation of the Great Qing Code* (Da Qing lüli huizuan) explained why they incorporated case precedents in their book: "As for the cases that do not perfectly fit any statute and substatute, we must weigh and consider the specific situations to decide sentences. Case precedents are used to assist statutes and substatutes. . . . Thus here we specially select case precedents that are extremely essential and important but do not rigidly adhere to the statues and substatutes. We include them in our compilation . . . for readers' reference."[49]

Similar statements were ubiquitous in the "General Editorial Principles" of commercial editions of the Code. Generally speaking, editors selected case precedents based on two basic principles. First, as in the above example, case precedents should not "rigidly adhere to the statutes and substatutes"; otherwise it would be redundant to include them in the Code. Most case precedents appear to define specific circumstances and corresponding sentences that statutes and substatutes did not clearly explain. Second, editors announced that they would include only case precedents that "do not contradict the statutes and substatutes" (*yu lüli bubei*). Rejecting cases deemed "too strange" or "too exceptional," editors intended to establish the texts of case precedents in the middle register as a reliable and coherent legal reference work, helping judges decide sentences for difficult cases and broadening readers' perspectives on the law.[50]

Some case precedents in the middle register represented changes in the judicial application of some old statutes, instructing readers to pay close attention to recent judicial practice rather than rigidly following the literal meanings of statutes. An example was the case precedent attached to the statute of "Marrying Someone with the Same Surname." Established as early as the Tang period (618–907), the statute strictly banned marriage between two people with the same surname: "In every case of marriage between two people with the same surname [the one in charge of the marriage, together with the man and woman] will each receive 60 strokes of the heavy bamboo, and the marriage will be dissolved."[51]

The centuries-old statute had survived various revisions and was kept in the Code throughout the late imperial period. However, the case precedent attached to the statute, which was printed in the middle register above the statute, indicates changes in judicial practice. In this 1789 case precedent, Tang Huajing killed his wife, Tang *shi*, in a fight. Because both he and his wife had the same surname, their marriage was void according to the statute. Tang Huajing should therefore have been sentenced according to the article "Engaging in an Affray [and Killing] or Intentionally Killing Another," which dealt with murder of a person with no family connection in a fight, the punishment for which was decapitation after the autumn assizes. However, officials of the Board of Punishments were not satisfied with the original sentence and argued that Tang Huajing and Tang *shi* were living together and had children, so their marriage was valid, even though it violated the law. Thus, Tang Huajing should be sentenced according to the statute on a husband killing his own wife in a fight, the punishment for which was strangulation after the autumn assizes, two degrees lower than the original sentence.

The board further explained in the case precedent that in "remote and backward places" (*qiongxiang pirang*) marriages between two people who had the same surname were quite common. "We should not abolish the established rules of the law simply because people frequently violate the law out of ignorance;" the board officials wrote, "but we should also not disregard the obligation of marriage between a husband and a wife [*fufu mingfen*] only because they committed the minor offense of 'marrying someone with the same surname.'" Officials of the board thus neither intended to abolish the law nor were willing to strictly apply it to every case in judicial practice. Editors of commercial editions incorporated the case precedent in the middle register right above the statute, preceded by a comment reminding readers to follow the principles of the case precedent, rather than the outdated statute: "What the Great Board [i.e., the Board of Punishments] has discussed makes perfect sense. Yamens that have judicial responsibilities should follow it. Thus we especially attach [this case precedent] for readers' reference."[52] Case precedents such as the above provided important and practical legal information for judges. They were important supplements and updates of imperially promulgated statutes and substatutes from the Code, which readers would not know about if they read only the imperial editions of the Code.

Private commentaries played a similar role to leading cases in defining various circumstances that original statutes and substatutes did not specify. In many cases, private commentaries also set out specific rules for the application of statutes and illustrated key concepts and key terms of the Code. Editors usually put commentaries before case precedents in the middle register, indicating that commentaries were of greater importance. In the bottom register, private commentaries were printed together with imperially authorized "small commentaries." The narrative of private commentaries sounded decisive and authoritative. Although private commentaries were subservient to statutes and substatutes and did not intentionally challenge the authority of the imperially promulgated laws,[53] they gave detailed interpretations of statutes and substatutes, sometimes defining and redefining the circumstances and potential applications of the laws. For example, in article 366, "Fornication," the statute mentioned "selling one's wife to her adulterous lover" (*jiamai yu jianfu*): "As for consensual fornication [*hejian*] . . . the adulterous wife will be sold or married to another according to her husband's wishes. If he wishes to keep her, he may. If she is married or sold to the adulterous lover, the adulterous lover and the real husband will both receive 80 strokes of the heavy bamboo."[54] The statute gave the husband the right to sell his adulterous wife to someone else but strictly banned him from marrying or selling her to her adulterous lover.

The middle-register commentaries printed above the statute, however, redefined the prerequisite of this statute: "This 'marrying and selling to the adulterous lover' only applies to those whose adulterous behavior has already been formally prosecuted. As for the husband who does not accuse his wife's adultery in court but marries or sells his wife to the adulterous lover . . . it should refer to the statute 'Facilitating and Tolerating the Wife's or Concubine's Fornication.' . . . The real husband will receive 100 strokes of heavy bamboo. The punishment that the wife and the adulterous lover receive will follow the original statute."[55] Although the original statute and the following substatutes did not confine the boundary of the "marrying and selling to the adulterous lover" law, the commentary specifically defined that the law could only be applied to those who went through judicial procedures and then married or sold convicted wives to adulterous lovers. For those who married or sold wives to adulterous lovers without formally prosecuting the adulterous behavior, the commentary stipulated that the husband would receive one hundred strokes of heavy bamboo according to another article in the Code, rather than the original eighty strokes in this article. Similar redefinitions or reinterpretations by private commentaries on the laws were prevalent in commercial editions of the Code.

In many cases middle-register commentaries provided updated explanations for old statutes and told readers to adapt obsolete statutes and substatutes to conform with contemporary judicial practice. For example, article 112, "Forcibly Taking in Marriage the Wife or Daughter of an Honorable Family," said, "In all cases where a person who is influential and strong [haoqiang shili zhi ren] forcibly takes the wife or daughter of an honorable family, and wrongfully makes her his wife or concubine, he will be punished with strangulation with delay."[56] The original statute emphasized that the law was only applied to those who were "influential and strong." The middle-register commentary, however, completely overthrew this prerequisite: "As for cases nowadays, no matter what kind of person he is, if he forcibly takes another person's wife or daughter as his own wife, he should be sentenced according to this statute. It is not necessary to that he be influential or powerful."[57] By denying "being influential and powerful" as a prerequisite of the statute, the commentary redefined the boundary of the contemporary application of the statute. Sometimes middle-register commentaries also reminded readers of updates to the laws. Because the Qing updated substatutes more frequently than statutes, old statutes kept in the Code sometimes contradicted newly established substatutes. Commercial editors reminded readers of this in the middle register by adding commentaries such as "there are new substatutes" above old statutes. In this way, they hoped readers would not easily make the mistake of citing outdated statutes when sentencing legal cases.

While readers of commercial editions of the Code did not have the same freedom as readers of late Ming multiregister printed literary works to choose preferred texts among different registers, there remained a sense of competition among the texts of different registers among Qing readers. Printing private commentaries and case precedents together with imperially authorized statutes and substatutes enhanced the authority of commentaries and case precedents, especially after the rise of *Comprehensive Integration* editions, when commercial editions formed a well-accepted standard for selecting commentaries and case precedents. In other words, commercial editions of the Code published after the late Qianlong period established a standardized database of commentaries and case precedents that leading legal experts deemed authoritative and applicable in judicial practice. Private commentaries and case precedents played an increasingly important role in judicial practice as a "source of law" in the Qing period.[58] The popularity of commercial editions of the three-register-per-page printing format might have contributed to this change in the Qing judicial administration. Commercial editions contained a well-accepted database of private commentaries and case precedents as supplements and instructions to the imperially promulgated laws. Together they formed a common foundation of the laws that would be applied in judicial practice. The multiregister printing format enabled Qing readers to connect additional legal information to the imperial laws, compare it with the imperial laws, and choose the most exact and applicable legal information.

Another salient feature of commercial editions of the Code is that they were designed to enable readers to quickly search and locate certain information, in a way similar to that of modern dictionaries and reference books. Commercial editions usually have a clear and well-organized general index. Moreover, in the margin of each page, commercial editors usually printed the title of the book, chapter (*juan*) number, chapter name, respective *juan* and article page numbers, and article title. Readers could thus find brief information without reading the text and could conveniently locate the pages they needed to consult. In "General Editorial Principles," editors said they expected their readers would search for information in their books by jumping from one section to another or quickly turning pages. They used terms to describe their readers' reading pattern, such as "turning over the leaves and reading" (*fanyue*), "searching" (*sousuo*), "searching and reading" (*jianyue*), and "looking for" (*xunqiu*).[59] Both the design of the book and the terms used by editors indicate that readers were expected to browse the Code quickly, looking for useful information.

The cross-index printed in the upper register was another convenient tool for locating statutes and substatutes. In the Code, it was common that similar or related statutes and substatutes were compiled into different chapters. For example, although article 292, "Killing in Play, Mistaken Killing; the Unintentional Killing or Injuring of Another," in "Laws relating to the Board of Punishments" mentions the general definition of and punishments for accidentally killing someone, statutes and substatutes for accidental killing in specific circumstances are dispersed in other chapters of the Code, such as "killing someone in public construction work because of using bad materials" and "drowning someone in a ferry because of ignoring strong wind and big waves," respectively in the "Laws relating to the Board of Works" and the "Laws relating to the Board of War." If a reader used only article 292 to deal with accidental killing cases, he might cite the wrong statute. The cross-index reminded readers to refer to all of the related statutes and substatutes scattered in different chapters of the Code and helped them find the most relevant law according to the circumstances of a case. For example, in article 292, commercial editors added a cross-index to the upper register that included at least fourteen items, enumerating all of the other statutes and substatutes relating to accidental or unintentional killing in various chapters.[60] Thanks to the cross-index, readers without specific legal training could easily locate all of the related statutes and substatutes, compare them with one another, and choose the most relevant one. This made Qing judicial officials' and legal advisors' task of looking for the best statute or substatute when sentencing cases much less difficult.

CONCLUSION

It has been argued that although a reading revolution resulting from the rise of silent and extensive reading was associated with the printing revolution in early modern Europe, a similar phenomenon did not occur in late imperial China because the Song and Ming printing revolution had only a limited impact on the Chinese literati's reading experiences, in which reading aloud and intensively were commendable behavior and essential to the literati's cultural identity.[61] In terms of reading Confucian classics and literary works, this argument is well founded and convincing. Reading experiences became increasing diverse in late imperial Chinese society, however, due to the development of the publishing industry and the rise of various genres of printed books. Reading methods and experiences of readers of the Qing Code were relatively sophisticated. Commercial editions of the Code functioned as two different kinds of texts in terms of reading practices: portions of the text were to be read through by officials to provide an overview of certain important sections of the Code; then the Code could be used as consultative or reference texts—that is, the readers, having gained a sense of basic information about the laws, could rely on the paratextual aids provided by the publishers to examine more closely specific portions of the text that were relevant to their cases. No evidence indicates that Qing readers read the Code aloud. Qing readers did not need to intensively read all parts of the Code and carefully recite the content of the book. The Code was widely available and affordable and thus did not need to be memorized and recited.

Reading the Code was the most important means for officials to obtain legal knowledge. Commercial editions not only provided up-to-date legal information but also made it easier for readers to read, understand, and apply that information in judicial practice. The commercial publishing industry provided a whole range of printed books, including all of the books that formed the core bibliography of Qing legal and administrative knowledge. The government emphasized that officials must read the Code and become familiar with the laws before they assumed office and established various tests and regulations of newly appointed officials' legal knowledge. Qing scholar-officials also generally thought that the laws and legal information were quite useful in terms of being a capable official and fulfilling one's official responsibilities. They published handbooks, instructing fellow officials on why and how they should read the Code. Even though officials did not receive any formal dedicated legal training, there is ample evidence that they had every opportunity, though commercial editions of the Code—supplemented with useful commentary and case examples—to learn the law and judicial practice.

Officials and legal advisors had access to commercial editions of the Code, enabling them to rely on the Code in sentencing. Commercial editions that used the three-register-per-page printing format and included the cross-index, private commentaries, administrative regulations, and case precedents, fundamentally transformed Qing people's reading experience as well as their understanding and application of the laws. Commercial editions of the Code deciphered legal knowledge, making it accessible and understandable for people without professional legal training. They provided detailed interpretations of the statutes and substatutes, reminded readers of updates and contemporary applications of the laws, and enabled readers to quickly locate related statutes and substatutes from different chapters. Commercial editions made it much less intimidating for readers to read, understand, and apply the laws. Moreover, commercial editions offered readers choices, from either the imperial laws or additional legal information incorporated by commercial editors or both. Commercial editions fundamentally changed the relationship between the imperially promulgated laws and legal information that was not authorized by the state. The judicial authority of private commentaries and case precedents was enhanced, and their function as a source of law was increasingly recognized. Qing judicial officials and their legal advisors often referred to private commentaries and case precedents in legal reasoning and judicial sentences. Editors of commercial editions of the Code used their expert knowledge and access to print to shape legal culture independent of the state. To some extent, therefore, commercial editions defined and redefined both the laws their applications in judicial practice.

4 LAW AND LEGAL INFORMATION IN POPULAR HANDBOOKS

IN THE EARLY JIAQING PERIOD, A COMMONER NAMED CHENG Xiangzhi traveled from a remote and mountainous county named Lushan, Henan, all the way to Beijing. His purpose was to file a capital appeal to the Censorate accusing clerks and runners in his county of corruption and overtaxation. Following the standard procedure of the capital appeal, the case was sent back directly to the Henan governor's office for investigation and trial.[1] During the investigation, the governor found that Cheng's accusation was completely fabricated. It turned out that Cheng's true purpose in filing the appeal was to avoid being prosecuted and having to pay his debts. He had previously acted as a middleman for his friend to borrow fifty taels of silver from a local rich man. Then the friend returned the money to Cheng and asked him to pass it on to the creditor. Cheng somehow embezzled it and denied that he had received any money. A lawsuit against Cheng was filed in the county court, and apparently, Cheng lost the case. Clerks and runners then fiercely pressed Cheng to pay the money back.

Since Cheng had no means to pay such a large amount of money, he turned to his younger brother, Cheng Xiuzhi, for help. After some discussion, the Cheng brothers decided to fabricate an accusation and file a capital appeal. Xiuzhi drafted an accusation against the clerks and runners. Xiangzhi then took the accusation to Beijing. They hoped that the capital appeal would scare off the yamen underlings and that the complicated investigation procedures involved in the capital appeal would delay the clerks and runners by putting them in prolonged detention. Xiangzhi would thus be free from their harassment. However, the provincial officials detected their scheme. When searching the Cheng brothers' home, the officials found four volumes of *The Thunder That Startles Heaven* (*Jingtianlei*, abbreviated as *Thunder* hereafter)—a notorious "litigation masters' secret handbook" strictly prohibited under the law. Under harsh interrogation and torture, the Cheng brothers insisted this was the first time they had written such an accusation. Nonetheless, the governor sentenced them to permanent exile based on the "Habituated Litigation Hooligans" (Jiguan songgun) substatute. The governor argued that "since they possess officially banned litigation books, they must have instigated other litigation cases." When the Jiaqing emperor read the case summary, he was enraged that the Cheng brothers owned the forbidden book. The emperor underlined the book's title and commented: "This is detestable!"[2]

To Qing officials also, litigation masters' secret handbooks were indeed detestable. They blamed these books for conveying destructive knowledge, inciting litigation, impeding social harmony, and adding to the caseload of the already overworked judicial system.[3] But for numerous litigants like the Cheng brothers, these handbooks were an important source of legal and litigation information. Although commercial publications of the Code flourished in the Qing and expanded access to the law, especially for elites, the Code was far too abstruse for most commoners to read and was too expensive for them to buy. Litigation masters' secret handbooks, on the contrary, targeted the lower end of the book market. These handbooks translated elite forms of legal knowledge into practical information useful for non-elite readers. These handbooks were sold in the book market despite the government's efforts to suppress them.

Scholars who have researched the origin, content, evolution, and usage of popular legal handbooks have tended to use them as a window to investigate litigation masters and their role in local judicial practice. They thus emphasize the availability of practical litigation knowledge (i.e., knowledge regarding how to compose litigation documents and how to participate in litigation) and marginalize the importance of legal knowledge (i.e., knowledge regarding statutes, substatutes, and regulations). They criticize legal information in these handbooks as unrefined, vulgar, and misleading and thus not worth serious study. These studies usually focus on several important editions printed in the late Ming, generally overlooking Qing editions, viewing them simply as low-quality replicas of late Ming editions.[4]

"Litigation masters' secret handbooks" were one of the most important genres of popular legal literature in early modern China. These handbooks included selected and simplified statutes and substatutes from the Code, legal knowledge in the rhyming-song style (*gejue*) and question-and-answer style (*wenda*), and so on. Sixty-five different editions of litigation masters' secret handbooks, including the nineteen *Thunder* editions published in the Qing and early Republican periods, inform the following analysis. Compared with the lengthy and intimidating presentation of legal information in the Code, popular representation of legal knowledge was deliberately more accessible, closer to everyday life, and easier to understand and remember. Qing legal handbooks usually contained much more accurate legal information than those from the late Ming. The flourishing trade in popular legal imprints brought legal knowledge to tens of thousands of households. Popular legal imprints fundamentally transformed the common people's access to and understanding of the law, and to some extent (and as the government feared!) encouraged them to go to court to solve their problems.

EVOLUTION OF POPULAR LEGAL HANDBOOKS: FROM LATE MING TO QING

Although scholars use the term "secret handbooks for litigation masters," in accordance with the terminology used by the Qing government when it banned the handbooks in 1742, these books were anything but secret. They circulated openly in the book market and were for the most part easily available to ordinary readers from the late Ming to the Republican period. Most readers were probably lower literati and commoners in need of legal and litigation knowledge. Therefore, "popular legal handbooks" is a more appropriate term for this genre.

Despite the Qing state's prohibition, popular legal handbooks flourished in late imperial society. Among the 65 different editions I have collected, 18 are from the late Ming period, 32 from the Qing, 6 from the Republican, and the remaining 9 editions do not have exact publication dates.[5] These 65 extant editions probably represent only a small portion of popular legal handbooks produced after the late Ming. The quality of these popular legal handbooks is usually low; many were cheaply made. Bibliophiles in the Ming and the Qing probably did not value these books and thus did not collect and protect them. Moreover, the government ban in 1742 also may have led to the destruction of some editions.

Popular legal handbooks matured as a genre in the late sixteenth century. Representative editions include *Newly Cut Golden Notes for the Legal World* (Xinqie falin jinjian lu), published in 1594, and *Newly Cut Notes Left by Xiao and Cao* (Xinqie Xiao Cao yibi), edited by Zhulin Langsou with a 1595 preface.[6] Although late Ming editions varied in content and printing formats, most shared the following four elements: general instructions on the litigation process and on how to compose litigation documents, sample litigation documents such as accusations (*gao*) and counteraccusations (*su*), collections of litigation phrases, and simplified or summarized law and legal information.[7]

Scholars usually view the late Ming as the golden age for popular legal handbooks, as a variety of editions of relatively high quality were produced during this time. They see the Qing as a period when the genre was in decline. Qing editions are criticized as less original, less diverse, and of lower quality than late Ming editions. Many Qing editions did recycle materials from late Ming editions. Qing editions also usually have similar basic content, structure, and printing format as Ming editions. It is unfair, however, to view Qing editions merely as reprinted copies of Ming editions. Many Qing editions incorporated significant changes. The most salient change was the increasing portion of legal knowledge. Some influential Qing editions, including *Thunder*, contained many statutes and substatutes quoted directly from the Code. In contrast, few late Ming editions contained such detailed legal knowledge.

The late Ming book market for popular legal handbooks was diverse and competitive. Many different editions that had distinct content and printing formats were sold on the book market. The genre itself was still fluid: some handbooks were oriented more toward lower-level officials and clerk than litigants, while others took the story format and read more like court-case fiction than practical legal manuals.[8] Qing editions, however, often have similar structures and printing formats. Qing editions usually took the two-register printing format, with litigation instructions, sample laws, and sample litigation phrases printed in the upper register and sample litigation writings printed in the lower register. The *Thunder* editions began to dominate the book market starting in the mid-Qing, and these comprised more than half of Qing printed editions. The lack of variation among Qing editions might be a sign of decline—legal experts were reluctant to produce new compilations due to the government ban. But it might also reflect a standardization process, similar to the standardization process for commercial editions of the Code after the rise of *Comprehensive Integration* editions. Qing readers seem to have accepted this as a basic format for the circulation of litigation and legal knowledge and thus publishers reproduced similar texts to meet readers' expectations.

LAW IN POPULAR HANDBOOKS 115

The thirty-two extant Qing editions outnumber the eighteen Ming editions. Compared with Ming editions, more recently published Qing editions apparently have a higher survival rate, as one might expect. The 1742 ban also destroyed many Ming and early Qing editions. Among the thirty-two Qing editions, twelve have an exact or approximate publishing date. Only one Qing edition published before the Jiaqing period seems to have survived the mid-Qing ban.[9] As was the case for commercial editions of the Code, the publication of popular legal handbooks revived in the Jiaqing period and flourished in the late Qing, due to the relaxation of the government prohibition. At the same time, the demand for legal and litigation knowledge in popular legal handbooks also probably increased because of some government policies in the Jiaqing-Daoguang period, such as "reopening of channels of communication," "all capital appeals being accepted," and "cleaning up accumulated legal cases."[10] These policies help explain the rise in the publication of legal handbooks in the Jiaqing period (two editions) and the Daoguang period (four editions). Commercial publishers continued to print legal handbooks in the late Qing and Republican periods. At least five editions were published from the Tongzhi reign to the end of the Qing.

The majority of extant editions of popular legal handbooks are published printed editions. Publishers mainly used woodblocks to print popular legal handbooks. Of the 18 Ming editions, 16 are woodblock imprints, as are 22 of the 32 Qing editions. Most popular legal handbooks belong to the category of low-quality reprints. The printing quality of late Ming editions is slightly higher than that of Qing editions. While many Ming editions have prefaces, usually printed in calligraphy style with large character size, few Qing editions have prefaces. Some Qing editions even do not have a table of contents. Qing editions also used smaller character sizes than Ming editions did. Publishers usually crammed each page with text and printed on inexpensive low-quality paper. Many woodblock cutters seem to have been unskilled, even illiterate, and obviously there was no proofreading process. Mistaken and miswritten characters are ubiquitous in Qing editions. These changes suggest that Qing editions oriented more toward the lower end of the book market than Ming editions did. Most popular legal handbooks are quite short—they usually have fewer than eight chapters, organized into two or four volumes. Compared with commercial editions of the Code, popular legal handbooks are significantly smaller, shorter, of lower quality, and thus much less expensive. Clearly, the printing of popular legal handbooks did not cost much. Although no information about the price of these books is available, we can estimate that they were sold at prices affordable to ordinary readers in Qing China.[11]

In the late Qing and Republican periods, some publishers used newly introduced lithography technology to print popular legal handbooks. There are at least nine extant lithographic editions. Six of them are *Thunder* editions. Most of these were from Shanghai, the lithographic printing center in the late Qing and Republican periods. The Shanghai Jinzhang Book Bureau (Shanghai Jinzhang Tushuju) published at least three lithographic editions of *Thunder* after 1915. Since the civil portions of the (revised) Qing Code were in operative and Qing litigation practice continued in local society in the early Republican period, knowledge in popular legal handbooks was still useful.[12] Some Republican readers also read popular legal handbooks for curiosity and entertainment. Thus, there was still a market for popular legal handbooks after the fall of the Qing.

Popular legal handbooks also circulated in unpublished manuscripts. Seven of the sixty-five extant editions in my sample are manuscripts: two from the late Ming and five from the Qing. Historian Gong Rufu collected four of these five Qing editions during his field research in Jiangxi and Hunan. These manuscripts are usually collections of real and sample litigation documents—mostly accusations and counteraccusations. The compilers were probably local litigation masters who gathered these documents in litigation practice. The compilers saved these documents for their personal use, not for publication and circulation. The other extant Qing manuscript edition is a handwritten copy of *Thunder*. The copyist carefully reproduced the entire text from a printed edition of the book on pages with pre-printed registers. He also followed the original two-register structure of the text. This is a clean copy, without any corrections or scribbles.[13] It seems that this copy may have been produced for sale rather than personal use.

Most popular legal handbooks lack information about their editors or publishers. Even before the government ban in 1742, few authors or editors were willing to reveal their identities, probably because they feared printing popular legal handbooks would incur government prosecution or divine retribution (*yinqian*). Litigiousness had long been condemned by the ruling elites, and instigating accusations was legally punishable under the Ming and Qing Codes.[14] Printing was associated with the accumulation of merit in late imperial Chinese popular religion. People believed that the mass production of texts could be powerful and sometimes dangerous. People who printed meritorious texts, such as Buddhist sutras and medical books, would accumulate merit. People who printed evil texts, however, would accumulate *yinqian*, thereby harming themselves and their offspring. In the late Ming, legal books were thought to belong in the category of evil texts because people feared they might "incite litigation," disrupt social harmony, and even imperil the cosmic balance. Although none of the authors of popular legal handbooks explicitly explained why they had concealed their real identities, we can find clues from a paragraph written by Wang Kentang, a renowned jurist in the late Ming. In his preface to *Annotations and Explanations on the Statutes and Substatutes* (Lüli jianshi) Wang explained his concerns: "I planned to publish it a long time ago. But Mr. Yuan Liaofan said that publishing and disseminating legal books [*falü zhishu*] would incur *yinqian*. When I heard about this, I was frightened and dropped [the plan]."[15] Late Ming authors like Wang even felt reluctant to publish commentaries on statutes—orthodox legal texts that did not necessarily lead to litigation. Probably for similar reasons, the authors of popular legal handbooks were extremely reluctant to include their own personal information in the books.

Authors and editors of popular legal handbooks usually used aliases to conceal their identity. They referred to themselves as mountain man (*shanren*), unconstrained man (*sanren*) and old man (*sou*), in sobriquets such as Mountain Man Who Knows Errors (Juefei Shanren), Unconstrained Man of Rivers and Lakes (Jianghu Sanren), Wandering Old Man of the Bamboo Grove (Zulin Langsou), and Reclusive Old Man of Clear Waves (Qingbo Yisou). These aliases imply that these editors viewed themselves as men outside ordinary social boundaries, who were reclusive, itinerant, and rootless. The content of legal handbooks suggests that most of these authors and editors had a level of familiarity with the law and litigation practice. They were probably lower-level literati with access to some legal and litigation knowledge, such as litigation masters and clerks working in local government.

Several major publishing centers in the late Ming and the Qing participated in printing and marketing popular legal handbooks, most notably Jinling (Nanjing) in Jiangsu and Shulin (Jianyang) in Fujian in the late Ming and Shanghai in the late Qing. Publishers in Nanjing produced several influential editions in the late Ming, including the *Newly Cut Golden Notes for the Legal World* (1594) and the *Newly Cut Notes Left by Xiao and Cao* (1595). Some late Ming editions proclaimed their Nanjing origin by featuring information like "revised from the original woodblocks in Jinling" in the salient place in the cover page or even in the title.[16] These imply that Nanjing was a printing center for popular legal handbooks and enjoyed a reputation of producing high-quality editions. Jianyang, the famous printing center in northern Fujian, produced at least three editions. *A Newly Carved New Book for Legalists* (Xinke fajia xinshu), published in 1826 and 1862, announced that its editors were two Nanjing men and its publisher was Zhu Tingzhen of the Yugengtang in Jianyang.[17] One edition of *Legalist Cold Penetrating the Gall Bladder* (Fajia toudan han) printed "Briefs of Administration in Longyan" (Longyan zhenglue) on the cover page. Longyan County was adjacent to another influential printing center, Sibao, in western Fujian. The book was probably also published in Fujian and had some connections with Sibao publishers.[18]

Full evidence for the sale and accessibility of popular legal handbooks is difficult to come by, but the existence of national bookselling networks supports speculation that they could circulate quite widely. These books were obviously easy to purchase in the areas near the major publishing centers—Jiangsu, Fujian, and Shanghai. Books printed in these publishing centers were also sold in other places through publishers' bookselling networks, including wholesalers, traveling booksellers, and branch stores.[19] For example, a bookstore named Yonghetang in Shengjing (Shenyang), Manchuria, sold an edition of *Thunder* printed in Jiangsu in 1888. The bookstore informed readers that it bought books from Jiangsu publishers and retailed them in Shengjing. Similar, another bookstore in Shengjing sold *The Heavenly Oil of the Legal Brush* (Fabi tianyou), which was also from Jiangsu.[20]

Evidence indicates that readers could obtain popular legal handbooks outside these major publishing centers and beyond their distributing networks. The Cheng brothers bought their copy of *Thunder* from a random bookseller in Lushan, Henan. Historian Gong Rufu's research also indicates that popular legal handbooks circulated in rural areas in Jiangxi and Hunan in the Qing period.[21] Most legal handbooks did not provide information about their publishers and printers. Many editions without publishing information might have been printed in local "character-cutting shops" (kezidian) or by itinerant woodblock cutters who found printing these handbooks profitable. Li Rulan (1684–1747), the Sichuan judicial commissioner who suggested the ban on popular handbooks to the Qianlong emperor, mentioned that these books were easily available in bookshops in Sichuan. When he attempted to ban these books in Sichuan, he found that people still could buy handbooks printed in other provinces. He complained, "if we destroy [these handbooks] in one place, other places will print and sell them!"[22]

Popular legal handbooks drew a much broader audience than the Code. They were much shorter and simpler as well as much less expensive than the Code. Litigation masters were undoubtedly the main target readers of popular legal handbooks. Historian Melissa Macauley argues that litigation masters were "a broad category of legal facilitators ranging from professional plaintmasters to simple literate men to whom people incidentally turned for legal help," and most of them were lower literati who were educated but who had failed in the civil service examinations. Litigation masters and litigants would turn to popular legal handbooks for litigation skills and legal knowledge. Other likely readers included lower literati and commoners who were interested in the law, clerks, runners, private legal advisors, and even officials. Many editions of popular handbooks clearly indicated that they targeted beginners who were not familiar with the laws.[23] Legal and litigation knowledge in popular handbooks was usually presented in simplified and easy-to-understand formats—even people without background knowledge of the laws could understand the texts well. Some readers might also read them for leisure or pleasure. Many sample lawsuits in these books involved family conflict, violence, sex, revenge, and crime—just the kind of "ripped from the headlines" stories that readers would have found attractive.

THE THUNDER THAT STARTLES HEAVEN: ITS STRUCTURE AND CONTENT

In 1742 the Qing government banned popular legal handbooks. The ban became a substatute and was formally incorporated into the Code in 1743. The substatute, under article 340, "Instigating Litigation" (Jiaosuo cisong), read: "Litigation masters' secret handbooks printed by bookstores, such as *The Thunder That Startles Heaven, Disputations* [Xiangjue], *A New Book for Legalists* [Fajia xinshu], and *The Punishment Platform of the Qin Mirror* [Xingtai Qinjing], and all other books that will incite litigation, should be banned and destroyed. Sales should be prohibited."[24] The substatute listed *Thunder*, together with the titles of three other popular handbooks, as examples of "books that would incite litigation" and thus should be prohibited and destroyed. This is why the Jiaqing emperor was enraged when he learned that the Cheng brothers in the false capital appeal case had hidden

Thunder—the most notorious handbook explicitly prohibited in the Qing law—in their house.

That the Cheng brothers possessed a copy of *Thunder*, however, was far from exceptional. As a matter of fact, various editions of *Thunder* flourished in the Qing period despite the government ban. Fifteen different editions of *Thunder* produced in the Qing remain extant, including twelve woodblock editions, two lithographic editions, and one hand-copied edition. The real number of editions produced in the Qing is probably far greater than that. The *Thunder* editions comprise nearly half of all thirty-two extant Qing editions of popular legal handbooks. The earliest editions may have been edited and published in the early Qing, but most extant editions were published since the Daoguang period. The government prohibition in the mid-Qing might have enhanced the status and credibility of *Thunder* as a typical popular legal handbook, which made its editions the most noticeable and widespread popular legal handbooks.

None of the *Thunder* editions have information about authors or editors. Only a few late Qing and Republican editions convey the information about their publishers or bookstores, including the Shulin Xiyuan in Fujian, the Yonghetang Bookstore and the Wenxing Deji Bookstore in Shengjing, and the Jinzhang Book Bureau in Shanghai. Most editors and publishers were apparently reluctant to reveal their identity because of the state ban. Some publishers even changed their book titles in order to avoid prosecution. For example, *The Heavenly Oil of the Legal Brush*, sold by the Wenxing Deji Bookstore, is obviously reprinted from the two-chapter version of *Thunder*.

The contents of different *Thunder* editions are not consistent. Generally speaking, *Thunder* editions can be categorized into two different types: the short version, which usually consists of two or four chapters, and the long version, which consists of six or eight chapters. The long version is not simply an extended edition of the short version. Although both versions share the same structure, printing format, and the types of legal and litigation information, they have different sets of legal and litigation instructions and sample litigation writings. The two versions might originate from two different popular legal handbooks in the early Qing: the short version possibly came from original editions of *Thunder* published before the Qianlong ban; the long version was possibly revised from *The Punishment Platform of the Qin Mirror*, another popular early Qing edition that the Qing law explicitly mentioned and banned. The content of eight-chapter editions of *Thunder* printed in the late Qing is similar to an extant edition of *The*

Punishment Platform of the Qin Mirror published in 1673.[25] The long version became more popular than the short version in the late Qing and Republican periods. The long version is also more comprehensive and contains much more detailed legal knowledge—including a large number of statutes and substatutes from the Code—than the short version does, which might contribute to its popularity among late Qing readers.

The Thunder That Startles Heaven looks like an encyclopedia of legal and litigation information that the common people could use in litigation practice. The language used in *Thunder* was simple classical Chinese, which was straightforward and not difficult to read or understand. The book combines long-established legal and litigation instructions and sample documents, most of which originated from the late Ming editions, with some new Qing factors—namely newly added statutes and substatutes from the Qing Code. Take the eight-chapter version of *Thunder* for example.[26] The first chapter of the book focuses on introducing basic legal knowledge. The upper registers print "Direct Explanations of the Names and Punishments," which is a collection of seventy-nine terms (with explanations) related to punishments, and "Comprehensive Rhymed Song of [the Laws Relating to] Fornication" (Fanjian zongkuo ge). The lower registers include a foreword, "Punishments and Laws of Previous Dynasties," "Notes for the Ten Rules," "Questions and Answers for Sentencing Crimes according to the Eight Laws" (Balü kezui wenda), and "Comprehensive Rhymed Song of Statutes and Substatutes" (Lüli zongkuo ge).

The second chapter focuses on litigation instructions. "A Prose Poem about Legal Specifications" (Jinke yicheng fu), printed at the beginning of the upper registers, discusses some perplexing situations about the laws that the Code did not specify. After the poem, there are several paragraphs of general instructions on litigation: "Guide for Trying Legal Cases" discusses several fundamental principles of writing accusations; "Ten Old Taboos" is about ten easily made mistakes in writing litigation documents; "Going to Court" provides instructions on how to file lawsuits beyond routine channels. In the lower registers are printed two short paragraphs of moral warnings and general instructions for people who want to participate in litigation. "Fine Instructions on Composing Ten-Section Plaints with Fixed Formats and Direct Explanations" occupies most of the space in the lower registers. This section provides step-by-step instructions on how to compose accusations as well as more than sixty-five different phrases commonly used in litigation. Nothing seems new or original in the second chapters.

All the legal information and litigation instructions can be traced back to late Ming editions of popular legal handbooks and everyday encyclopedias. *Thunder* simply gathered and recycled these old materials and assembled them together in one book.

The third chapter includes three essays that explain some fundamental legal concepts, printed in the upper registers. "A Guide to Punishments and Laws" gives definitions and explanations of various punishments used in the Qing legal system. The other two essays explain several key legal terms regarding killing (*sha*) and illicit goods (*zang*) in the Code. The lower registers featured three sample memorials (*zouben*). The author of the first memorial was a late Ming censor who impeached the notorious corrupt grand secretariat Yan Song (1480–1567). The second memorial is an impeachment written by a grand coordinator (xunfu) to accuse a county magistrate of corruption and malpractice. The author of the third memorial is a female poet named Li Yuying. Her stepmother accused her of adultery and had her put in prison. She wrote this memorial in prison to express her grievance, pointing out that her stepmother abused her and her siblings after the death of her father, murdered her younger brother (not born by the stepmother), and framed her for adultery to get rid of her. Li Yuying's memorial seems to be more fictional than real, but it was widely circulated in the late Ming period and even was mentioned in collections of popular fiction including *Stories to Awaken the World* (Xingshi hengyan).[27] Although these memorials are not directly related to commoners' litigation writings, they provide excellent examples of the terms, logic, structures, and grammar of formally written official documents. They are also expressively written and entertaining to read.

Chapters 4 through 7, which are the core of *Thunder*, feature many statutes and substatutes from the Code, sample legal and litigation phrases, sample accusations, counteraccusations, and sentences. The text is grouped into nine categories covering most types of lawsuits that commoners might encounter: marriage, fornication, homicide, theft and robbery, households and corvée service, inheritance and establishing heirs, fields and houses, graves and mountains, corruption and deception, and merchants. In each category, the author first lists dozens of sample legal and litigation phrases (*eryu*), probably copied from earlier editions of popular legal handbooks. Then he provides newly added phrases (*xinzeng suiyu*) and a large number of newly added statutes and substatutes of the Great Qing (*xinzeng Da Qing lüli*). All the phrases and laws are printed in the upper registers, with sample litigation writings in the lower registers. Each sample set usually contains three paragraphs, including an accusation, a counteraccusation, and a sentence. Beside sample litigation writings, the lower registers usually have an additional section of Qing laws, noted as "additional statutes and substatutes" (*bushang lüli*). The laws, legal and litigation phrases, and sample litigation writings always correspond to one another. The upper register and lower register arrangement also help readers locate related laws and litigation phrases when they read sample accusations and counteraccusations.

The last chapter—the eighth—contains basic forensic knowledge and miscellaneous writing samples regarding the common people's requests toward local governments. The upper registers of this chapter print forensic information selected from various forensic manuals, including *The Washing Away of Wrongs*, the official forensic manual of the Qing judicial system. It details the appearance and injuries of corpses from various causes of death, such as death by strangulation, burning, drowning, poison, and so on. Forensic information seems to be relatively new and exceptional—few other popular legal handbooks contain such information. Unlike the other chapters, the content of the lower registers here is not related to that found in the upper registers. The lower registers of this chapter include writing samples submitted by commoners to the local government for business such as exonerations from crimes, petitions for famine relief or tax exemption, and requests for certificates of remarriage and inheritance, and so on.

In conclusion, *Thunder* is a comprehensive collection including materials related to various aspects of legal, litigation, administrative, and forensic knowledge. Although most of the information in the book is recycled from late Ming editions, it has some new content, including a large number of statutes and substatutes from the Code and forensic information, which few previous popular legal handbooks contain. The author marks this new information as "newly added" and "additional" in the section titles as a form of distinction and advertisement. The most salient feature of *Thunder* is that the portion dealing with legal information in the book is significantly increased relative to the material related to litigation. General instructions and explanations of the laws and the legal system, as well as specific statutes and substatutes cited from the Code that directly correspond to sample litigation writings, occupied nearly half of the entire content of the book. Although almost all popular legal handbooks contained some legal information and instructions, the laws in *Thunder* are more comprehensive, more detailed, more accurate, and closer to the common people's needs than other editions.

WHY LAW MATTERS

Law and legal knowledge played an important role in local litigation practice. In his pathbreaking research on Chinese civil law, historian Philip Huang argues that "formal law played a major role in the lives of the majority of the population." He estimates that "one in every ten households had someone involved in litigation" in a twenty-year period. Although legal historians have proved that the cost of litigation was not as intimidating as previously estimated, bringing a lawsuit to court was still an important legal decision as well as a considerable commitment of money, time, and reputation.[28] Those who filed lawsuits needed assurance that the laws would largely support their accusations—otherwise, they would have little chance to have the court accept their cases, let alone win the lawsuits. As a well-known paragraph of litigation advice printed in *Thunder* pointed out, there were three essential factors that comprised "the way of pursuing litigation" (*zhisong zhidao*): *qing* (feeling or human compassion), *li* (principles), and *fa* (law). A successful plaint must reflect true feelings, embrace principles, and observe the laws—the absence of any of these factors would lead to failure or even disaster in litigation.[29]

A reference (explicit or implicit) to the laws might significantly enhance the possibility of a plaint being accepted in local courts. The Qing legal system was notoriously understaffed and overburdened. Case backlogs had been rampant in local and provincial courts since the mid-Qing. In 1759, for example, Fujian alone had a total of 22,800 unresolved lawsuits accumulated in courts. The situation became even worse in the late Qing, despite the government's frequent efforts to clear backlogged cases. Overworked officials were extremely reluctant to accept new cases, especially those regarding civil disputes and minor criminal offenses and those with messy stories and unclear evidence. The Dan-Xin Archives indicate that the court rejected more than 36 percent of the plaints after the initial review process.[30] The acceptance rate in the newly discovered late Qing Huangyan litigation archives in Zhejiang is astonishingly low—the magistrates rejected nearly 91 percent of civil cases submitted in the court.[31] Only clearly written plaints with strong evidence and obviously supported by the laws could pass this harsh initial review process.

Although litigants often did not cite the laws specifically, it was quite common for them to narrate their stories in plaints based on certain statutes and substatutes.[32] Instructions in popular legal handbooks emphasized that writing plaints needed to follow the meaning of the laws. For example, the "Guide for Plaints and Litigation" (*Cisong zhinan*) in a four-chapter edition of *Thunder* reminded its readers: "When writing plaints, you must first fully consider the actual facts, situations, and principles. . . . After that, you must use the meaning of the laws [*lüyi*]. Consider which article fits [the situation], and then pick up some essential words from that article and apply them in writing plaints so that people will know your grievance from their first glance at your plaints."[33] The author clearly knew that legal terminology would draw officials' immediate attention. Writing plaints based on laws was also an effective way of organizing evidence and clarifying facts and made it easier for officials to judge and sentence—such cases would have better a chance to be accepted in the court and plaintiffs would have a better chance to win. The "Fine Instructions on [Composing] Ten-Section Plaints" (Shiduan jin), a well-known text explaining how to compose plaints that many Ming and Qing popular handbooks contained, also instructed readers to make use of law in plaint writing. It argued that law should be clearly mentioned in the conclusion sections of plaints: "Every word must be in accord with the laws, and every character must be incisive. . . . If you have this conclusion in your plaint, it is called 'closed door.' Then it is easy for county and prefecture courts to sentence. If you do not have this conclusion, it is called 'open door.' Then your opponents can easily dispute your plaints." The instruction emphasized again in the "Ending" (*jiewei*) section that a reference to the law must be included: "Here you need to clarify the laws [*chanming lüfa*]!"[34]

Generally speaking, Qing editors emphasized the importance of law more than late Ming editors did. The inclusion of detailed legal information became a selling point for many Qing editions. Advertising sentences such as "The statutes and substatutes of *The Great Qing Code* are included inside" and "The statutes and substatutes of *The Great Qing Code* are added" were frequently printed saliently on the cover page of Qing editions.[35] Few Ming editions printed such information. The increasing importance of legal information in popular legal handbooks from the late Ming to the late Qing might reflect the rising demand for such information among readers, probably because of factors such as the wider circulation of accurate legal information, the more legally savvy population, and the higher rejection rate of plaints in local courts. Beside the necessary litigation knowledge, Qing people needed practical information about the laws when going to court to solve their problems. Popular legal handbooks provided one of the important channels for ordinary people to get access to the laws.

LEGAL INFORMATION IN *THE THUNDER THAT STARTLES HEAVEN*

What kinds of legal information were included in popular legal handbooks? In the eight-chapter version of *Thunder*—the most representative Qing editions of popular legal handbooks—for example, law was represented in a variety of formats, ranging from catchy jingles of extremely simplified legal information to long verbatim replications of statutes and substatutes from the Code. The most important four formats were rhymed songs, question and answer sets, interpretations of legal terms, and replications of the laws from the Code.

RHYMED SONGS

Thunder included two rhymed songs, the "Comprehensive Rhymed Songs of [the Laws Relating to] Fornication" and the "Comprehensive Rhymed Song of Statutes and Substatutes." The former contained 88 lines and covered 5 statutes in the "Fornication" chapter in the Code. The latter was longer—it contained 128 lines and mentioned at least 50 different statutes.[36] The songs were loosely rhymed, following the standard of traditional poetry with five characters to each line. The songs converted complicated and intimidating representations of laws in the Code into simple, straightforward, and unpolished jingles so that even less educated readers were able to understand and remember them. For example, the first lines of the "Fornication" song focused on the "Fornication" statute (article 366). It translated the law as follows:

> *Nannü hejian zhe, ge gai zhang bashi.*
> Men and women committing fornication with consent, each shall be punished with eighty strokes of the heavy bamboo.

> *Youfu ruo hejian, jiadeng zhang jiushi.*
> For a married woman committing fornication with consent, the punishment will be increased to ninety strokes of the heavy bamboo.

Diaojian yin chuwai, ge zhang yibai zhi.
For *diaojian* that seducing women to go outside [their home to fornicate],
    the punishment is one hundred strokes of the heavy bamboo.

Qiangjian wu fuming, jianfu dangni jiao.
Rape tarnishes the woman's reputation; the rapist shall be punished
    with strangulation.

Qiangjian ruo weicheng, zhangbai liu sanqian li.
For attempted rape, the punishment shall be one hundred strokes of the
    heavy bamboo and exile to three thousand *li*.[37]

The language in the song was simplified, but the information was relatively comprehensive and accurate, closely matching the text of the Code. In addition to specifying the punishments, the song also explained potentially difficult legal terms. *Diaojian* (fornication by seduction), for example, was a legal term seldom used in everyday language. The song added *yin chuwai* (seducing to go outside) into the line, indicating that *diaojian* was a form of fornication in which the adulterer seduced the woman into leaving her home.

The laws in the "Comprehensive Rhymed Song of Statutes and Substatutes" were even more simplified than the "Fornication" song. Take the first lines for example:

Qiangdao wei decai, yili ni liuzui.
Committing robbery without taking property, the punishment is life exile
    according to the law.

Kanfa fenyuan shu, jiandeng zhang jiushi.
Cutting down trees in someone's graveyard, the punishment is reduced
    one degree to ninety strokes of the heavy bamboo.

In these two lines, the song mentioned two statutes—article 266, "Theft with Force," and article 263, "Stealing Trees from Tombs."[38] The original statutes in the Code had several long paragraphs of texts, which specified various conditions of the crimes and their corresponding punishments. The song converted the complicated statutes into two short lines with only twenty characters—it retained the main crimes and punishments, deleting numerous variations of the crimes and nuances of punishments. In the same fashion, the song converted at least forty-eight other statutes and regulations into simple catchy lyrics in the song. Most laws mentioned in the song were cited from the "Laws relating to the Board of Revenue" and the "Laws relating to the Board of Punishments" chapters in the Code, which contained most of the penal and civil laws that commoners would encounter. The song, therefore, gave readers basic ideas of crimes and punishments relating to "useful" civil and penal laws. Through deleting the details, the song made the otherwise complicated and obscure law much clearer and easier for readers to understand and memorize. Simplification also enabled the song to include as many statutes as possible in the limited space afforded by popular legal handbooks.

QUESTION AND ANSWER SETS

"Questions and Answers for Sentencing Crimes according to the Eight Laws" in *Thunder* contained twenty-five sets of questions and answers. Using question-and-answer format to explain the laws had a long history in China. *Annotations and Discussions on the Tang Code* (Tanglü shuyi), the law code of the Tang dynasty promulgated in 653, contained about 178 questions and answers in its "Annotations and Discussions" sections.[39] Popular legal handbooks apparently borrowed this question-and-answer format: in each set, a question—usually on a confusing or difficult point of the laws unclarified in the Code—was posted, then an answer followed with detailed explanations responding to this question. All question and answer sets in *Thunder* were copied from late Ming editions of popular handbooks. *Thunder* reduced the original forty-four sets of question and answer to twenty-five, omitting outdated and less useful ones.

Laws discussed in the question and answer sets covered a wide range of civil and penal laws related to the common people, such as laws regarding beating relatives, cursing wife's parents, husbands abandoning wives, treating wives as concubines, fornicating with former wives after divorce, catching adulterous lovers, establishing orphans as legal heirs, and so on. For example, one question asked: "If one's wife gives birth to a son, his concubine gives birth to a son, his maidservant [*tongfang*] gives birth to a son, and he also has a son born through fornication, how should these four sons inherit and divide his property?" This was a rather difficult—and important—question about inheritance law. How should sons born by mothers of different status in the family inherit the father's property? The following answer offered an informative solution:

> There are no differences between the son born by the wife and the son born by the concubine [in terms of inheriting property]. The question of whether the son was born to the wife or the concubine is only salient with the regard to the hereditary official rank. The son born through fornication cannot receive the hereditary official rank, nor can he be established as the legal heir [with regard to property]. In terms of dividing up family property, it should be divided into three and a half shares. The sons born by the wife, the concubine, and the *tongfang*—It is said that a maidservant is called *tongfang*. Her status is lower than that of the concubine. But [her son's status] should be viewed as equal to that of the son born by a concubine—each should get one share. The son born through fornication should get half a share.[40]

The answer not only provided information on how to allocate family property among sons of different status but also mentioned who would be entitled to receive the hereditary official rank.

This question and answer set articulates the general principle of household division and inheritance in late imperial Chinese law—the equal division of family property among the sons, even if they were born by mothers of different status (the only exception, however, was the son born through fornication—he would get only half of the share). The question and answer clearly referred to an imperial edict by the first Ming emperor Zhu Yuanzhang (r. 1368–1398) in 1369, which later became a regulation in the *Collected Statutes of the Great Ming* (*Da Ming huidian*) and a substatute in the Qing Code.[41] Other question and answer sets also indicated that the legal information was from a variety of sources, including the Code, the *Huidian*, imperial edicts, and statutory commentaries.

The question and answer sets provided readers a valuable opportunity to obtain in-depth legal knowledge that the Code often did not directly mention. Compared with the rhymed songs, the knowledge in question and answer sets was more accurate, complex, and difficult. It seems that it targeted more advanced readers than the songs did. The questions and answers not only provided insight into particular problems but also modeled legal reasoning and problem-solving. Compared with directly advancing legal explanations, proposing a hypothesized situation in the question and providing the solution in the answer made for a livelier and more memorable account. The hypothetical situations allowed readers to imagine comparable problems that they might encounter in their own lives.

INTERPRETATIONS OF BASIC LEGAL TERMS

Some sections in *Thunder* focused on providing interpretations to terms relating to law, punishments, and the judicial system. These interpretations included "Direct Explanations of the Names and Punishments," "A Guide to Punishments and Laws," "Differences among the Six Types of Illicit Goods," and "Regulations for Seven Types of Killings." They provided definitions and explanations on many key legal concepts. For example, "Differences among the Six Types of Illicit Goods" introduced the six types of illicit goods and theft—supervisors and custodians stealing, ordinary persons stealing, theft, illicit goods obtained through subverting the law, illicit goods obtained without subverting the law, and illicit goods obtained through malfeasance. "Regulations for Seven Types of Killings" explained the differences among the seven types of killing—killing in a robbery, premeditated killing, intentionally killing, killing in an affray, mistaken killing, killing in play, and unintentionally killing.[42]

The "Guide for Punishments and Laws" was a comprehensive introduction on the five punishments used in the late imperial Chinese legal system, including the two degrees of death penalty, three degrees of exile, five degrees of penal servitude, five degrees of beating with the heavy bamboo, and five degrees of beating with the light bamboo. When explaining the beating with the light bamboo, the author wrote: "Beating with the light bamboo refers to the punishment imposed if someone commits a minor crime and is beaten with a small *vitex negundo* [*jingzhang*]. There are five degrees of severity: from ten to fifty strokes. Every ten strokes will be considered one degree of punishment."[43] The explanations were quite comprehensive and understandable. Most information in the interpretations could be located in the Code, especially in the "Diagrams" (*zhutu*) chapters at the beginning. These legal terms were ubiquitous in the Code and were fundamental for readers hoping to understand the laws and punishments. The comprehensive and accurate interpretations of key legal terms would greatly enhance the readers' ability to read and understand the laws.

STATUTES AND SUBSTATUTES FROM THE CODE

The most impressive legal information in *Thunder* was a large number of statutes and substatutes copied from the Code. The book contained at least eighty-two statutes and forty-five substatutes, which covered a large percentage of civil and penal laws that the common people would be interested in and could use in litigation practice. The author loyally kept most of the original text of statutes and substatutes in the Code and even kept the original sequence. In many occasions, he also included official small commentaries (*xiaozhu*) along with the main body of text of statutes in the Code. The author was selective when choosing statutes—he only chose the laws from the "Laws relating to the Board of Revenue" and the "Laws relating to the Board of Punishments" chapters. He completely skipped the "Civil Office," "Rites," "War," and "Public Works" chapters because the laws in these chapters were often related to administration, imperial rituals, military, and public projects that did not concern the common people. From the "Revenue" chapters in the Code, he chose at least 33 statutes and 14 substatutes. He seemed particularly interested in the marriage laws and included all 17 statutes from the "Marriage" chapter. In addition to statutes, he selected 7 substatutes from the marriage law. He also copied many statutes that pertained to taxes and services (e.g., article 80, "Inequality of Land Taxes and Service," and article 84, "Fleeing to Avoid Compulsory Service"), property disputes (e.g., article 93, "Theft and Sale of Fields and Houses," and article 95, "Conditional Purchase of Fields and Houses"), inheritance (e.g., article 78, "Establishing a Son of the Official Wife [as One's Successor] Contrary to the Law"), and markets (e.g., article 154, "Monopolizing the Market"). These statutes and substatutes comprised the main portion of civil laws that Qing litigants would refer to in civil lawsuits.[44]

Besides laws relating to civil affairs, the author also paid close attention to the penal laws in the "Laws Relating to the Board of Punishments" chapters. He chose at least 49 statutes and 31 substatutes from these chapters in the Code. He copied the entire section of the "Fornication" chapters in his book, which was comprised of 10 statutes pertained to sex and sexual offenses, such as "Fornication" (article 366), "Fornication between Relatives" (article 368), and "To Buy a Person of Honorable Condition as a Prostitute" (article 375). He also included 20 of the 28 statutes in the "General Public Disorder and Theft" chapters and 18 of the 20 statutes in the "Homicide" chapters, including the laws regarding rebellion, treason, robbery, theft, murder, and so on. In sum, the laws in *Thunder* focused on "useful" civil and penal laws, with particular emphasis on property, marriage, sex, and violence. When selecting the statutes and substatutes, the author probably not only considered the practical value of these laws in litigation but also measured the entertaining factors that would satisfy the readers' curiosity about sex, violence, and the related harsh punishments in the judicial system.

How accurate was the legal information in *Thunder*? Compared with other genres of law books, such as the Code, collections of substatutes and regulations, and official handbooks, *Thunder* was less accurate. The legal information in popular legal handbooks was usually not updated efficiently or in a timely way. Laws in the rhymed songs, question and answer sets, and interpretations of legal terms were usually based on Ming laws. The statutes and substatutes were Qing laws, but they were possibly from editions of the Code published before the 1740 revision. Although the Qianlong ban did not eliminate popular handbooks, it discouraged legal experts from revising and updating them. Many late Qing editions thus contained some old statutes and substatutes from the late Ming and early Qing. There were also some inaccuracies in numbers and specific punishments in *Thunder*. For example, the "Rhymed Song on [Laws relating to] Fornication" stated that having sex with girls under thirteen years old would be viewed as rape, but the correct age should have been twelve.[45] In the "Fornication" category, *Thunder* mentioned the "Facilitating and Tolerating the Wife's or Concubine's Fornication" statute (article 367) and recorded the punishment for the husband who facilitated his wife's or concubine's fornication would be one hundred strokes of the heavy bamboo. The correct punishment in the Code, however, was ninety strokes of the heavy bamboo.[46]

Generally speaking, these inaccuracies were minor problems that would not significantly affect readers' understanding and use of the laws. For one thing, most legal information in *Thunder* originated from statutes, which did not change significantly from the Ming to the Qing. Almost all the Ming statutes mentioned in *Thunder* were still effective in the Qing. For another thing, potential readers of popular legal handbooks, such as litigants, litigation masters, commoners, and lower literati, usually did not care much about various situations of crimes and their specific punishments. After all, they were not officials and legal advisors, who relied on the laws to sentence legal cases. Even composing accusations and counteraccusations did not require details of specific crimes and punishments. What common readers needed was general ideas and principles of the laws, and popular legal hand-books such as *Thunder* were one of the most convenient channels for them to get access to this information.

The Code was obviously the most important source of legal information in *Thunder*. Statutes and substatutes in the book were directly copied from the Code, and the rhymed songs, questions and answers, and interpreta-tions of legal terms also clearly referred to the laws in the Code. Besides the Code, the authors also referred to a variety of sources, including the *Hui-dian*, imperial edicts, statutory commentaries, and other legal treatises. Although most of these law books were also available in the book market, they were usually beyond the reach of ordinary readers due to their high cost and difficulty of reading. Popular handbooks popularized the laws by converting complicated representations of the laws in the Code to simpli-fied and easy-to-understand jingles, questions and answers, and interpre-tations. They also abridged the laws by deleting complex situations and numerous variations of punishments and including only the sections that concerned the common people. Popular legal handbooks, therefore, reached to lower classes of readers than those of the Code and greatly contributed to the dissemination of legal knowledge from officials and legal experts to the common people in late imperial society.

Combining legal information with sample litigation documents (i.e., accusations and counteraccusations), popular legal handbooks illustrated how to use, and sometimes to manipulate, laws to win a lawsuit. Laws in these books were no longer intimidating presentations of strict regulations and harsh punishments; they became effective means common people could use and even abuse to achieve their own ends. The two-register printing for-mat used by most of the *Thunder* editions put statutes and substatutes in the upper registers and corresponding litigation documents in the lower registers. This arrangement allowed the audience to read these two types of information together and encouraged them to think about how laws could possibly be used in litigation. Cases in sample litigation documents also illustrated how to exaggerate and reinterpret scenarios of cases (often dis-guising "trivial" civil disputes as serious criminal cases) to draw officials' attention and get accepted in court. For example, a sample litigation in the marriage category in *Thunder* was a marriage dispute between a widow and a man. The widow lived with her two young sons after her husband died. Because the family needed a capable male laborer to sustain their livelihood, her brother arranged a marriage between her and a recently widowed man, who would move to her house and help with the work. The widow at first agreed to the marriage, but later she regretted it. She filed a lawsuit in the court and accused the man of forcibly taking her as his wife (*qianghun*). In the accusation, she described the man as a rich, powerful, and fierce man and herself as a poor, powerless, and chaste widow. The accusation continued: "Taking advantage of his wealth and power, this villain plotted to marry me, and I refused. On the eleventh day of this month, he found out I was alone at home. He gathered thirty or so hooligans. They attacked my house and attempted to take me by force. My sons and I were scared and ran away. They took the chance to steal my clothes and jewelry. My neighbors are witnesses of the crime."[47] Then she pleaded the judge to punish the man according to the laws (*ru lü fa jiu*). Although the accusation did not specifically cite any statute, the scenario apparently referred to the "Forcibly Seizing Wives or Daughters of Honorable Families" statute (Qiangzhan liangjia qi'nü), printed in the upper registers in the same chapter.

The counteraccusation from the man, however, told a completely different story. He maintained that he had made a formal marriage contract with the widow under the supervision of her uncle and brother. The widow also accepted a gold hairpin as the bride price. He claimed that he never thought she might be having a secret adulterous relation with a local rogue, who hated the marriage arrangement because it would cut off their relationship. The rogue then persuaded the widow to file a false accusation against him so that they could continue with the love affair. If the judge interrogated the widow's uncle and brother, he claimed, all the truth would come out. The counteraccusation was sharp, logical, and based on the law. The man's major argument was that his marriage with the widow was legitimate—he had a written marriage contract, established under the agreement with the widow's senior male relatives, and he had already sent the bride price. These factors were important proof of a legitimate marriage contract acknowledged by the "Marriage between Men and Women" statute, printed in the upper registers right above this sample litigation. He was an innocent man, falsely accused by the widow only because she wanted to continue her adulterous relationship with another man. Both accusations and counteraccusations skillfully employed the marriage laws. Litigants clearly tailored or even made up the stories according to what the laws regulated to attack opponents, to impress judges, and to win lawsuits. Similar examples were ubiquitous in popular legal handbooks. Combining law and litigation skills empowered readers, which enabled and encouraged them to use and abuse the laws and the legal system.

THE STATE BAN

In contrast with the utilitarian perspective on law in popular legal hand-books, Qing rulers believed that the common people should revere the law and stay away from the judicial system. Although many Qing elites sup-ported popular legal education, they did not want commoners to actually use their legal knowledge in litigation. Instead, they hoped that if common-ers knew strict laws and harsh punishments, they would not dare to com-mit crimes. As the Yongzheng emperor wrote in his preface to the 1725 imperial edition of the Code: "Establish laws and promulgate them clearly to both officials and the common people. . . . When the commoners know the laws, they will not commit crimes, and thus disputes will be settled and customs will be transformed."[48] Law was an educational method to prevent crimes, maintain order, and transform customs, not a tool people could use to fight with one another in court. It was thus no wonder that Qing ruling elites found popular legal handbooks troublesome and dangerous.

The Qing court launched a nationwide campaign to ban and destroy popular legal handbooks and all other "books that would incite litigation" in 1742. The ban was thorough and strict: Those who compiled popular handbooks and who cut new woodblocks would be punished by one hun-dred strokes of heavy bamboo and permanent exile of three thousand *li* (roughly one-third of a mile). Those who hid old woodblocks and printed books from them would be punished by one hundred strokes of heavy bam-boo and penal servitude for three years. Those who sold the books would be punished by one hundred strokes of heavy bamboo. All the woodblocks must be destroyed. Those who hid old woodblocks would get the punish-ment one degree lower than those who printed the books, by one hundred strokes of heavy bamboo. Governors-general and governors in each prov-ince would supervise their subordinates to search and destroy the wood-blocks and books. If officials failed to find and destroy the books, they would be fined or demoted.[49] The ban was a serious effort for Qing rulers to regu-late commercial legal publications. It reflected the court's tightening con-trol over the circulation of legal information in the high Qing. The ban seems to have been effective in the Qianlong reign. Few early Qing editions

survived—I have seen only one extant Qing edition printed before the Jiaqing period.

Despite the strict ban and harsh punishments, popular legal handbooks
were not eliminated. The court never reiterated the prohibition after the
Qianlong reign—the ban seems to have eased in the Jiaqing period, and
these handbooks resurged and flourished in the market in the late Qing.
Moreover, the Qianlong campaign mainly targeted published editions.
Manuscripts proved more difficult for the government to find and destroy.
Xue Yunsheng (1820–1901), the famous late Qing jurist, commented on the
effectiveness of the ban: "Although printed editions can be banned, manuscripts cannot be banned. Many people still circulate and study these books
in private. They are just like pornographic novels that can be banned but
cannot be eradicated."[50] Therefore, it is unlikely that the Qianlong era ban
had any more than a temporary impact on the production and circulation
of the popular legal handbooks.

LEGAL KNOWLEDGE IN LITIGATION PRACTICE

Knowledge is power. When late imperial Chinese people obtained legal
knowledge and litigation skills, they were willing to use (and often abuse)
them for their own ends. Qing county-level legal archives have a large number of lawsuits indicating that commoners were familiar with the laws, and
they used their legal knowledge and litigation skills to write accusations and
counteraccusations, to get their cases accepted in local courts, and to solve
disputes. Woman Lin's case in the Dan-Xin Archives was a representative
example of how Qing litigants used the laws in litigation. In 1887 Woman
Lin, a sixty-four-year-old widow, filed a lawsuit in the Xinzhu County Court
against her fourth son, whom she accused of stealing money and beating
her. In the accusation, Woman Lin first put herself on the moral high
ground, claiming she was a hardworking wife and a filial daughter-in-law.
She gave birth to six sons and raised them after her husband died young.
Her fourth son, Fan Huosheng, however, was extremely unfilial and frequently committed crimes:

> My fourth son, Huosheng, is not only unfilial but also condones his wife
> to offend and humiliate me. He even had the audacity to steal two hun-
> dred *yuan* from me to spend extravagantly on prostitution and gambling.
> When I tried to ask him to return the money, he began to hold a grudge

against me and frequently came to my house to make trouble. He helped his wife Liao *shi* insult and curse me. They acted violently, attempting to grasp me and hit me. My clothes were torn and I only escaped with the help of my neighbor. . . . This unfilial villain not only insults and bullies me—his own mother—but also steals from me. This is severely against the law [*da gan lü jiu*]![51]

Woman Lin then asked the magistrate to arrest and interrogate the son and punish him according to the law (*anlü chengban*). In her accusation, Woman Lin clearly indicated that her son's behaviors violated the laws and deserved punishments. Indeed, cursing and beating parents were severe crimes in late imperial China; both were punished with the death penalty. Since the accusation mentioned capital crimes, it drew the magistrate's immediate attention—he accepted the lawsuit and asked for additional evidence of the son's crimes.

Around two weeks later, a counteraccusation was filed in the court. The counteraccusation, however, told a completely different story: Although Woman Lin gave birth to Fan Huosheng, he was adopted by his fourth uncle at a young age because the uncle did not have a son. The uncle established Huosheng as his heir. When dividing the Fan family property, Woman Lin's five other sons were angry that they could each get only one-fifth of a share of their late grandfather's property, while their brother Huosheng, as the only heir of the fourth uncle, could enjoy a whole share by himself. The five brothers then seized the family property and refused to give Huosheng his proper share. The counteraccusation acclaimed that the Fan brothers fabricated a completely false accusation, filed under the name of Woman Lin, that attempted to frame Huosheng for capital crimes. They clearly intended to get rid of Huosheng to swallow up his share of the property. In the hearing held by the magistrate, Woman Lin admitted that the fourth uncle had adopted Huosheng. The magistrate scolded Woman Lin for the false accusation, but he did not punish her because the Qing law pardoned parents' false accusations against their children.[52] After several rounds of following-up accusations, counteraccusations, and petitions, Woman Lin and Huosheng reached an agreement on the family division through the mediation of local gentry and lineage elders. They then withdrew the case from the court.

This lawsuit indicates how Chinese litigants manipulated the law and applied their legal knowledge in litigation practice. Woman Lin and her sons, or the litigation master hired by them, was clearly aware of the laws regarding children cursing and beating their parents. After all, this legal information was widely available. The related statutes appeared in different editions of popular legal handbooks and were frequently mentioned in community legal lectures. For example, two lines in "Comprehensive Rhymed Song of Statutes and Substatutes," included in many different editions of popular handbooks such as *Thunder*, read: "A son or daughter beating his/her father or mother, this violates the law and should be punished by slow slicing. . . . A son or grandson curses his senior relatives, he would undoubtedly be punished by strangulation."[53] Although the information in the song was not entirely accurate, it spelled out the severity of the crimes and the potential for harsh punishments. Woman Lin clearly fabricated her story based on the knowledge of this law, turning a civil dispute on inheritance among brothers into a severe criminal case of a son beating his mother. As for Woman Lin and her sons, this was a smart strategy of "hitting three birds with one stone": their case would more easily be accepted in the court because it concerned capital crimes; Fan Huosheng would be severely punished if they won the case; and they would not be punished even if the magistrate found out that it was a false accusation. The accusation, therefore, evidently implied their (or their litigation master's) familiarity with the laws and judicial practice in local courts.

Another lawsuit in the Dan-Xin Archives also vividly illustrates how Qing people manipulated their legal knowledge to achieve their own ends. In 1843 Jiang Tengjiao's grandfather bought a piece of land from the brothers Zhang Youqing and Zhang Tianding. Around twenty-seven years after the transaction, Zhang Youqing's son, Zhang Guo, intended to request to increase the sale price (*zhaoxi*), probably due to the increase of land value.[54] In fear that Jiang Tengjiao would not agree to pay the increased price to him, Zhang Guo first borrowed twenty yuan from Jiang's father and then refused to return the money. Zhang wanted to keep the money as the add-on price of the land transaction. Jiang was enraged and furiously pressed Zhang to pay the money back. One night, Zhang dug a fake grave on Jiang's land. The next morning, Jiang noticed that some of his crops were trampled and that a grave had appeared. Without much thought, Jiang notified the local headman and destroyed the grave. Two days later, Zhang led a dozen men and swarmed into Jiang's house. They accused Jiang of destroying their ancestral grave and asked him to return the bones of their ancestors to them. They threatened that if Jiang did not return the bones, they would not leave Jiang's house and "even one hundred taels of silver would not settle this issue."[55]

Jiang then realized that he had fallen into a trap. Zhang Guo clearly knew that digging up grave was a serious crime. According to article 276, "Uncovering Graves" (Fazhong): "Everyone who digs up another's grave and causes the coffin to appear will receive 100 strokes of the heavy bamboo and be exiled to 3000 *li*. If he has opened the coffin and the corpse appears, he will be strangled with delay." Many popular legal handbooks included the "Uncovering Graves" law and related sample lawsuits. *Thunder*, for example, not only recorded the details of the article but also included around thirty sample litigation phrases and five sample lawsuits regarding the "Uncovering Graves" law.[56] In the Code, the law was in the "General Public Disorder and Theft" chapter in the "Laws relating to the Board of Punishments" Section. In *Thunder*, however, the law was put into the "Laws relating to the Board of Revenue" chapter, printed together with other civil disputes on lands, property, and inheritance. Through relocating the "Uncovering Graves" law, *Thunder* reminded readers that they might consider using this law in civil disputes regarding land and property. Zhang Guo intended to use (or more precisely, abuse) the law to solve his dispute on the land and debt with Jiang. After Jiang destroyed the fake grave, Zhang gained considerable advantages: he could accuse Jiang of digging up his ancestral grave and exposing the bones—a capital crime according to the law, and he could use the potential lawsuit and harsh punishments to force Jiang to pay more money or make a compromise on the debt.

When Jiang realized he had fallen into Zhang's litigation trap, he and his family became frightened. After consideration, Jiang decided to file a lawsuit in the county court first. In the accusation, Zhang narrated the facts about the land transaction, the debt, Zhang Guo's intention of seeking an additional price for the land, and the grave incident. In his comments on the accusation, the magistrate scolded Jiang of destroying the grave without reporting it to the government. He wrote, "Now Zhang Guo has an excuse and gets together his sons and nephews to go to your house and request their ancestors' bones. You really bring the trouble to yourself!" But the magistrate seemed to side with Jiang that the true dispute was the land rather than the grave. He asked Jiang to provide the contract of the land transaction in 1843 for further investigation. A few days later, Zhang Guo's nephew filed a counteraccusation in the court. He claimed that the transaction in 1843 was a conditional sale (*dian*, which meant that the seller could ask an increase in sale price or request a redemption after the transaction), rather than a finalized sale (*mai*). When he had saved enough money, he wanted to redeem the land back. But Jiang refused and began to hold a grudge against him. Jiang then destroyed the Zhang family's ancestral grave as a revenge. In his comments on the counteraccusation, the magistrate simply ignored Zhang's accusation against Jiang of uncovering the grave. Instead, he treated the lawsuit as a civil dispute on land and asked Zhang to provide the contract of the land transaction. After the hearing, the magistrate found that the transaction was indeed a finalized sale, as Jiang had claimed. He punished Zhang with a light bamboo beating, but he asked Jiang to forgive Zhang's debt (twenty yuan of silver) as a compromise. Both sides seemed to be satisfied with the settlement. No further accusation was made after the sentence.[57]

Woman Lin's lawsuit and Zhang Guo's lawsuit were not exceptional. After examining local archives, historians have found that Qing litigants often disguised civil disputes about debts, land boundaries, marriage, and inheritance as more serious criminal cases involved with charges of stealing, robbery, kidnapping, abduction, rape, gambling, homicide, and so on. Scholarship on litigation masters also indicates that Qing litigants often made false or exaggerated accusations as a strategy of judicial access because they believed that magistrates would not be interested in their petty complaints in civil matters.[58] When writing accusation and counteraccusations, it was common for litigants to fabricate and exaggerate their stories based on one or several statutes in the Code and asked officials to sentence their cases according to the laws, as seen in Woman Lin's case. Some litigants even manipulated their legal knowledge to set up a legal trap, as seen in Zhang Guo's case, to convert petty civil disputes into weighty criminal matters to gain leverage in litigation.

Late imperial Chinese officials were well aware of the prevalence of false or exaggerated accusations in litigation practice. An official commented about these exaggerations in litigation as follows: "If there is a fight on the street during the day, the accusation must say robbery; if someone goes to another's house and has an argument, the accusation must say breaking into the houses and taking property by force; if someone has a small argument or a fight with a woman, the accusation must say rape; if there is a dispute on the boundary between graveyards, the accusation must say digging up tombs and exposing the corpse."[59] Since many litigants brought criminal accusations with civil goals, it was crucial for magistrates to make a judgment on the true purpose of the litigation, which was usually hidden behind the narratives of crimes and suffering in accusations and counteraccusations.

In both Woman Lin's case and Zhang Guo's case, the magistrates clearly decided to deal with the cases mainly as civil disputes, even though the original charges were involved with serious crimes.

Popular legal handbooks substantially influenced local litigation patterns in Qing China. Historians such as Fuma Susumu, Guangyuan Zhou, and Deng Jianpeng find clear connections between popular handbooks and litigation writings in Qing local archives. These connections included:

Similar terms: Accusations and counteraccusations usually borrowed terms from the litigation phrases (*zhuyu*) sections of popular legal handbooks. Qing litigants used these borrowed terms in the title of their accusations to exaggerate the severity of lawsuits and attract officials' attention. For example, they described an inheritance dispute as "losing all the property due to fornication" (*yinjian dangchan*) and property dispute as "violently occupying and beating" (*chengxiong ouda*).[60]

Similar writing styles: Following the strategies in popular legal handbooks, litigants usually described themselves as the poorer, weaker, and helpless party and their opponents as the stronger, richer, and more resourceful party. The structure of accusations and counteraccusations often followed the instructions in popular legal handbooks. The language and the tones were also similar between the samples in handbooks and the real ones in the archives. The only difference between real accusations and sample litigation writings in popular handbooks was the length—real accusations were longer than the samples.[61]

Similar strategies of using and abusing the laws: Popular handbooks such as *Thunder* printed the laws, sample litigation phrases, and sample litigation writings together. Both the instructions and sample litigation writings indicated the importance of using laws in litigation. Accusations and counteraccusations in Qing local archives indicated that litigants adopted a utilitarian attitude toward the laws of popular handbooks. Litigants used the laws as weapons to defend their own interests and to attack opponents. They chose the laws that would serve their own ends, carefully wrote (or fabricated) stories according to the laws, and on many occasions, they explicitly asked officials to sentence cases according to the laws. They did not have to specifically mention the laws in accusations or know the details about various conditions and levels of punishments of the laws. Even simple legal knowledge, such as "beating parents or grand-parents deserves the death penalty" and "excavating tombs and exposing bones will be strictly punished," could be very powerful. Knowledge about the laws and how to use them in litigation obviously eased litigants' access to the court. Not only did popular legal handbooks disseminate legal knowledge from experts to common readers, but also, more importantly, they transformed popular views of the law and fostered popular legal awareness in late imperial China.

CONCLUSION

When the governor asked the Cheng brothers where they bought *Thunder*, they replied that they simply got the book from a random bookseller whose name was unknown to them. The memorial also mentioned officials found "four volumes" of the book from the Cheng brothers' houses—which indicates that the book probably was the long (eight-chapter) version of *Thunder*.[62] It seems that it was not difficult for the Cheng brothers, who lived in the remote mountainous county of Lushan in Henan, to obtain *Thunder*. Although Lushan was not near any major printing center, itinerant book peddlers could reach towns and villages through trade routes. The Cheng brothers probably bought the book from one of these book peddlers. It is possible that they bought the book because they planned to use it in litigation or that they initially bought it only out of curiosity or for entertainment, and when they got into trouble, they thought of a "solution" based on what they learned from the book.

Many Qing people also possibly got popular legal handbooks as the Cheng brothers did and used what they had learned from the books in litigation. Similar to the wide circulation of forbidden novels such as *The Plum in the Golden Vase* (Jin ping mei) and *The Water Margin* (Shuihu zhuan), the strict state ban did not eliminate popular legal handbooks. On the contrary, the ban aroused readers' curiosity about popular legal handbooks. Evidence indicates that popular legal handbooks were circulated in Qing society and available on the book market. These books brought relatively accurate legal knowledge and litigation skills to the lower end of the society. Most readers, like the Cheng brothers, were lower literati and literate commoners.

Most legal information in popular legal handbooks originated from statutes and substatutes from the Code—in other words, popular legal handbooks imparted orthodox legal knowledge to readers. Books like *Thunder* directly copied texts from the Code. However, through combining this orthodox legal knowledge with litigation skills, these books successfully transformed the meanings and usage of the laws. Law was no longer an intimidating symbol of control and order established by the state; it became a tool, a weapon that anyone could use and even manipulate to achieve his or her own ends and to attack enemies. Through selecting, simplifying, and categorizing texts, popular legal handbooks translated the laws from elite texts written by and for officials to popular texts that licentiates and even commoners could read and understand. The two-register printing format used by most Qing editions efficiently organized and categorized the laws and litigation writing samples, which greatly facilitate readers to locate useful information in the book. When the Cheng brothers decided to accuse local clerks and runners of corruption and overtaxation, they could easily find more than one hundred different sample phrases in "Established Phrases and Selected Sentences of Accusing Clerks and Runners" (*Gao yayi taoyu zhaiju*) in *Thunder*.[63] They could also find useful laws and sample accusations about the corruption and malpractices of clerks and runners in the "Corruptions and Deception" section and those about overtaxation in the "Households and Corvée Service" section.

The most salient change from late Ming editions of popular handbooks to late Qing editions was the increase in accurate legal information. *Thunder* contained a large number of statutes and substatutes selected and replicated from the Code. Few Ming editions had such detailed and accurate legal information. The rising portion of accurate legal information in popular legal handbooks responded to the rise of interest and need among readers toward such information. Under the pressure of case backlogs, local courts were reluctant to accept lawsuits in which the accuser's claims were not clearly supported by law. Qing local legal archives also proved that litigants frequently mentioned or implied the laws in their stories in accusations and counteraccusations. Legal and litigation knowledge would greatly enhance litigants' accessibility to local courts. Many people—such as the Cheng brothers, murderer Du Huailiang, Woman Lin, and Zhang Guo— were Code-smart and were not reluctant to use and abuse the laws and the legal system for their own interests.

5 POPULAR LEGAL EDUCATION

AN EMPIRE-WIDE MARKET IN BOOKS MEANT THAT PEOPLE COULD easily buy legal books, including the Code, a variety of legal treatises, and popular legal handbooks. Literate people who could afford to buy books thus had access to accurate and up-to-date legal information. But most of the Qing populace—arguably 70 percent of the male population and more than 90 percent of the female population—were illiterate.[1] Were there other forms of legal information circulating in Qing society? Could illiterate people get accurate information about the law?

Previous research suggests that there was no effective popular legal education in the Qing and that the general public had no access to accurate and up-to-date legal information. Most commoners received only "fragmented and usually imprecise" legal information through sources such as novels, plays, and operas.[2] However, community lecture manuals and a variety of imperial and local documents show that the Qing state and many officials made serious efforts to educate the common people with the laws. The most important vehicle for legal education was the community lecture system. Although formerly understood as moral indoctrination, this system incorporated not only moral lectures but also legal lectures on statutes and substatutes from the Code. Lecturers usually read these statutes aloud and explained them in colloquial language to the audience. Laws were carefully selected and imparted to men and women, young and old, literate and illiterate, Han and non-Han, around the Qing empire. These lectures enabled people with limited education to understand basic laws and legal principles. Common people had unprecedented access to written laws and punishments, in the form of texts, speeches, and lectures, thanks to commercially printed editions of the Code, popular legal imprints, and community lectures.

POPULAR LEGAL EDUCATION: ATTITUDES AND POLICIES

Most Qing rulers embraced the idea that the populace needed to know state-authorized legal principles and basic statutes from the Code. Qing emperors and their officials believed that a benevolent government should promulgate its laws to its people, establish popular legal education, and tell the people about the potential harsh punishments for those who dared to violate the laws. In this way, the people would be forewarned and less likely to commit crimes, which would contribute to the building of ideal society. The idea of fostering popular legal education can be traced back over two thousand years. *The Rites of Zhou*, one of the five Confucian classics, specified the responsibilities of the legal minister of the Western Zhou: "On the first day of the first month [of each year], [the minister of justice] starts to promulgate the rule of punishments in cities and towns of the kingdom. He puts up images of the punishments and laws on the wall of the high towers outside the palace gate for all the people to see."[3] The Western Zhou government depicted in *The Rites of Zhou* symbolized the ideal benevolent government in Confucian discourse. The book thus indicated that an ideal benevolent government ought to publicize its laws and punishments and let everyone in the realm know them.

This story about the Zhou's popular promulgation of the laws may be legendary, but it served as a model for subsequent ruling elites to apply to popular legal education. Qing rulers frequently cited this passage to legitimatize their efforts in publicizing and promulgating laws to the general public. For example, in his preface to *The Great Qing Code*, the Yongzheng emperor cited the story and noted that the Code should follow the Zhou precedent to promote popular legal education: "From large cities and towns to remote lands and poor villages, every magistrate should follow the institution of reading the laws recorded in *The Rites of Zhou* and constantly expound [the laws to local people]. They should also order men in local communities to teach each other the laws. In this way, the people will learn to respect the laws and value themselves. Officials will make wise judgments; people will cease to engage in litigation. Customs will be rectified; rituals and comity will be restored."[4] In the emperor's eyes, popular legal education was an essential means of perfecting social customs. Similar discourse was prevalent in Qing genres that supported popular legal education and promoted the dissemination of legal knowledge in local society.

Some Qing ruling elites, however, doubted the effectiveness of popular legal education in transforming customs and stabilizing local society.[5] They worried about the danger of over-educating the populace in the laws. Viewing law and legal knowledge as a threat to morality and social stability had its roots in early Chinese thoughts. In *Analects* (Lunyu), Confucius praised rule by morality (*de*) and ritual (*li*) over that by regulations and punishments: "Lead the people by regulations, keep them in order by punishments, and they will flee from you and lose all self-respect. But lead them by morality and keep them in order by ritual and they will keep their self-respect and come to you."[6] Although *The Rites of Zhou* indicated that the government should promulgate its laws to the general public, some other early Confucian texts warned that popularizing legal norms would be fraught with moral and political danger. *The Chronicle of Zuo* (Zuozhuan) recorded a sharp criticism from a minister of the state of Zheng on the promulgation of Zheng's *Books of Punishment* (Xingshu), known as the first codes of written law in Chinese history: "When the people know that there is a code, they will not be in awe of their superiors. All together, they bicker, appeal to the code, and seek to achieve their goals by trying their luck. They cannot be governed. . . . When the people have learned how to contend over points of law, they will abandon ritual propriety and appeal to what is written. Even at chisel's tip and knife's edge they will contend. A chaotic litigiousness will flourish and bribes will circulate everywhere."[7] The minister argued that promulgation of written law would threaten the people's respect for ritual and authority, which would inevitably lead to moral decline and political disorder.

The Qing judicial system faced many troubles and challenges, especially after the mid-Qianlong period. Case backlogs piled up on magistrates' desks and false accusations flooded in, despite frequent prohibition. In this troublesome era, some Qing ruling elites began to reconsider the popular education policies. They thought that the people were already too litigious, and teaching them law would do more harm than good to society. In this context, the discourse on the potential danger of legal knowledge was resurfacing. For example, although he did not openly oppose legal education in community lectures, the Jiaqing emperor frequently rejected his officials' suggestions on the popularization of legal information through other channels. In 1812, aiming to prevent the people from engaging in unorthodox religions, an official suggested that the court should print and disseminate the statutes and substatutes about "teaching and practicing unorthodox religions." The emperor responded sternly in an edict:

Our state establishes law and punishments. When there is a public execution, officials post proclamations that list the convicts' names and their
crimes. We do so in order to make commoners hear and watch, and then
they can generate fear and get caution. But the people still violate the laws
one after another. Is it that we can stop the evil and prevent the violence
merely by printing and disseminating the texts of the statutes? Moreover,
the statutes have their profound meanings. They are the foundation of our
dynasty's judicial administration. Are they things that illiterate commoners of every household can thoroughly understand? The suggestions in the
memorial are impractical.[8]

In the Jiaqing emperor's eyes, educating the people on the laws could not
help prevent crimes and transform social customs. He indicated that most
people had already obtained some basic knowledge of legal principles, and
it was also impossible for them to understand thoroughly the complicated
laws in the Code. Popular legal education could contribute little to their
understanding of the laws, let alone restraining their behavior.

Therefore, Qing rulers held complicated attitudes toward popular legal
education. Some ruling elites, such as the Yongzheng emperor, embraced
the idea that educating the people about law could transform social customs
and reduce the number of people who committed crimes. Others, such as
the Jiaqing emperor, sometimes expressed doubts about the effectiveness of
popular legal education in transforming local customs and maintaining
social order. They indicated that the common people already knew the laws
well, and further legal education provided by the state would do more harm
than good. But none of them questioned the legitimacy and effectiveness
of community lectures—the main vehicle of popular legal education in
the Qing.

THE COMMUNITY LECTURE SYSTEM

The Qing community lecture system played an important role in state-
sponsored popular legal education. The precedent for community lectures
was the community compact (*xiangyue*) of the Northern Song period
(960–1127). Promoted by leading Confucian scholars, the community compact in the Song symbolized a voluntaristic community organization that
emphasized "mutuality, reciprocity, and cooperation among community
members." By establishing the community compact, Song elites intended

to build self-regulating local communities without the state's interference and to assert their local leadership. They also aimed to implement popular moral education by "bringing to life the moral potential of the compact members" rather than applying stiff moral indoctrination.[9] The community compact declined during the Yuan period. When it revived in the late Ming, the community compact began to be associated with more imperial control and moral indoctrination. Specifically, it was usually local officials rather than gentry who initiated the community compact in the late Ming. All community members were required to join the community compact and perform the five bows and three kowtows ritual to a wooden tablet bearing Ming Taizu's Six Edicts (Liuyu), whereas in the Song they usually kowtowed to Confucius's image. Reading and expounding Taizu's Six Edicts, sometimes together with a number of statutes from *The Great Ming Code*, became the center of the community compact. Moreover, the community compact also became fused with *baojia* surveillance units, designed to suppress social and political unrest.[10] Thus the essential feature of the organization was gradually transformed from voluntaristic, gentry-led, local community self-regulated compacts to compulsory, official-led, state-sponsored lectures in the Ming and Qing.

The community lecture system had several new features in the Qing. First, the central government asserted more control over community lectures, especially in the early and mid-Qing period. Qing emperors established detailed regulations on how the lectures should be organized and performed and also issued imperially authorized manuals for community lectures to local officials. The content of Qing community lectures also emphasized the state's power and imperial authority more than their Song and Ming counterparts had. In 1670 the Kangxi emperor promulgated *The Sixteen Maxims of the Sacred Edict* (Shangyu shiliu tiao), which later became the outline of the content of Qing community lectures. The *Sacred Edict* was adapted from Ming Taizu's Six Edicts. The *Sacred Edict* consisted of the following sixteen maxims:

1. Esteem most highly filial piety and brotherly submission, in order to give due importance to the social relations.
2. Behave with generosity toward your kindred, in order to illustrate harmony and benignity.
3. Cultivate peace and concord in your neighborhoods, in order to prevent quarrels and litigation.

4. Recognize the importance of husbandry and the culture of the mulberry tree, in order to ensure a sufficiency of clothing and food.

5. Show that you prize moderation and economy, in order to prevent the lavish waste of your means.

6. Give weight to colleges and schools, in order to make correct the practice of the scholar.

7. Extirpate strange principles, in order to exalt the correct doctrine.

8. Lecture on the laws, in order to warn the ignorant and obstinate.

9. Elucidate propriety and yielding courtesy, in order to make manners and customs good.

10. Labor diligently at your proper callings, in order to stabilize the will of the people.

11. Instruct sons and younger brothers, in order to prevent them from doing what is wrong.

12. Put a stop to false accusation, in order to preserve the honest and good.

13. Warn against sheltering deserters, in order to avoid being involved in their punishment.

14. Fully remit your taxes, in order to avoid being pressed for payment.

15. Unite in hundreds and tithings, in order to put an end to thefts and robbery.

16. Remove enmity and anger, in order to show the importance due to the person and life.[11]

Ming Taizu's Six Edicts overwhelmingly emphasized the people's proper behavior and responsibilities on the family and community level rather than their relationships with the ruler or the state.[12] The Kangxi emperor's *Sacred Edict* indicated a clear ideological continuation of the "Six Edicts" in terms of family and local community, but it significantly extended to the realm of the people's legal and political obedience to the state. As historian William Theodore de Bary argues, the *Sacred Edict* "would serve to enhance state power and imperial authority: namely the enforcement of dynastic law, obedience to the state, crime prevention, punishment for deserters, payment of taxes and tithes, banning heterodoxy, etc."[13]

The Kangxi emperor and his successors made serious efforts to promulgate the *Sacred Edict* and rebuild the community lecture system to educate commoners with the moral principles in the *Sacred Edict* and basic legal knowledge from the Code. In 1679 the Kangxi court issued copies of an imperially authorized manual for community lectures to prefectures, counties, and villages in the empire. The manual instructed lecturers to read the *Sacred Edict*, its colloquial explanations, and a number of statutes from the Code to local people. In 1686 the emperor ordered officials to promote the lectures in the military and in southwest regions where non-Han people dwelled.[14] In 1700 he ordered teachers to read and expound the *Sacred Edict* to students in local schools. In the Yongzheng reign, the court continued to institutionalize the community lecture system. In 1729 the emperor issued an imperial edict that established community lectures in every community and large village. Local officials or officially appointed compact leaders (*yuezheng*) took charge of giving the lectures on the first and fifteenth day of each month.[15] This imperial edict defined *xiangyue* as reading and expounding the *Sacred Edict*. Following this edict, the Qing court began to take direct control over the institution: the imperial court regulated the content of the lectures and gave local officials the power to choose compact leaders, who had been publicly selected (*gongju*) by community members in the past. In the Yongzheng reign, therefore, *xiangyue* formally became state-dominated moral and legal lectures aimed at inculcating ethical orthodoxy in local people as well as strengthening central political control over local society.

After the Yongzheng reign, the Qing court continued to emphasize the importance of community lectures in the people's moral education and ordered local officials to make real efforts to implement them. The Qianlong emperor issued at least fifteen edicts to support and to regulate community lectures. He told officials to give the lectures in remote villages and in frontier regions where non-Han people dwelled. He also encouraged lecturers to use colloquial language when expounding the *Sacred Edict* and to teach imperial laws and regulations to the people in the lectures.[16] The Jiaqing emperor issued about ten related edicts, and the Daoguang emperor issued at least five. Even in the Tongzhi and Guangxu reigns when the dynasty was on the verge of collapse, the court still issued a number of imperial edicts and stressed that lectures were fundamental in the people's moral education, and officials and schools should regularly deliver the lectures.[17]

Beside the imperial control, another salient feature of Qing community lectures was that the ritual ceremony was diminishing, and at the same time, moral and legal lectures played an increasingly important role. The late Ming community compact usually had lengthy ritual ceremonies. All of the participants performed the five bows and three kowtows ritual—identical to the ritual carried out by officials at an imperial audience—in the late Ming community compact. Many Ming gentry believed that the ritual would uphold social hierarchy and transform the local people's morality.[18] In the early Qing, however, the ritual of community lectures had been simplified. Although commoners were ordered to kneel when officials kowtowed to the imperial tablet, they no longer had to perform the court audience ritual. In the late Qing lectures, commoners just gathered and stood around the lecture altar, and no kneeling was required (figure 5.1). While many late Ming and early Qing lecture manuals painstakingly described how the ceremony should be conducted, late Qing manuals usually did not mention such ritual ceremonies at all. In some places, even officials and lecturers did not have to kowtow to the imperial tablet anymore.

Some late Qing lectures were held on a daily basis. In late Qing Guangzhou, for example, local officials hired lecturers, set up tables at local markets or busy roads, and let the lecturers read and expound the *Sacred Edict*,

FIG. 5.1. A lecture on the *Sacred Edict* in Suzhou in the late Qing. Lithographic print. In *Dianshizhai huabao* (1884–1898); reprinted by Guangdong Renmin Chubanshe (1983), vol. 5: 74.

the laws, and meritorious books to the local populace every day.[19] The orderly, serious, and ritualistic ceremony of community lectures in the late Ming and first half of the Qing dynasty became increasingly like a crowded and noisy storytelling party in the late Qing. A lithographic painting in the *Dianshizhai Pictorial* (Dianshizhai huabao) depicted a late Qing lecture in Suzhou: a lecturer—apparently an official—was speaking, and the audience, including both men and women, stood around. Some were listening; some were talking with others; some were running (figure 5.1). The whole picture looks dramatically different from the depiction of a well-regulated community lecture ceremony in an early Qing woodblock illustration (figure 5.2).

As the ritual's popularity declined, Qing officials and gentry incorporated more and more oral indoctrination into community lectures. The focus of the lectures, therefore, gradually shifted from the ceremony to moral doctrine and legal knowledge that lecturers imparted to local people. One part of the lectures significantly extended in the Qing was "reading the statutes and substatutes from the Code." Although some lecturers began to

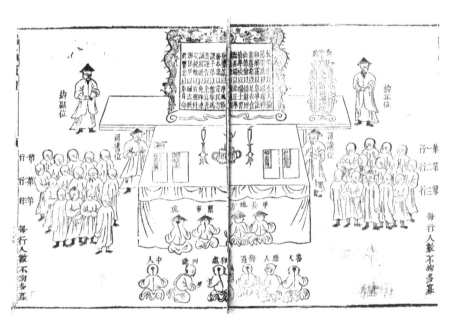

FIG. 5.2. The community lecture ceremony in Lianshan. Woodblock illustration. In Li Laizhang, *Shengyu xuanjiang tiaoyue* (1705 ed.). Courtesy of the Harvard-Yenching Library.

POPULAR LEGAL EDUCATION   153

introduce law in the late Ming, the Qing lecturers incorporated a much larger number of statutes and substatutes. Moreover, the colloquial explanations of the *Sacred Edict* in the Qing lectures were longer and closer to everyday language and included more details and examples than those in the Ming lectures.[20] Qing officials and gentry generally thought that only through carefully teaching the people moral principles (telling them what they should do), legal knowledge (warning them about the potential punishments), and religious ideas (binding them with ideas of retribution) could they be truly touched and transformed. Previous scholarship on Qing moral education shows that leading philosophers embraced a "ritualist approach to moral cultivation"—that is, employing ritual ceremonies to educate the populace and transform social customs.[21] In terms of community lectures, however, the role of ritual ceremony gradually declined, and moral and legal lectures simultaneously increased from the late Ming to the late Qing. Therefore, there was a plurality of approaches to moral education in the Qing. While some Qing thinkers might have advocated the ritualist approach, many officials and gentry adopted a much more didactic approach in the practice of popular moral cultivation.

The performance of community lectures varied according to time and place, but many shared the following similar procedures. In cities magistrates usually personally led the "reading and expounding the *Sacred Edict*" ceremony on the first and fifteenth day of each month. They could choose their own yamen's hall, the Confucius temple (*wenmiao*), Buddhist or Taoist temples, or another spacious place as the lecture location. The ceremony started in the morning, around ten o'clock. The magistrate and his fellow officials wore formal official robes and performed the ceremony of kowtowing to the tablet bearing the *Sacred Edict* in the lecture hall. The local people gathered outside the lecture hall, lining up according to their ages and kneeling when officials performed the ceremony to the imperial tablet. Then everyone rose, and the magistrate himself or a hired lecturer started to choose one or several maxims from the *Sacred Edict* and read them aloud in Mandarin (*guanyu*; lit., "official language"). He then explained the maxims in colloquial language. In some southern areas, the lecturer explained in local dialect (*tuyin*). After explaining, he usually read a number of statutes and substatutes from the Code that were related to the content of the maxims he had just expounded and cautioned the people on the potential punishments if they dared to violate the laws. At the end of a lecture, local officials, gentry, and lecturers again kowtowed to the imperial tablet, and other listeners were required to kneel down. Then yamen clerks carried the imperial tablet back to the magistrate's yamen, and the lecture was over.[22]

In villages the lecturers, usually hired by local officials, led the reading ceremony. The lecturer, his assistants, and local gentry performed the roles in a village that a magistrate and other officials performed in city lectures. The village lectures were usually not conducted as frequently as those in cities. For example, villages in Henan in the Yongzheng period held the lecture only in the second month, the ninth month, the tenth month, and the eleventh month of a year. Lecturers and local gentry usually chose temples or lineage shrines as the place for the lectures; in some locations where those were not available, they built a temporary wooden stage, like those used in village opera parties. The ceremony and the content of the lectures in villages, as many records indicate, were similar to those in cities.[23]

Some previous studies have argued that community lectures were not seriously carried out in local society in the Qing.[24] However, sources in local archives, official handbooks, and lecture manuals show that Qing community lectures were influential and effective, though they were more seriously carried out in some places and periods than others. As historian Victor Mair points out, "a large number of the populace were exposed to and, in some cases, thoroughly familiarized with the *Sacred Edict* through the village lecture system." Qing officials frequently mentioned or cited sentences from the *Sacred Edict* in their writings, and students often quoted the text from the *Sacred Edict* in the civil service examinations. Some late Qing newspapers recorded the *Sacred Edict* and the community lectures. Western missionaries commented on the community lectures and recorded the details of structure and content of those they had attended, and some even borrowed the format for preaching to the Chinese audience.[25] The *Sacred Edict* was also often used as the textbook to teach students about standard Mandarin pronunciation in schools. The text of the *Sacred Edict* even appeared in popular word games in the late Qing and early Republican periods. Evidence from Qing genealogies further proves the popular acceptance of the *Sacred Edict*: many quoted sentences from the *Sacred Edict*, and many used words from the *Sacred Edict* as their clan titles (*tanghao*).[26]

In the early and mid-Qing, the imperial state and officials were the major force to implement community lectures. Many provincial and local officials made serious effort to compile manuals and uphold the lectures in local society.[27] In the Daoguang and Xianfeng periods, when the officially sponsored community lecture organizations were in decline, local gentry began to advocate and fund the lectures. Even during the Taiping War, community lectures were not totally abandoned. Local activists in Jiangnan, such as Yu Zhi (1809–1874), embraced the lectures as a fundamental means of awakening the listeners, eliminating evils, and avoiding the catastrophe of war.[28] After the Taiping War, the ruling elites saw community lectures as an effective instrument to restore social and cultural order. Late Qing gentry not only organized, regulated, and financed the local community lectures but also transformed the lectures by simplifying the required ceremony and incorporating stories from meritorious books, which made the lectures more appealing to local people. Their endeavors in reforming community lectures usually won local officials' endorsement and support. In the last years of the Qing, community lectures, at least in some places, could still attract a large group of listeners.[29] Therefore, thanks to the efforts of the imperial state, officials, and gentry, community lectures were long-lived. Few other programs reached its influence and popularity in disseminating orthodox ideas, moral principles, and legal knowledge in society.

LEGAL INFORMATION IN THE LECTURES

Qing community lectures not only taught orthodox Confucian moral principles but also introduced legal knowledge. Previous scholarship on community lectures, however, largely neglect this perspective.[30] The reason is probably that the original text of the *Sacred Edict* itself has little legal information. Only a few of the sixteen maxims mentioned law and litigation. For example, number 3, "Cultivate peace and concord in your neighborhoods, in order to prevent quarrels and litigation," told people that they should establish good relations with their neighbors and should not get involved in litigation. Number 8, "Lecture on the laws, in order to warn the ignorant and obstinate," encouraged people to gain some legal knowledge. People who knew the laws and punishments would not dare to commit crimes. Although these maxims mentioned the laws and litigation, they provided no specific legal information.

Many lecture manuals, however, included a large amount of accurate legal information. These manuals were widely used in practice as instructions for local officials and lecturers to conduct community lectures. The most influential manual in the early Qing was the *Complete Book of the Sacred Edict and Community Lectures with Statutes* (Shangyu helü xiangyue quanshu), first published in 1679. It was also one of the earliest manuals that contained detailed legal information from the Code and the *Substatutes in Current Use*. The author was a prominent Manchu official named Chen Bingzhi (d. 1686). When working as Zhejiang governor, Chen published the manual and issued copies to magistrates and community leaders in his province. Chen also asked the emperor's permission to promote the manual in other provinces. When the emperor ordered all governors to print and issue the manual as the guide for community lectures, it gained nationwide influence.[31]

Chen's preface pointed out that the lectures on the *Sacred Edict* were a fundamental means of "transforming the people and perfecting moral customs" (*huamin chengsu*). He explained each maxim in colloquial language so that even "illiterate men and women in remote lands and poor villages" would be able to easily understand the profound meanings of the *Sacred Edict*. Chen noted that moral education was much more important than legal punishments, but if the government taught people the basic principles of the laws and the harsh punishments that could result from crimes, even the most ignorant and obstinate people would comply with the laws. So Chen attached to each maxim's explanation a number of the current statutes and substatutes. Chen hoped that "the people would be able to know that they should do good things and that they should not violate the laws."[32]

Chen Bingzhi wrote that all the people were educable, but that officials needed to use different approaches to educate people of different intellectual levels. As for those who were wise and reasonable, the *Sacred Edict* would help them establish themselves (*lishen*) and cultivate their morality, but for those who were stupid and stubborn, the moral instructions in the *Sacred Edict* were less effective. When positive instructions from the *Sacred Edict* failed to touch their hearts, Chen argued, fear of punishments would at least stop crime. The laws, though less desirable, were useful in popular moral education.[33] By teaching the laws in the lectures, Chen intended to generate public awe and fear of the punishments and the state's legal power. For example, for maxim number 1, "Esteem most highly filial piety and brotherly submission, in order to give due importance to the social relations," Chen first provided detailed explanations and examples of the proper behavior regarding filial piety and brotherly submission, and then he incorporated the "Reading the statutes" (*dulü*) section:

> You, the people, must know that filial piety [*xiao*] and brotherly submission [*di*] are the fundamental principles of human beings. If you can

perform *xiao* and *di*, you are the top-grade good people in the world. For those who don't follow the principles of *xiao* and *di*, let's try to read the following laws from the Code:

If someone curses his grandparents or parents, or if the wife or concubine curses her husband's grandparents or parents, the punishment will be strangulation.

If someone curses an elder brother or sister, the punishment is one hundred strokes of the heavy bamboo.

If a younger brother or sister strikes an elder brother or sister, the punishment will be ninety strokes of the heavy bamboo and penal servitude of two and half years. If there is an injury, the punishment is one hundred strokes of the heavy bamboo and penal servitude of three years. If there is fracture, the punishment is one hundred strokes of the heavy bamboo and exile to three thousand *li*. If the injury is made with a knife, or if there is fracturing of a limb, or the blinding of one eye, then the punishment is strangulation. If the victim dies, all will be beheaded.

Chen continued to list five other statutes and substatutes that were related to the crimes of violating the rules of filial piety and brotherly submission, such as murdering one's parents or grandparents, violating parents' or grandparents' orders, and failure to take care of one's parents or grandparents. At the end of the section, Chen concluded: "Reading these texts from the Code, you should always be alert at any time and always be fearful. Definitely do not do things that violate the rules of *xiao* and *di*, and throw yourself into the net of the dynasty's law."[34]

Chen cited the statutes and substatutes directly from the Code but abbreviated many complicated legal definitions and simplified the language. Chen's short version of the laws did, however, keep most of the original terminology of the laws, and the crimes and punishments he mentioned were mostly accurate and not hard to understand. According to Chen's design, the Code should be read aloud to the local people after officials and lecturers had explained the maxims.

Similarly, Chen's manual provided laws that related to each of the remaining fifteen maxims: altogether about 39 statutes and 12 substatutes from the Code and 8 regulations from *The Substatutes in Current Use* and imperial edicts (table 5.1). The laws that Chen selected to introduce in the lectures had several features.

TABLE 5.1. Statutes from the Qing Code in Chen's Manual

Article No.	Title	Chapter
30	Distinguishing Principals and Accessories in Joint Offenses	Names and General Rules
61	Explaining and Reading the Laws and Regulations	Official Rules
87	Establishing Separate Household Registration and Dividing the Family Property	Household and Services
97	Uncultivated Lands	Fields and Houses
101	Marriage of Men and Women	Marriage I
102	Selling or Hiring out Wives and Daughters	Marriage I
105	Marrying or Taking in Marriage during Mourning	Marriage I
107	Marrying Someone with the Same Surname	Marriage I
119	Collecting Grain after the Established Time-Limits	Granaries and Treasuries I
162	Prohibitions Concerning Sorcerers and Sorceresses	Sacrifices
175	Violating the Rules on Clothing and Houses	Rules of Demeanor
179	Concealing Mourning for Parents or Husbands	Rules of Demeanor
181	Burial	Rules of Demeanor
182	Village Wine-Drinking Rituals	Rules of Demeanor
225	Privately Exporting by Going Beyond the Land Frontiers or by Sea in Violation of the Prohibitions	Law of Control Pass
254	Plotting Rebellion and High Treason	General Public Disorder and Theft I
266	Theft with Force	General Public Disorder and Theft II
268	Wrongful Taking in the Daytime	General Public Disorder and Theft II
269	Non-Manifest Theft	General Public Disorder and Theft IV
270	Stealing Horses, Cattle, and Other Livestock	General Public Disorder and Theft V
278	Harboring Thieves and Robbers	General Public Disorder and Theft VII
282	Plotting to Kill Another	Homicide I
284	Plotting to Kill Paternal Grandparents and Parents	Homicide I
289	Making or Keeping Gu Poison for Killing People	Homicide I

Article No.	Title	Chapter
290	Engaging in an Affray and Killing or Intentionally Killing Another	Homicide II
302	Affrays and Blows	Affrays and Blows I
311	Striking the Master from Whom One is Receiving Instruction	Affrays and Blows I
316	Striking a Relative of the Same Surname	Affrays and Blows II
317	Striking a Superior or Older Relative of the Third Degree and Below	Affrays and Blows II
318	Striking a Superior or Elder Relative of the Second Degree	Affrays and Blows III
319	Striking Parental Grandparents or Parents	Affrays and Blows III
324	Cursing Another	Cursing
328	Cursing Superior or Older Relatives	Cursing
329	Cursing Paternal Grandparents and Parents	Cursing
333	Making a Written Anonymous Accusation of an Offense against Another	Procedure I
336	False Accusations	Procedure I
337	Offending against One's Status Obligations and Violating Duty	Procedure II
338	Violation by Children or Son's Children of Orders	Procedure II
378	Gambling	Miscellaneous Offenses

Note: Translations of titles are based on Jones's translations of *The Great Qing Code*. Chen's manual has no names or article numbers of the statutes. I looked up article numbers in the Code according to the content of the statutes and added their names and numbers so that readers can easily locate them in the Code.

First, Chen included a lot more statutes than substatutes and other regulations. In his time, the Code had almost an equal number of statutes and substatutes (459 statutes and 449 substatutes), but he obviously preferred statutes, which conveyed fundamental and constant principles of the laws, rather than the more practically applicable substatutes. He was after basic legal principles.

Second, the laws Chen included in the manual were carefully selected for their relevance to the lives of common people. The fifty-one statutes and substatutes selected from the 908 in the Code covered a variety of scenarios that the common people would encounter. He focused on the laws dealing with commoners' usual crimes, including laws regarding marriage, robbery, theft, homicide, fight, and judicial procedure. Chen chose only one statute from the "Name and General Rules" chapters, one from the "Civil Office" chapters, and one from the "War" chapters, but he included twelve from the "Revenue" and the remaining twenty-four statutes all from the "Punishments" chapters.

Third, the laws that Chen included in the manual were up-to-date. He not only closely followed the latest edition of the Code when compiling the manual but also incorporated some substatutes and regulations that had not yet been compiled into the Code. At least seven substatutes Chen mentioned in the book had been established or revised in the Shunzhi or Kangxi period. Chen sometimes noted "new substatute" at the beginning of a substatute. For example, in the number 6 maxim's "Reading the Code" section, Chen cited a substatute issued in 1673, which banned licentiates from filing complaints: "There is a new substatute. In recent years, the common practice of licentiates has been greatly deteriorating. . . . From now on, if licentiates dare to come to Beijing . . . to file false complaints or submit unauthorized memorials, we will not only reject their complaints or memorials, but also deprive them of their licentiate titles. We will also send them to the Board of Punishments for more severe sanctions." Judging from the tone of language, it seems that Chen cited the paragraph from a memorial or an imperial edict, not from the Code. When tracing the history of this substatute, I found that although the ban was issued in 1673 and became a substatute in the same year, it was only formally incorporated into the Code in 1727.[35] Chen's inclusion of new substatutes that had not been compiled into the Code guaranteed that the laws in his book were up-to-date.

The legal information in Chen's manual was designed to be read aloud together with the maxims in the bimonthly lectures on the *Sacred Edict*. In this way, even illiterate people, Chen hoped, would "know the statutes and substatutes, think them through, and understand each of them thoroughly."[36] Of course, Chen's aim of upholding popular legal education was to boost moral education and prevent the people from committing crimes, not to encourage the people to use this knowledge in litigation. He specifically explained the function of the Code to his audience in the colloquial explanations of maxim 8: "You, people, listen. Do you know why our dynasty establishes *The Great Qing Code*? It is because we are afraid that you people take chances of doing evil things and committing crimes. . . . There are a lot of harsh punishments in the Code. . . . We want you people to see the laws and generate fear, so that you dare not go with bad people or have evil ideas. You should be always vigilant and cautious and behave as good, respectable, common people." Under the sponsorship of the throne, copies of Chen's manual were issued to prefectures, counties, and villages in the empire. For example, Huang Liuhong, Chen's contemporary and a county magistrate in Shandong, mentioned that he received Chen's manual and adhered to it when conducting community lectures in his jurisdiction.[37]

In 1868 the imperial court endorsed a new manual on community lecture, compiled by Xia Xin (1789–1871), a renowned Confucian scholar who worked as an instructor in several county and prefecture schools in Jiangxi and Anhui. Xia's manual, *Sixteen Maxims of the Sacred Edict with Statutes and Simple Explanations* (Shengyu shiliutiao fulü yijie) also contained detailed information about the law.[38] After Xia finished compiling the manuscript, his friend Hu Zhaozhi (1807–1871), vice minister of the Board of Civil Office, recommended the book to the throne. The throne was pleased with the manual, praising it for "inheriting the ancient ideas that taught the people to read the laws in *The Rites of Zhou*" and "extremely useful when used in community lectures." The throne then decided to promote the manual as the authorized instruction for community lectures, and asked the Wuyingdian to publish the manual. In 1869 the Wuyingdian reported that it had finished printing the book and would issue copies to governors-general, governors, prefects, and educational intendants (*xuezheng*) as well as generals in Shengjing, Jilin, and Heilongjiang. The Wuyingdian also sold the manual through its Book Circulation Bureau to the public at the price of only 0.15 taels.[39] Several provincial governments reprinted and republished the book. For example, the Jiangsu Provincial Book Bureau (Jiangsu Shuju) republished the book in 1870. Provincial officials in Xinjiang even translated the manual into Uyghur language, published it, and issued the book to local officials and community leaders. In the late Qing and Republican periods, readers around the country could easily buy the Jiangsu edition of the manual for 0.185 yuan through a mail order catalog.[40] Xia's manual, therefore, was widely circulated in the late Qing period under the sponsorship of the imperial court and provincial officials.

Similar to Chen's manual and many other manuals for community lectures, Xia's manual attached simple explanations in colloquial language and explicated the laws related to each maxim of the *Sacred Edict*. Although the structure and the content of Xia's manual are similar to Chen's manual, it has two distinct features. First, Xia's manual did not mention the ritual ceremony of community lectures at all, while Chen's manual explained precisely how the ritual should be properly conducted, including providing illustrations and detailed descriptions on the arrangement of the lecture hall (fig 5.2) as well as the step-by-step process of the ceremony. Second, Xia's manual contained more detailed and accurate legal information than Chen's manual did. Xia included seventy-five statutes and substatutes in his manual, compared with Chen's fifty-one. Seen from Xia's manual, therefore, popular legal education played an increasingly important role in the moral education program, while the role of ritual performance was declining.

In the manual Xia elucidated why popular legal education was necessary. He argued that the people could be divided into three groups and that officials should use different methods to instruct them. The superior people (*shangdeng ren*), Xia wrote, could understand the teachings of the sages— that is, they could fully understand the profound meanings of the *Sacred Edict* and receive instructions from it. As for the medium people (*zhongdeng ren*), officials and lecturer could reach their hearts and transform their morality by telling religious stories about karma and retribution. The inferior people (*xiadeng ren*), however, were extremely stupid and obstinate. Neither the *Sacred Edict* nor meritorious books could enlighten them. The only method, therefore, was to restrain them by the laws and punishments. Xia explained in the manual, "Although these inferior people are ignorant and stubborn, they all fear the laws and the pain of punishments. If we teach them clearly what the laws and punishments are, they will surely take them as a caution and abstain from committing crimes. . . . Therefore . . . the laws not only are used for punishing violence, but also are used for driving the people to do good things." Xia admitted that it was impractical to teach the people all the legal knowledge in the Code. He pointed out that officials should give lectures on simplified statutes and substatutes frequently. As for local people, besides learning the laws from community lectures, in a family, the father or elder brother should teach his sons or younger brothers the laws. Similarly, in a community, educated people should instruct to those who were illiterate in the laws.[41] In this way, everyone in a community, young or old, literate or illiterate, could know and understand the *Sacred Edict* and the laws.

Almost all the laws that Xia cited in the manual were statutes and substatutes from the Code. Compared with Chen's Kangxi-era manual, Xia included fewer laws and regulations beyond the Code. While Chen cited eight such laws and regulations, Xia only cited three.[42] Xia also incorporated more substatutes—twenty-two—in his manual than Chen did with his twelve. By the Tongzhi reign, when Xia's manual was published, the Qing legal system had undergone several changes: first, the Code played a greater role in later Qing legal practice, as discussed in chapter 1, whereas in the early Qing substatutes issued separately from the Code had been more important. Second, Qing legislators had increased the substatutes from 449 in the Kangxi reign to 1,892 in the Tongzhi reign.[43] Xia's manual mirrored these changes. Moreover, Xia also simplified the language and deleted many confusing circumstances of the statutes and substatutes, while trying, like Chen, to maintain the key terms and the original meanings of the laws. Legal information in Xia's manual, therefore, was accurate and straightforward. When read to the audience, Xia hoped, even the people with no formal education could understand easily.

Xia carefully chose the statutes and substatutes relevant to the common people. Like Chen Xia emphasized that the common people should be familiar with the laws in the "Revenue" and the "Punishments" chapters, which included many core statutes and substatutes of civil and penal law in the Qing period. Among the 51 statutes and 22 substatutes in Xia's manual, 45 statutes and 19 substatutes were from these two sections. The laws Xia chose from the "Revenue" chapters were generally about marriage, taxation, business, land and property, and inheritance. The laws he selected from the "Punishments" chapters were generally about rebellion, homicide, theft, robbery, affray, fight, cursing, rape, adultery, and violations on litigation procedures. He also incorporated several statutes and substatutes regarding mourning, burial, clothing and housing rules, public road, and sorcery from the rest chapters.

Xia did not mention whether he referred to Chen's manual when compiling his own manual, but he and Chen included many similar statutes and substatutes in their manuals. Although they apparently used different editions of the Code, Xia cited at least 25 statutes that Chen also included in his manual—nearly half of Xia's statutes (25 of 51) and more than 60 percent of Chen's statutes (25 of 39) were the same. This indicates that Xia and Chen agreed upon "the core legal knowledge" that the common people should have. These 25 statutes included six statutes (articles 87, 97, 101, 105, 107, and 119) from the "Revenue" chapters, three (articles 162, 175, and 181) from the "Rites" chapters, and the remaining sixteen (articles 254, 266, 269, 278,

282, 290, 302, 311, 317, 318, 319, 324, 328, 329, 332, 336, and 338) from the "Punishments" chapters. These statutes regulated the fundamental principles of proper behavior in family and community, such as those regarding marriage, inheritance, and funerals, as well as the punishments if one violated these principles, such as punishments for theft, rioting, gambling, homicide, and rebellion.

Despite many common statutes, Xia obviously emphasized more economic and sexual offenses than Chen did in his manual. Xia did not explain the reason, but it could be a response to social and economic changes. Qing law changed as the economy became increasingly commercialized, and traditional social relations and sexual order had been threatened by overpopulation and an increasing number of single men who could not afford a wife. For example, in maxim 10, "Labor diligently at your proper callings, in order to stabilize the will of the people," Chen only cited three statutes and regulations on gambling, robbery, and swindling.[44] Xia listed six, including "the Salt Laws" (article 141), "Monopolizing the Market" (article 154), and "Privately Casting Copper Cash" (article 359). At least twelve of Xia's additional statutes were the laws and regulations on business, market, property, and transportation (articles 78, 93, 96, 141, 149, 154, 187, 233, 271, 359, 412, 435), which were relevant to the common people's economic and financial life. Another sharp difference between Xia and Chen was that Xia introduced at least six statutes about offenses related to sex. Xia included several core statutes of rape and adultery, such as "Fornication" (article 366), "Facilitating and Tolerating the Wife's or Concubine's Fornication" (article 367), "Fornication between Relatives" (article 368), and "Killing the Adulterous Lover" (article 285).

Both Chen's and Xia's manual contained a substantial amount of accurate and up-to-date legal information. These two manuals are typical examples of how much legal knowledge was taught to the public through the community lecture system in the Qing. Some other lecture manuals, less widely used, also contained detailed legal information. For example, the *Amplified Instructions with Statutes and Case Precedents* (Guangxun fulü cheng'an), a community lecture manual published in 1745, contained not only statutes and substatutes but also a large number of related case precedents. Another manual published in 1857 in Suzhou translated the statutes and substatutes from the Code into the local Wu dialect, Wuyu.[45] The Qing court strongly supported local officials and lecturers teaching the laws in community lectures. Many common people could gain legal information by attending community lectures, and Qing local society might have been more sophisticated in its awareness of the law and more Code-smart than we previously assumed.

LEGAL EDUCATION IN FRONTIER REGIONS

Qing officials also promoted lectures on the *Sacred Edict* and the laws in frontier regions. The Qing was an expanding multiethnic empire. The goals of giving the lectures in China proper were to transform customs, maintain social stability, and cultivate people's morality. In frontier regions where non-Han ethnic groups dwelled, the goals were similar but also conveyed the purpose of acculturation—to transform indigenous people through moral and legal education as well as to establish the state's cultural and judicial hegemony in frontier communities. Qing officials believed that educating indigenous people, who were usually non-Han ethnic groups, Qing laws could transform (*hua*) their "backward" and "brutal" local customs, "civilize" them, and nourish law-abiding subjects. In some regions, the Qing state contested with the local power, and Qing laws largely based on the Han Chinese traditions contested with local customs or laws of minority ethnic groups. Therefore, disseminating and propagandizing orthodox principles and imperial laws was important for the Qing state to establish and stabilize its control in frontier regions.

Many non-Han ethnic groups, such as Miao, Yao, and Zhuang, lived on the southwest frontier. Although the region had been nominally a part of China's territory since the Han period, the central government did not attempt to establish direct control until the late imperial period. In the Ming and especially the Qing, the imperial state gradually replaced indirect control through native headmen with direct bureaucratic administration. The Qing court established the regular bureaucracy, along with the tax system, household registration, and the legal system similar to those in China proper. In the process of the empire's expansion, many Qing officials assigned to frontier areas considered their first and foremost mission to "transform the indigenous people and perfect local customs" through promoting education in local society. Some officials, such as Chen Hongmou in Yunnan, focused on building community schools to teach local children Chinese culture and Confucian values.[46] Others employed the community lecture system for propagating basic Confucian principles and the imperially authorized laws to the local populace.

Take magistrate Li Laizhang's (1654–1721) endeavor in Lianshan for example. Lianshan was a remote and mountainous county on the border of Guangdong, Guangxi, and Hunan, where more than 80 percent of the local population was Yao and Zhuang people. As Li recalled his first impression of the county when he arrived in 1704: "There are only seven villages and two thousand Han people. All of the other people are Zhuang and Yao. They have five large villages and seventeen small villages. Their population is over ten thousand. There are mountains after mountains. Stones are thin and cliffs are steep, as if they are cut by knifes. Only ten percent of the land can be cultivated. Even though people are working hard all year, what they can get is slim."[47] The poverty and remoteness of the county, however, did not stop Li's ambition to transform local society. Embracing Han-Chinese-Confucian cultural and moral superiority, Li criticized that customs of non-Han ethnic groups in Lianshan were "savage," "primitive," and "brutal" and thus should be completely reformed. Li believed that although these indigenous people were "stupid" and "stubborn," they were educable because most of them were by nature good. He listed four fundamental methods to control the indigenous people. The first and foremost was education (*jiao*); the other three were respectively nourishing and cultivating (*yang*), military control (*bing*), and punishments (*xing*).[48]

The educational policies through which Li intended to reform various aspects of the Yao people's social and cultural life were comprehensive. He established the Lianshan Academy to teach the Confucian classics to local talents. He launched a campaign to collect and openly burn Yao books that he thought were "evil," "vulgar," "absurd" and "inciting rebellion." He painstakingly taught the Yao people how to plant tea and mulberry trees and how to cultivate farmland.[49] Li also made considerable efforts to implement community lectures in local communities. In his first year, Li published a community lecture manual titled the *Sacred Edict with Illustrations and Additional Commentaries* (Shengyu tuxiang yanyi). Two years later, he published another manual—*Trimetric Songs of the Sacred Edict with Additional Commentaries and Vernacular Explanations* (Shengyu yanyi sanzige sujie)—designed to help local children read and recite the *Sacred Edict*. He himself gave the lectures in the county seat and several nearby large Yao villages, and he hired Confucian scholars to conduct the lectures in remote Yao villages.[50]

Li's lectures were similar to community lectures given in other areas in the Kangxi period. He provided the sixteen maxims, their colloquial explanations, and related statutes and substatutes from the Code in the lectures. Compared with other lecture manuals, community lectures in Li's manual had several features designed specifically for the local non-Han audience. For each maxim, Li divided the speech into five sections—colloquial explanations, principles and regulations, statutes and substatutes, popular songs, and instructions for the Yao people. Regular lectures in other regions usually only had two sections—colloquial explanations and reading the laws. In the principles and regulations segment, Li propagated the proper behavior of a good subject according to Confucian Chinese (Han) values. He taught rhymed songs in the popular songs segment to help local people remember the maxims and related principles. He also provided particular instructions for the Yao people whose customs and culture were different from those of the Han, attempting to draw their attention to their specific "bad customs" and to provide instructions on how to rectify them. He donated his own salary to build the lecture pavilion (*shengyuting*) in each of the five large Yao villages and hired Confucian scholars as lecturers. He asked them to live in the villages, leading the bimonthly lectures and teaching Yao children.[51]

In the community lectures, Li enthusiastically introduced the state's laws to local people. He included about 30 statutes, 22 substatutes, 2 regulations outside the Code, and 4 substatutes from the *Substatutes for Arresting Escapees* (Dubu zeli).[52] The total number of the statutes and substatutes from the Code in Li's manual was 52, similar to the 51 in Chen Bingzhi's manual of 1679. Li chose many different statutes and substatutes from Chen, but he similarly focused on the "Revenue" chapters and the "Punishments" chapters, with a slightly greater preference for the former. It seems that he intended to introduce laws about tax, land, household, and marriage to the local non-Han audience in order to "transform their customs."

Li noted that teaching the people law was an effective way to protect the common people and reform local society. He pointed out that the state established law to punish crimes and violence, but many good common people unintentionally violated the laws out of ignorance. These people were like unfortunate blind men walking on the road and accidentally falling into traps. Li felt pity for these people. Similarly, he observed that the Yao people committed many wrongs and even crimes, such as stealing, robbing, and killing, mainly because they did not know about the state's laws. Teaching them laws, therefore, was the first and foremost method to prevent crimes, restrain local people, and reform Yao customs. Li pointed out that everyone in local communities should learn the laws. Even though "illiterate people in villages" (*cunzhong yumin*) could not know every statute, they could choose to learn the laws related to household and marriage, land and property, cursing, affrays, fights, and so on that were relevant to their lives. Moreover, they should follow new substatutes. Once there was a new substatute, officials should let local people know about it. Li even promoted popular legal education beyond the community lecture system. He sent one copy of his manual to each village school in his county and asked teachers to teach local children the laws in it. He also emphasized that women must learn the laws because they were usually "emotional and ignorant" and inclined to commit suicide. Many did so in the vain hope that they could get revenge against someone by involving them in capital cases. To solve this problem, Li hired women who were more than sixty years old or old blind men in villages. He taught them basic laws and tales of the virtuous and the filial, and they then could go to each household and teach local women the laws and stories.[53]

Li reported that the moral and legal education in Lianshan was effective. During his eight-year tenure (1704–1712) as magistrate, the county's local customs were transformed. Several years after he established the community lectures in Yao villages, he wrote that most Yao children could recite the *Sacred Edict* and explain its basic meaning. He also claimed that the lectures successfully touched the hearts of Yao men and women. The author of his biography also praised Li Laizhang for having made the non-Han people in Lianshan believe in essential Confucian values such as loyalty, sincerity, and honesty. Talented Yao men who graduated from the academy Li established pursued examination degrees, and the valleys of the county were "filled with sounds of local children chanting books."[54] Although these writings almost certainly exaggerated the changes, Li did try to promote moral and legal education in Lianshan's local Han and especially non-Han communities. By his report, legal education changed local attitudes toward the state's law and opened their access to the legal system. Li reported that there were an increasing number of lawsuits filed by the Yao people in the local court during his tenure. While this might have displeased magistrates in the heartland, on the border it was a step up. The Yao people, as Li observed, had formerly solved local conflicts themselves, usually in violent and brutal ways. Several years after he launched his reforms, in cases of conflict that could not be resolved through mediation by the Yao headmen, the Yao would file a complaint to the court in the county seat. Li proudly wrote, "now, all of the conflicts in the Yao villages are solved in the county court." Rather than viewing these lawsuits as burdens, Li viewed them as a sign of social and cultural transformations among local people.[55]

Community lectures in Lianshan was not exceptional. The Qing state implemented similar popular moral and legal education in Xinjiang, but only quite late. When the Qing troops conquered this vast inner Asian land in the mid-Qing period, the Qing court did not rush to establish the regular bureaucracy and the legal system. It seems that the court was comfortable limiting itself to the military and commercial control of the region rather than spending money and energy in establishing formal administrative and judicial institutions to govern non-Chinese Xinjiang natives. In the eighteenth and early nineteenth centuries, two legal systems operated simultaneously in Xinjiang. The one was the Qing legal system based on *The Great Qing Code*, administered by Manchu, Mongol, and Han officials in the Urumchi area. The other was Xinjiang's local customary laws based on the Muslim law of the Hanafite School, administrated by the native East Turkestani bureaucracy.[56] Generally speaking, the two legal systems were applied based on ethnic groups: Han, Manchu, and Mongol people were subject to the Qing law, while local Muslims were under the control of Islamic law.[57] It seems that the Qing court did not establish the community lecture system in Xinjiang in this period.

The Qing state changed its policy in Xinjiang dramatically after the Dungan revolt (1862–1877). When the court restored its control over Xinjiang after 1877, it took more aggressive measures to build up its political control and legal hegemony as well as to whittle the authority of local headmen and religious leaders. In 1884 the court incorporated Xinjiang as a formal province, transplanting administrative and legal institutions from China proper to this vast northwest frontier region.[58] Along with this process, officials in Xinjiang (most of them Han) enthusiastically established regular lectures on the *Sacred Edict* and systematically propagated Chinese moral values and laws to Xinjiang Muslims. They viewed the lectures as one of the most efficient ways to "transform their strange customs and acculturate them to our Chinese traditions" (*hua bi shusu, tong wo Huafeng*).

Zhang Yao (1832–1891), a Han general who was then in charge of Xinjiang's military affairs, hired scholars to translate Xia Xin's community lecture manual into the Uyghur language, republished the book in Xinjiang, and issued the book to local lecturers. In this translated edition of Xia's manual, the editor retained the original Chinese text and added Uyghur translations between the lines.[59] Liu Jintang (1844–1894), another Chinese general who took charge of southern Xinjiang's military and administrative affairs, reprinted Zhang Yao's translated version of Xia's manual in large numbers and issued copies to public schools and native headmen (*begs*). He also ordered local *begs* to read and explain the *Sacred Edict* and laws attached to the edicts in the book to Muslim communities. At the same time, officials strictly banned local nobles and religious leaders from judging legal cases based on the *Quran*. Each and every criminal case in Xinjiang, no matter whether it involved Han, Manchus, Mongols, or Muslims, should go through the state's judicial system and should be sentenced according to *The Great Qing Code*.[60] Through propagating Qing laws and weakening local leaders' judicial power, the state attempted to establish its legal authority and judicial hegemony in Xinjiang in order to strengthen its control over this newly established province.

Many records of local lectures on the *Sacred Edict* and the laws survive in Xinjiang's local gazetteers published in the late Qing periods. These records give us the details of community lectures in Xinjiang. For example, in Luopu County—an oasis in the Hotan region where the overwhelming majority of the population was Turkic-speaking Muslims, the Qing officials built at least five "platforms for lectures on the *Sacred Edict*" (*shengyu xuanjiang tai*) in several local bazaars. They also appointed local scholars (*mawali*) who were familiar with Chinese language as lecturers and paid them monthly salaries. These lecturers went up on the platforms and expounded the *Sacred Edict* and Qing laws to local people. The lectures were conducted at seven-day intervals, when local bazaars opened. The manual used in the lectures was Zhang Yao's edition of Xia Xin's manual with Uyghur translations. Officials also offered cash rewards to local people who attended the lectures and could explain the main points. To reach a broader audience with Xia Xin's manual, officials in Luopu County not only gave free copies of the book to lecturers but also distributed them to local elementary schools and local headmen.[61]

Above two examples—Lianshan and Xinjiang—were only a small sample of the popular education programs in the form of community lectures that Qing officials launched in frontier regions. Evidence indicates officials delivered similar community lectures for the Qiang people in the Sanqi area (a frontier region on the border of Sichuan and Tibet), Chinese-speaking Muslims (Hui) in Shaanxi and Gansu, the Miao people in Guizhou, the Yao people in Guangxi, and so on.[62] The real impact of such moral and legal education on local community and culture is hard to evaluate, and most evidence we now have was left by Qing officials and thus inevitably conveys their own moral bias, imperialistic ambitions, and cultural chauvinism. The effectiveness of such education programs largely relied on local officials' efforts and whether or not local people were interested. It is safe to conclude, however, that many Qing officials accepted community lectures as an essential means for "transforming" and "acculturating" local native people through exposure to Confucian principles and legal information. The popular moral and legal education sponsored by the Qing state usually went hand in hand with the empire's expansion and the establishment of regular administrative and legal systems in frontier regions. Local non-Han populations could access accurate legal knowledge, and in some areas, officials encouraged local people to go to court to solve their conflicts rather than turn to native elites for mediation or to solve their conflicts through violence. By teaching local people laws and encouraging them to go to court, officials intended to establish the state's judicial authority and stabilize their control over frontier regions.

OTHER FORMS OF POPULAR LEGAL EDUCATION

Common people in the Qing period could get access to legal knowledge not only through attending community lectures but also through several other state-sponsored channels. For example, under an imperial edict issued in 1737, local people participating in the community wine-drinking ceremony (*yinjiuli*) should read the laws together after performing the ritual. On execution grounds, officials usually explained the crimes and punishments after reading out the names of the convicted. The officials took this chance to propagate law and educate the crowd watching the execution.[63] The government also frequently printed and posted proclamations (*gaoshi*), promulgating newly established laws and local regulations and explaining certain statutes and substatutes that local people were likely to violate. Such proclamations were ubiquitous in Qing official handbooks and local archives.

Some local officials even initiated their own version of popular legal lectures beyond the community lecture system. For example, in 1864 a Manchu official named Zhihe (1823–1883) who worked as vice minister of Shengjing's Board of Punishments at the time, published *Brief Explanations on the Selected Important Penal Laws of the Great Qing* (Da Qing xinglü zeyao qianshuo)—a detailed manual for popular legal lectures. The aim of publishing the book, as Zhihe pointed out in his preface, was to boost popular legal education in his jurisdiction. In the book Zhihe and his preface contributors (most of whom were also officials working in Shengjing) all agreed that many people committed crimes because they did not know the laws well. These people caught by "the net of law" were like beasts, birds, and fish that fell into hunters' snares—all did so because of their lack of knowledge (wuzhi).[64] It was extremely immoral that officials strictly punished the people who violated the laws without teaching them the laws and warning them about the potential harsh penalties in advance. Officials of a benevolent government should not set up strict law while providing little legal education for the people. What they needed to do was to nourish and educate the people, rather than "trapping" them with harsh laws and punishments. Therefore it was officials' responsibility to promote popular legal education in local society.

Zhihe and his fellow officials acknowledged that disseminating legal knowledge—even the orthodox legal information from the Code—was potentially dangerous. Popular legal knowledge might "incite litigation" among local people and aggravate the judicial burden on local government. But they believed that the gain outweighed the loss. As Zhihe wrote in the "General Editorial Principles" of the book:

Some people . . . worry that when we publish this book, pettifoggers will have more excuses. I think, however, if we make correct judgments and give exact sentences that are not too heavy or too light, why should we worry about the threat posed by pettifoggers? Let's try to think that each time statutes and substatutes are promulgated, our dynasty declares them openly and publicly, so that people in and out of the empire can read them through and think about them thoroughly. Is it that our dynasty intends to keep the laws as a secret, and to "trap" [xian] those who do not know? In ancient times, people put up the image of the laws on the palace's gates, and read the laws on the first day of the first month. They did not worry about it: Why? When there is an advantage, there must be a disadvantage. . . . Should we give up eating for fear of choking? No, this is not what I know.[65]

Despite the risk that some people might abuse their legal knowledge, Zhihe insisted that officials should uphold popular legal education and let the people know the laws and punishments. Zhihe argued that this was the correct and honest way to govern the people and would save many people's lives.

The content and quality of Zhihe's book matched his announcement on promoting popular legal education in the prefaces. This book provided the largest number of statutes and substatutes, the most accurate texts from the Code, and the clearest explanations of the laws among the manuals for popular legal education that I have seen thus far. Zhihe included thirty statutes and fifty substatutes in the manual and divided them into eight categories:

1. "Rebellion and disobedience to superior orders" (Fanshang), including three statutes (Article 254, 310, and 306) and five substatutes (Article 336.17, 306.02, 268.11, 267.02, and 267.01). All the laws in this category concerned various political crimes that were related to common people challenging officials' authority and threatening the state's security, such as rebellion, treason, beating local officials and government deputies, and breaking into prisons.

2. "Crimes committed against other family members" (Fuzhi). Zhihe incorporated seven statutes (Article 319, 318, 315, 311, 329, 328, and 338) and six substatutes (Article 319.12, 299.09, 338.01, 338.03, 319.08, and 299.10), all dealing with crimes that threatened proper family hierarchy and patriarch authority. He especially emphasized the crimes that children committed toward parents or grandparents, or wives or concubines toward their husbands, such as cursing and beating parents or grandparents or senior relatives, a wife or concubine beating her husband, and violating orders from parents or grandparents.

3. "Fornication" (Fanjian). Here Zhihe listed four statutes (Article 366, 367, 368, and 285) and five substatutes (Article 366.02, 366.03, 366.04, 319.06, and 299.17) about crimes related to sex, such as adultery and rape. These laws dealt with the violations of sexual order of a family and society.

4. "Homicide" (Renming) included four statutes (Article 287, 282, 290, and 292) and seven substatutes (Article 287.07, 287.17, 289.01, 290.01, 290.19, 290.15, and 383.02). Specifically, Zhihe mentioned the laws about general murder, murder by poisoning, intentionally killing in an affray, killing in play (*xisha*), mistaken killing, killing three persons from one household, and arson.

5. "Gambling" (Dubo) included five substatutes (Article 378.02, 378.14, 378.15, 378.08. and 378.05) from the same statute (Article 378) on gambling.

6. "Robbery and theft" (Zeidao). This is the largest category of the laws in Zhihe's book, which included seven statutes (Article 266, 278, 257, 259, 269, 270, and 271) and fourteen substatutes (Article 266.02, 266.19, 278.04, 260.02, 263.02, 263.03, 270.01, 263.06, 269.18, 269.22, 270.04, 270.06, 270.10, and 281.01). Here Zhihe listed detailed laws about a variety of categories of thefts, such as theft with force (*qiangdao*, i.e., robbery), "non-manifest theft" (*qiedao*, i.e., theft), stealing horses and other livestock, and stealing rice and wheat from fields.

7. "Uncovering graves" (Fazhong). This is the smallest category in the book, which only contained one statute (Article 276) and one substatute (Article 276.02).

8. "False accusation" (Wugao). Zhihe listed four statutes (Article 336, 369, 337, and 340) and seven substatutes (Article 336.08, 336.09, 336.14, 336.19, 340.09, 340.06. 336.15), including several major statutes and substatutes about false accusation and instigating litigation. Zhihe put this category of the laws in the end of the book in order to prevent the people from engaging in litigation, especially involving false accusations, after receiving the legal education he provided in the book.

All the statutes and substatutes provided in the book were from the last section of the Code—chapters on the Board of Punishments. Zhihe emphasized penal laws more than Chen Bingzhi and Xia Xin, who had included statutes and substatutes from the "Revenue" and the "Rites" chapters. Zhihe included many more substatutes than statutes, which indicates he emphasized laws in practices more than legal principles. The laws in Zhihe's book are not only up-to-date and relevant to local people but also accurate—he usually kept whole sentences from the Code. By propagating the laws, Zhihe intended to reduce crimes and sustain social and political order.

The most salient feature of the manual is that Zhihe translated every statute and substatute in the book into colloquial language mingled with words from Shengjing's local dialect. Zhihe announced that the book was not written for officials or clerks but for men, women, and children of villages and local communities, and that was why he picked up many vulgar (*cusu*) words and why the language in the book was pervaded by "old women's tone" (*pozi qi*).[66] The colloquial translations in Zhihe's book were accurate, colorful, easy to understand, and close to judicial practice. For each statute and substatute, he first cited and abbreviated original text from the Code, then attached a translation in the vernacular. He also interpreted many legal terms he came across and provided vivid explanations for some confusing concepts. For example, Zhihe provided a detailed colloquial interpretation of *diaojian* (fornication brought about by deception), a legal term that was seldom used in daily language: "If you seduce another person's wife or daughter to go someplace in order to commit adultery, this is called *diaojian*. Or if someone sees a woman committing adultery, he also wants to have sex with her, but the woman does not agree. He then threats her to tell others about her adultery. The woman has no choice but to have sex with him. This is also called *diaojian*."[67] The Code provided no explanations of the term. Zhihe might have referred to some legal handbooks or commercial editions of the Code that included commentaries to define the term.

Zhihe also picked up the terms that had different meanings in the Code from everyday usage, explained them, and reminded readers of the difference. For example, while the original text of article 254, "Plotting Rebellion and High Treason," did not explain what "rebellion" and "high treason" were, Zhihe provided explicit and vivid colloquial explanations for the terms:

Plotting rebellion [*moufan*], in our daily language, is "making rebellion" [*zaofan*]. This "making rebellion" does not only include things like recruiting an army, buying horses, and declaring oneself as an emperor or a king, as described in novels and operas. For example, if an official comes to collect taxes, you people argue with him about the amount. He sends clerks to bring you to the yamen, and you refuse arrest. You then gather some people, and go to the yamen to make trouble. The official comes to interfere, but you kill him. Officers and soldiers then come to capture you, and you gather some men to fight with them. For another example, you have some friends or relatives who are involved in a legal case and are put into a prison. You gather some people, break into the prison, and kill officials. Or you establish some evil religion, recruit disciples, gather many people, and arouse troubles. Officers and soldiers then come to capture you, and you fight with them. All of these are called rebellion and will be sentenced according to the statute.[68]

He provided word-by-word explanations for the rest of the statute in the same fashion.

Zhihe also provided punctuation for the texts to help readers with limited education read and understand the book. By the end of the interpretation of each statute or substatute, after narrating the penalties defined by the laws, Zhihe usually concluded the section with the same sentence: "You tell me! They are terrifying, aren't they?" By listening to the laws in lectures based on his manual, Zhihe hoped, local people would be forewarned and comply with the laws. Although I have not seen written records indicating how the popular legal education program proposed in his book was carried out in local society, his proposal did gain support from some prominent officials in Shengjing city and Fengtian prefecture. Zhihe and preface writers indicated that the content of the book would be disseminated in local society through both printed and oral channels. They would issue copies of the book to local schools as well as communities in cities and villages and let schoolteachers and community leaders read the book to local people. After hearing the lectures, local people could also tell each other what they had heard. Through this way, they wrote, all the local people would understand the laws well.[69]

CONCLUSION

Law played an important role in state-sponsored popular moral education in the Qing period. The state and officials organized and upheld community lectures, which usually conveyed a large amount of accurate legal information from the Code. They also posted proclamations about the current laws and regulations and propagated the laws through other forms of public speeches or lectures. The popular dissemination of legal knowledge was usually through oral channels—the laws and sometimes legal explanations were read to local people. The state-sponsored legal lectures, therefore, aimed to teach the laws to both literate and illiterate people. By attending the lectures and public speeches, even people from the lower classes who had received little education could grasp at least some basic meanings and principles of law. Officials not only implemented the legal lectures in China proper but also launched campaigns to propagate the laws and educate indigenous people (usually non-Han ethnic groups) in frontier regions on legal knowledge.

The goals of popular legal education were to let the common people know and understand fundamental legal principles and punishments to prevent the populace from engaging in illegal behavior. The ruling elites felt the tension between the need to provide legal knowledge (even if only by encouraging moral behavior through threats) and the fear that such knowledge would incite litigation. Although some officials disapproved of popular legal education, legal lectures in the community lecture system generally won the supports of the ruling elites. Many officials viewed the benefits of popular legal education outweighed the risks. In their opinion, a benevolent government should educate its subjects about the laws, and such education would warn the people about the harsh punishments, discourage them from committing crimes, and save lives. They viewed popular legal education as an instrument of social control and moral transformation and, in frontier regions, an instrument to transform local customs and acculturate indigenous people.

Because of the limits of the currently available documents, it is difficult to answer some essential questions about the exact impact of popular legal education programs on legal culture, such as how the people received the legal information from community lectures and how they used it in practice. But we do know that community lectures conveyed relatively accurate legal information to the populace. As we have seen from the murder Du's case, Woman Lin's case, and the fake grave case in previous chapters, legal knowledge could be powerful and might influence people's decisions and behaviors. The main content of legal lectures in the community lecture system was simplified statutes and substatutes from the Code. Although officials' purpose of teaching these laws in legal lectures was to warn the public of potential harsh punishments and to exhort them not to commit crimes, rather than to let people use these laws in litigation, officials could not control how people used the legal knowledge that they learned from community lectures. After all, people who were well informed with legal knowledge were more likely to go to court to solve their problems. Moreover, people could combine the knowledge about statutes and substatutes they gained from community lectures with other (more practical) legal and litigation information they could learn from other channels, such as popular legal handbooks, which would significantly enhance their ability to use (or even abuse) the laws. State-sponsored popular legal education was one of the major ways for the common people to receive accurate and authorized legal knowledge, especially for those who could not buy or read books. Printed legal books widely circulating in society as well as popular legal education sponsored by the Qing state contributed to popular understanding and use of the laws. The population, literate or not, had access to law and legal information thanks to the book market and state-sponsored legal education projects.

CONCLUSION

The Impact of Printing on Law and Legal Culture

PRINTING IS WIDELY RECOGNIZED AS "AN AGENT OF CHANGE" influencing culture and society in early modern settings. Although print's effect on legal culture has not drawn as much scholarly attention as has the history of books in religion, statecraft, and science, in recent years some historians have begun to study the impact of printing on law, finding that the print revolution brought pervasive and far-reaching changes to early modern legal world.[1] Take the impact of printing on early modern English law for example. After the fifteenth century, the printing revolution in England enabled the production of a larger number and a wider variety of texts related to law than what had been available in manuscript form. The availability of printed law books changed the training of lawyers and administrators and led to the collapse of the oral learning exercises in the inns of court. A wider audience gained access to accurate legal knowledge, which previously had been available only to a restricted coterie of experts. The dissemination of standardized legal texts contributed the spread of royal power and standardized administrative practice. Printing facilitated the formation of the modern notion of precedent. Through organizing and reorganizing legal texts, authors of printed law books brought order to the common law. State control and industry regulations on the printing press significantly influenced the way printing changed the law and legal culture in early modern England.[2]

Printing had transformative effects beyond early modern Europe. Although the legal system of Qing China was quite different from that of early modern England, the two legal systems experienced many similar changes as a result of the printing revolution. In China it was not techno-logical innovations (most publishers still relied on the "old" technology of woodblock printing) but an increasing volume of circulation, ease of production, and enthusiasm for consumption that brought about transformations.[3] Beginning in the 1550s, a revolution in commercial printing significantly transformed how legal information was communicated in China. Printed law books had a profound influence on the functioning of the judicial system, the training of legal officials and advisors, the development of legal consciousness, and the evolution of judicial practice.

DISSEMINATION

Printing undoubtedly contributed to the wider dissemination of legal information in early modern China. Before the commercial printing revolution, the state largely monopolized the production of law books, and accurate legal information circulated mainly within the bureaucracy. People outside the bureaucracy had limited access to updated and accurate legal information. As commercial publishing began to rise in the 1550s, commercial publishers began to publish more law books and made them available on the book market. Although the majority of commercially printed law books were designed for judicial officials and legal experts, there also were genres designed for commoners and non-experts. A great variety of legal information circulated in society, including statutes, substatutes, administrative regulations, case precedents, commentaries, abbreviation and simplification of laws, rhymed songs to help people memorize statutes, sample litigation documents, and so on. Commercial publishers often advertised that their books made accurate and updated legal information accessible to readers outside the government. Commercial legal imprints also made some "secret" legal knowledge and litigation skills, formerly "hidden under the pillows" of legal advisors and litigation masters, available to the general public. In sum, printing facilitated the dissemination of accurate legal information from state to society and from officials and legal experts to ordinary people.[4]

Compared with early modern England, Qing China had a broader, more competitive, and more dynamic market for law books in a less regulated environment. In England, most legal publishers were in London, and the law book industry was under strict state and industry regulations. The market for law books was a small and specialized niche market.[5] In China, publishers of law books were scattered around the empire. Law books were published not only by prominent publishers in large cities such as Hangzhou, Beijing, and Shanghai but also by less prominent printers in small towns and villages in places such as Jiangxi and Fujian. Copies of law books were sold through extensive bookselling networks and by itinerant book-sellers and thus became accessible to readers who lived outside major printing centers. The market for law books in Qing China was competitive. Because there were few state or industry regulations, and no notions of patent or copyright, unauthorized reprinting was rampant, and many publishers simultaneously sold similar editions of law books at similar prices. Reprinting and competition not only indicated that law books such as *The Great Qing Code* were in demand but also potentially lowered prices and eased readers' access to law books.

The state used printing technology to promulgate its laws, especially statutes, to the populace in early modern England. The state supported the dissemination of legal information, and English humanists advocated for making legal information available in service to an educated and informed citizenry. The humanists upheld popular legal education and viewed the printing press as a means of disseminating legal information that would contribute to the building of the common weal or good of the community. Some English elites, however, were against the dissemination of legal knowledge to the populace, arguing that popularization and vulgarization of law would inevitably invite miscommunication and misuse of legal knowledge, breed lawsuits and incite litigation, as well as multiply faction and impair political unity.[6] Qing elites held similarly contradictory attitudes toward the dissemination of legal information and popular legal education. Those who supported the dissemination of legal knowledge generally believed that a benevolent government had the responsibility to educate its subjects about its laws. Knowing about the harsh punishments encoded in the law would intimidate people from committing crimes. Appropriate legal knowledge among the populace would potentially reduce the number of crimes committed out of ignorance. Thus, popular dissemination of legal knowledge would reduce crimes, uphold morality, and contribute to the building of a well-ordered society. This was the main reason why the state promoted popular legal education by means of the twice-monthly community lectures. However, some elites were opposed to the popular dissemination of legal knowledge. They feared that people with legal knowledge were more likely to manipulate the laws and to abuse the legal system.

The dissemination of legal information was indeed a double-edged sword. The circulation of legal information was essential to the functioning of the judicial system. Many officials and legal advisors had a collection of law books, including the Code, administrative regulations, official handbooks, and legal treatises to refer to when making judicial decisions. Officials who owned the Code were more likely to sentence cases based on the laws than those did not have a copy. Printed law books in many ways influenced judicial decisions. Law books also facilitated legal education in Qing China. Since there was no formal legal education system for officials, many officials taught themselves by reading law books. The dissemination of legal knowledge also nourished popular legal consciousness, as knowledge about the law in many cases encouraged people to go to court to solve their problems and thus added more caseloads to the already overburdened legal system. Some people, such as murderer Du and Woman Lin, tried to manipulate their legal knowledge and abused the legal system to achieve their own personal ends.

CHANGING THE LAW

Printing not only disseminated information about the laws but more significantly brought changes to the content, organization, and presentation of the laws through the editing and printing process. In England publishers used tables, catalogs, indexes, and cross-references—innovations characteristic of print—to reorganize and systemize the disorganized body of the common law. The reorganizing process brought some order into the common law and facilitated the development of a logical framework and principles for applying the laws. The printing and distribution of law books, such as the *Year Books*, *Abridgements*, Edmund Plowden's *Commentaries*, and Sir Edward Coke's *Reports*, eased jurists' and lawyers' access to past cases, which built the foundation for the modern development of the common law system.[7]

In China printing changed the presentation and organization of the laws even more dramatically than it had in England. Due to the absence of state regulations, Chinese publishers had much more freedom than English publishers to alter, revise, and reorganize legal materials. Commercial publishers brought new content and new formats to the Code when they published it. They added a large amount of information that the state did not formally acknowledge or promulgate, including private commentaries and case precedents. Using the three-register format, commercial publishers printed these commentaries and precedents together with the imperially promulgated statutes and substatutes. This new format and content began to dominate the book market in the 1790s and had several impacts on the laws and judicial practice.

First, commercial editions of the Code enhanced the accessibility of commentaries and case precedents. The Qing central government did not formally publish case precedents, and most case precedents were stored in government archives and circulated among a small number of officials in the bureaucracy. Commercial editors made case precedents accessible to a much wider audience. Moreover, because editors carefully sorted these commentaries and precedents and printed them together with related statutes, readers could easily locate them when reading the Code.

Second, commercial editions enhanced the authority and reliability of commentaries and precedents. Commentaries and case precedents in commercial editions of the Code were selected and arranged by prominent legal experts, and the books were endorsed by high-ranking judicial officials. Commercial editions of the Code provided readers a clear impression that leading legal experts and judicial officials affirmed the reliability of these selected commentaries and precedents.

Third, accessibility and reliability increased the potential utility of private commentaries and case precedents in legal reasoning and judicial practice. As we have seen, it was quite common for judicial officials (and their legal advisors) to refer to private commentaries and case precedents when sentencing cases. Commentaries and precedents played an increasingly important role in Qing judicial practice and to some extent influenced the legislation and acted as a source of law.

Most editors of commercial editions of law books were private legal advisors. The rising popularity and authority of commercial editions of law books on the one hand reflected the rising power of these non-official legal experts in the Qing judicial system. Legal advisors often acted as de facto judges, who drafted legal documents and suggested sentences for cases in local and provincial courts. Officials acknowledged legal advisors' expertise in law, and the functioning of the judicial system relied on legal advisors' professional skills and knowledge. Therefore, works by prominent legal advisors were viewed as reliable, authoritative guides or even as canon for people working in the judicial bureaucracy. On the other hand, the commercial publishing industry provided legal advisors opportunities to promote themselves as learned men of law. The publication and circulation of their works, such as commercial editions of the Code, further enhanced legal advisors' authority.

In the literary field commercial printing revolution in the late Ming significantly influenced the cultural production. The expansion of the book market produced publicity for literary professionals whose authority over literary taste could rival and challenge that of officials in the field of civil service examinations. The flourishing publishing industry thus contributed to the creation of a new authority in the literary public sphere in the late Ming.[8] Similar effects occurred when commercial publishing and non-official legal experts entered into the legal field in the Qing. Commercial editors did not openly (and perhaps did not intentionally) challenge the state's legal authority. They often declared that the goal of their works was to make the state's law more accessible, understandable, and usable to readers. In the process of editing, commenting on, and reorganizing the laws and other legal information, however, commercial editors redefined what the laws were and how the laws should be applied in practice. Commercial editions of law books impacted legal reasoning and statutory interpretations, which consequently brought about changes in judicial decisions and sentences. Although private commentaries and case precedents did not directly challenge the authority of statutes in commercial editions of the Code, they brought new interpretations and updated usage of the laws to the attention of readers, which could considerably influence officials' choices of statutes and substatutes when sentencing cases. Whether a legal public sphere existed in the Qing is questionable because the judicial bureaucracy was under the strict control of the central government and people working in the legal system had much less flexibility than their counterparts in some early modern societies that nourished the public sphere or civil society. However, the book market did provide legal advisors with a platform through which to transmit their opinions on the law, which in turn challenged the state's authority over the interpretation and application of the laws.

Commercial printing not only transformed the laws as used by professionals but also changed popular perception of and engagement with the legal system. Officials opined that while commoners should know the basic principles of law, they should not actually use their knowledge of the law to pursue litigation. The state viewed legal information as a tool for moral education to intimidate commoners and prevent them from committing crimes. The official presentation of the laws was indeed intimidating, full of descriptions of crimes and harsh punishments. However, popular legal handbooks brought the laws and the legal system closer to commoners' everyday life. These popular legal handbooks successfully converted complicated statutes into simple lines and jingles, connected legal information with litigation skills, and bridged the gap between penal laws and punishments and civil lawsuits. In these books, law and the legal system were no longer intimidating tools to be used only by the state to maintain order and control society. Instead, they became tools available to everyone.

REGULATIONS AND CONTROL

The most striking difference between early modern England and Qing China in terms of the printing of legal materials was how the industry was regulated. In England the state imposed direct and effective control over the publication of law books. The Qing did not. The British state not only granted the King's printer the exclusive right to print statutes and proclamations but also allowed one of the printers in London to monopolize common law printing (i.e., the common law patent). By restricting the publication of law-related materials to selected printers, the state could ensure the consistency and reliability of content. In addition to the state, the trade organization of printers in London—the Stationers' Company—also established rules for law printers to protect the industry for the benefit of its members. Law printing in England thus was under both content regulation (what could be printed) and industry regulation (how printers carried on their trade). The regulations were largely effective until the 1780s, so law books in early modern England were well controlled and standardized in the interest of the state. The printing and dissemination of legal statutes was especially regulated, contributing to the spread of royal power and standardized administrative and judicial practices.[9] The strict state control and monopolistic business practices of law printers, however, eliminated healthy competition, inhibited creativities, and impeded the further development of law publishing industry. The monopoly not only pushed up book prices but also prolonged the lifespan of obsolete titles and made it extremely difficult to publish new works in the seventeenth and eighteenth centuries. Only until the 1780s, when the effectiveness of the law patent faded, did the law book market start to bloom fully.[10]

By contrast, neither the Qing state nor the book industry established effective control over legal publishing. The government did not build a close and cooperative relationship with commercial publishers, nor did it impose serious and systematic regulations on the book market. The state regulated law book publications mainly through two channels: the Wuyingdian Imperial Publishing House and book bans. The Wuyingdian was the main publisher of imperial editions of the Code and other law books. Imperial editions symbolized imperial judicial authority and assumed the responsibility to promulgate and disseminate standardized texts of the law in the empire. However, the Wuyingdian never enjoyed a monopoly on law printing. There were no monopoly or patent systems in Qing China for law books publishing. Publishers did not need the state's permission to edit, print, or reprint law books. Moreover, as an inefficient publisher, the Wuyingdian did not provide enough usable copies of law books and its editions were never popular among readers. Although there was no institutionalized censorship system in the Qing, the state did occasionally impose bans on books that were dangerous and against the interest of the state. The only genre of law books that the government seriously attempted to prohibit was popular legal handbooks. The ban, imposed in 1742, was well enforced in the Qianlong reign, but its effectiveness declined considerably in the nineteenth century. In sum, neither the Wuyingdian nor the book bans were effective ways to regulate the law publishing industry. The Qing state had not developed a long-lasting regulatory system to control the printing and the circulation of legal information.

RE-ENVISIONING QING LEGAL CULTURE

Scholars usually view the late Qing legal reforms of the early twentieth century, when Qing jurists attempted to reform traditional Chinese law and legal system based on Western models, as the starting point of the modernization of Chinese law. However, an examination of legal publishing and the dissemination of legal information reveals that law and legal culture underwent many dramatic changes in the Qing before the introduction of Western laws. Indeed, these changes in Qing law contained certain early modern features.

First, accurate and updated legal knowledge was being widely circulated through both textual and oral channels. Qing people had more convenient access to accurate legal information than people in previous dynasties, and many were familiar with the laws. The dissemination of legal knowledge nourished popular legal consciousness and encouraged people to use the legal system to solve their problems.

Second, non-official legal experts were experiencing rising authority. Private legal advisors were a new phenomenon in the Qing, and these well-trained legal experts played an important role in the judicial system as well as in publishing. Such men were the authors or editors of most law books commercially published. They established their fame and authority through editing and publishing law books. They challenged the imperial government's dominance in producing and circulating authoritative legal information. As seen from the history of commercial publications of the Code, leading legal advisors in Jiangnan formed their own consensus by the end of the eighteenth century on how to edit and organize texts in the Code, which was different from the imperial versions. They built their own identities as legal experts who made a living through their professional activities and believed that their work would benefit the state and society. Therefore, legal advisors practiced law as well as producing and disseminating legal knowledge. They helped transform the legal system and can be viewed as the originators of early modern legal professionalism in China.

Third, government control over legal knowledge and judicial practice was diminishing. The Qing state did not successfully establish control over legal advisors. Nor did the state seriously try to regulate the production and circulation of authoritative legal information. Legal advisors and commercial publishers produced a large percentage of legal information—much of it was viewed as reliable, if not authoritative. The state largely relied on the book market to equip its officials with updated editions of the Code and other law books. The government no longer exercised exclusive control over authoritative legal texts. Legal advisors and commercial publishers added their own thoughts on what the laws were and how the law should be interpreted and applied in practice into commercial editions of the Code, which in turn challenged the state's authority in statutory interpretation and judicial practice. Commercial editions of the Code also increased the flexibility and applicability of the laws. Private commentaries and case precedents printed in commercial editions often included updates on the application of statutes and substatutes in judicial practice, making the laws more adaptable to social and economic changes.

Finally, case precedents were rising in importance in judicial practice. The prevalence of commercial editions of the Code sheds new light on the recent debate about the nature of Qing laws. The Qing legal system has been viewed as a typical statutory law system dominated by imperially promulgated statutes and substatutes. In recent years, however, some Chinese legal historians have begun to question this assumption. By examining the application of case precedents in judicial practice, historians have found that case precedents profoundly influenced legal reasoning and judicial decisions. In addition to statutory laws, the Qing legal system also had a case law tradition, which was comparable to case laws in early modern England and France.[11] Commercial editions of the Code published after the 1780s almost universally included a large number of case precedents, which clearly illustrated the importance of these precedents to judicial officials and legal advisors. The imperial editions that only included statutes and substatutes fell out of favor with readers. Therefore, the history of commercial editions of the Code suggests that the Qing legal system should not be viewed as a pure statutory law system; instead, to some extent, it can be viewed as a hybrid system that combined statutory laws and case precedents. Commercial editions of the Code and collections of case precedents increased the circulation and accessibility of precedents and thus built the foundation for the application of precedents in practice.

In conclusion, the Qing state exercised limited control over the flow of legal information. Laws were flexible and in many cases were not created only at the top. They were adapted through interpretation, application, commentary, and precedents. The judicial system depended on the market for the timely promulgation of information. Legal advisors and commercial publishers gained considerable power and authority in the legal system. Commercial legal publications challenged the state's judicial authority and fostered popular legal awareness. Finally, officials and commoners had convenient access to accurate legal information thanks to commercial publications and community lectures, and many were familiar with the law. As a result of the publishing revolution, the Qing legal system was less centralized, less arbitrary, more flexible, and more commercialized than previous scholarship has led us to expect.

EPILOGUE

THIS BOOK BEGAN WITH THE STORY OF DU HUAILIANG, A FARMER who murdered both his own wife and his lover's husband by a method he hoped would help him avoid punishment. He clearly knew enough about the "Killing the Adulterous Lover" statute to think he might be exonerated. But how did he know? This study has shown how officials and commoners obtained legal knowledge, how the commercialization of legal information transformed judicial authority, and how popular dissemination of legal knowledge impacted litigation practice at the local level. We have seen the genres through which legal knowledge circulated and the effects of legal information on local society. I would like to end by returning to the case with which I began—and thus to one of the questions that inspired and animated this book: how could a peasant in Shandong come to know enough about a specific law that he thought he could kill his wife with impunity?

Du's case was not in fact exceptional; many cases informed by knowledge of the "Killing the Adulterous Lover" statute appear in Qing legal records and compilations. *The Conspectus of Legal Cases* (Xing'an huilan) features at least 146 cases categorized under the rubric of the "Killing the Adulterous Lover" statute.[1] For example, one such case report from 1789 records that Ou Meicheng knew his concubine was involved in an adulterous relationship with his nephew. One day he hid under the bed and caught them having sex. But both the concubine and the nephew managed to run away when Ou's wife and neighbors came to mediate a settlement. Ou caught the concubine the next day, tied her up, and dragged her to the nephew's house, where he caught the nephew. He tied the lovers together and pushed them into a river. Both were drowned. In a 1799 case, a man caught his wife and her lover while they were having sex. The irate husband killed the lover immediately. His wife ran away while the husband was hacking at her lover, but the husband was eventually able to catch her. He dragged her back into the house, tied her up, and killed her too.[2]

"Killing the Adulterous Lover" was a relatively new statute compared with long-established and well-known statutes in earlier dynastic codes. The Tang Code, from which a large percentage of Qing statutes originated, did not exonerate the husband who killed his adulterous wife. A case precedent in the Jurchen Jin period (1115–1234) noted that a commoner who killed his wife's lover was sentenced to the death penalty, but the emperor exonerated him to warn those who dared to commit adultery. This indicates that the formal law in the Jin still prescribed the death penalty for a husband who killed his adulterous wife or her lover but that rulers' attitudes had begun to change. The "Killing the Adulterous Lover" law was formally integrated into the Code in the Yuan period.[3] In the Ming and the Qing, the law was expanded and became more detailed and practical. Both the Ming and Qing statutes on "Killing the Adulterous Lover" emphasized three criteria that would lead to the complete exoneration of the husband killing his wife and her lover: (1) he had to kill both of them, not just one or the other; (2) he had to catch them at the place of adultery; and (3) he had to kill them immediately, while they were committing adultery. If he did not meet all three conditions, he would be subject to punishment.[4] Although the law was relatively new and had complicated prerequisites, Qing case reports indicate that people involved in "Killing the Adulterous Lover" cases—mostly commoners—understood the law well. They not only knew that the husband had the right to kill his adulterous wife and her lover without being punished but also generally knew at least one or two, if not all the three, of the prerequisites for exoneration. How did this knowledge circulate? How did people know that by killing both the lover and the wife, the husband could be exonerated?

Knowledge of the "Killing the Adulterous Lover" law could not easily be deduced from other well-known legal principles such as "He who murders pays the forfeit of his life" (Sharen changming). As a matter of fact, "Killing the Adulterous Lover" was an unusual statute and was incompatible with some important legal principles in late imperial China. For one thing, the right to execute criminals usually belonged to the state. Most capital sentences in the Qing required the emperor's final approval. This law unusually permitted the husband to kill without any permission from the state. Moreover, adultery was not a capital crime. The punishment for committing adultery was only eighty or ninety strokes of heavy bamboo. According to the Code, if someone killed another person who had committed a capital crime without permission, he would be punished by one hundred strokes of heavy bamboo. It was thus unreasonable, as some Qing jurists argued, for the law to completely exonerate the husband for killing his adulterous wife and her lover when their crime (adultery) was only a minor one according to the law.[5]

If they could not obtain the knowledge of the "Killing the Adulterous Lover" law through deduction from other well-known legal principles, there must be some concrete sources through which Qing people could learn the law. Popular legal imprints were among the important channels for literate commoners to obtain information about the law. Various editions of popular legal handbooks written in different formats such as simplified summaries, questions and answers, replications of the statute, sample cases, and stories mentioned the "Killing the Adulterous Lover" law. For example, *Newly Cut Notes Left by Xiao and Cao* (1595), an influential late Ming edition that continued to be published and circulated in the Qing, included a brief summary of the law: "There is no punishment for killing the adulterous wife and her lover."[6] Compared with Ming editions, Qing editions usually included more detailed discussions of the law. The eight-chapter edition of *The Thunder That Startles Heaven* replicated the entire statute from the Code. In the "Additional Statutes and Substatutes" section, under "Fornication," the book explained, "Whenever a wife or concubine commits adultery with another man, and the husband himself catches the adulterous wife and the adulterer at the place in the very act of adultery and immediately kills both of them, there is no punishment. If he merely kills the adulterous lover, the adulterous wife will be punished in accordance with the law on consensual adultery."[7] The information presented in the handbook was both comprehensive and accurate.

"Questions and Answers for Sentencing Crimes according to the Eight Laws," a section in many different editions of popular legal handbooks, included an interesting hypothetical discussion about the law:

> **Question:** If a wife or a concubine commits adultery and if not the husband but his relatives kill the adulterous lovers at the place of adultery, how should the case be sentenced?
> **Answer:** All the relatives within the five mourning degrees who live with the couple are allowed to catch the adulterous lovers.[8]

This question and answer set discussed a specific situation that the "Killing the Adulterous Lover" statute did not clearly define. It implied that the husband certainly could catch and kill the adulterous lovers with impunity and also that the same privilege applied to his close relatives. And indeed, a substatute under the "Killing the Adulterous Lover" statute in the Qing Code did allow the husband's relatives to catch and kill the adulterous lovers without being subject to the death penalty. But unlike the husband, they were subject to some punishment: one hundred strokes of heavy bamboo and three years of penal servitude.[9]

Many popular legal handbooks, such as *The Thunder That Startles Heaven* and *Cold Penetrating the Gall Bladder*, contained sample litigation cases about the "Killing the Adulterous Lover" law. Stories in these sample writings usually vividly and dramatically presented how the law was used in practice. These sample cases were not only informative but also entertaining to read. For example, one sample case in *Cold Penetrating the Gall Bladder* was titled "My Young Brother's Life Is Tragically and Wrongfully Taken." In this case, "The husband killed the adulterous lover immediately, and killed his own wife on the next day—it is neither at the same time nor at the same place." In the accusation, the plaintiff claimed that a local villain had long borne a grudge against the plaintiff's young brother because of some trivial disputes. One day, the villain brutally murdered the young brother by cutting off his head. Three days later, hoping that he might be exonerated, the villain killed his own wife, arguing that his wife had committed adultery with the brother. The accusation then clearly pointed out that this situation was against the law: "If this killing is to be decided based on the statute about 'killing the adulterous lover,' how can they be killed when they are not in the same bed?"

The accusation concluded that even if the wife was killed at the place where the brother was murdered, this was not a "legitimate" killing because the brother had not committed adultery with the wife. Ultimately, the accusation argued, the killing was a premeditated murder, not "killing the adulterous lover." The main evidence was that the brother and the wife were killed at difference places and at different times. In the counteraccusation, however, the defendant provided a rather different version of the story. He argued that he had caught the adulterous lovers having sex in his house. He was enraged and killed the plaintiff's brother immediately, but his wife took the chance to run away. When she came back home on the next day, he killed her too.[10] This sample case provided detailed information about the "Killing the Adulterous Lover" law, including the three prerequisites of exoneration. Through the vivid narrative of this dramatic story, the case reminded readers that if the husband did not kill both his wife and the adulterous lover immediately at the place of adultery, he might be accused of murder as a result of the litigation process. The story also provided some clues as to potential legal loopholes: if one man murdered another man, he could kill his own wife. By declaring that he had killed them both because of their adultery, he would have a chance of being pardoned.

Information about the "Killing the Adulterous Lover" law also spread in late imperial society through popular literature. Some stories in court-case fiction truthfully represented the law. For example, *Stories of Legal Cases of Various Departments in the Imperial Ming* (Huang Ming zhusi gong'an), a popular court-case fiction published in the late Ming, included a story titled "Censor Chen Allows [Yang Chong] to Kill the Adulterous Man" (Chen Xun'an zhunsha jianfu). In the story, a man named Zhan Sheng had been a close friend of Yang Chong since childhood. Both men were rich, but Yang indulged in gambling and prostitution and seldom stayed at home. Zhan took the opportunity to seduce Yang's wife. Yang's wife refused Zhan at first, but when she felt frustrated by her husband's frequent nights with prostitutes, she agreed to sleep with Zhan. After that, whenever Yang spent the night outside his house, Zhan came to sleep with Yang's wife. Later, Yang's mother found out the affair and told her son. Yang became furious and decided to kill both his wife and Zhan.

Yang discussed these matters with his parents and made up a plan. He spread the news that he would go to the city to sell a maidservant. He then brought a knife, hid under the bed, and waited. Yang's parents and uncles also secretly waited in another room. At night, Zhan came to sleep with Yang's wife. While the adulterous lovers cuddled and talked on the bed, Yang's parents and uncles rushed in. Yang also jumped out and immediately killed Zhan. Yang's wife, scared, knelt in front of Yang, and begged him to let her go. Yang had just killed one person, when he saw his wife begging, he felt pity for her and was reluctant to kill her. But his uncle pushed him to kill her and said: "You must kill this adulterous woman now! Otherwise, you will have to pay for Zhan's life with your own!" Having no choice, Yang drank wine to pluck up enough courage to cut her head off. The next morning, Yang brought the two heads to the court and filed an accusation:

> Killing the adulterers in order to uphold righteousness. According to
> the statute in the Code, if the husband catches his adulterous wife and
> her lover at the place of adultery, and kills them immediately, there is no

punishment! A lascivious rich man named Zhan Sheng has had an adulterous relationship with my wife Li shi for years. Their love affair is known among our neighbors. On the third night of this month, I myself caught them naked in bed. I was furious and killed them both. Here are their heads, and their bodies are still in my house. I report this case to the court and ask your honor's favor to accept the case in order to ban the licentious custom and establish principles.[11]

A few days later, Zhan's father filed a counteraccusation in the court and cried that his son's life had been wrongfully taken. He claimed that Yang was a local hooligan who loved gambling. Zhan had lent Yang eighty taels of silver, but Yang refused to return the money. When Zhan pressed for the repayment of the debt, Yang began to hold a grudge against him. On the night in question, Zhan came to Yang's house and asked for the money again, Yang murdered him and his own ugly wife to make it look like they were committing adultery when he killed them. After a thorough investigation, the official found that Yang was telling the truth. He exonerated Yang for the killing according to the "Killing the Adulterous Lover" law. This dramatic story not only contained fascinating factors that would appeal to readers, such as love, sex, money, and violence, but also conveyed real legal knowledge. It provided detailed causes, scenarios, and consequences of killing the adulterous lovers, as well as a sample accusation and counteraccusation. *Stories of Legal Cases of Various Departments in the Imperial Ming* clearly bridged two genres of literature—popular legal handbooks and court-case fiction.

A folktale, "Divine Retribution on a Litigation Master" (Songshi guobao), circulating in Qing society also conveyed detailed information about the "Killing the Adulterous Lover" law. Folklorist Qi Lianxiu has collected more than ten different versions of the story. His research indicates that this story circulated widely in local society in regions such as Shanghai, Jiangsu, and Hunan in late imperial and modern China, through both textual and oral channels.[12] According to one version of the story, a drunk farmer came home one night and encountered his wife having sex with another man. The farmer was outraged and immediately stabbed his wife to death, but the adulterous lover managed to run away. When the farmer sobered up, he regretted his actions and pondered the possible consequences: "I did not catch the adulterous lover and I have no evidence for the adultery that will justify my killing. Won't I forfeit my own life for my wife's life according to the laws?" He was scared and went to Mr. Yang, a local litigation master, for help. Yang soon made a plan for him—he told the farmer to go home immediately, open the door, and light a lamp in the room (according to the local custom, this was a sign that the homeowner welcomed travelers to stay overnight). When someone was lured into the house, the farmer could kill him and claimed that he was the adulterous lover—after all, a corpse would not talk! The farmer followed Yang's advice. Before dawn, someone went into the farmer's house, and the farmer immediately killed him. After the killing, the farmer went to Yang's house and asked Yang to help him file a report to the yamen. Yang followed the farmer to his house and examined the corpse, but he suddenly found that the dead man was his only son! It turned out that Yang's son was a sojourning merchant and did not know the farmer in person. When the son came back to his hometown to visit his parents, he was killed by the farmer, who was following his father's evil advice. In the end, Yang died of grief over the death of his son. The magistrate caught the true adulterous lover, and the farmer was punished by strokes of light bamboo and then was released.[13]

The theme of this story was that evil people would get retribution—Yang lost his only son because of his evil advice. The narrative also vividly presented how the "Killing the Adulterous Lover" law was understood and used in practice. The dark side of the story was also informative. If one killed his own wife for whatever reason, he could kill another man and claim that he caught and killed them when they were committing adultery. Then he could possibly use the legal loophole of the "Killing the Adulterous Lover" law to be exonerated. This story was not the only one that mentioned the legal loophole. *The Anthology of Petty Matters from the Qing* (Qingbai leichao) recorded another example. A drunk man was cutting meat with a knife, and his wife came to play with him. While they were playing, the husband pretended to put the knife on the wife's neck, but he missed and accidentally killed her. The man was scared and went to ask advice from a cunning litigation master. The litigation master told him: "You have a neighbor named Wang Dakui. He is crazy. You can lure him to your house and kill him. You put his corpse on the ground together with your wife's corpse. Then you bring their heads and surrender yourself to the yamen. You tell them that you killed your wife because of the adultery. You will not be harshly punished."[14] The story contained "dangerous" legal information—it reminded readers how to make use of the legal loophole in the "Killing the Adulterous Lover" law. Compared with the previous story, it lacked moral restrictions—neither the husband nor the litigation master was punished by law or by divine retribution. These stories were simple, attractive, and informative. Even illiterate commoners could grasp basic principles of the "Killing the Adulterous Lover" law when they heard such stories.

Community legal lectures also taught the "Killing the Adulterous Lover" law, which further contributed to the oral dissemination of knowledge about the law in Qing local society. For example, Xia Xin's *Sixteen Maxims of the Sacred Edict with Statutes and Simple Explanations*, a widely used and imperially approved manual for community lectures in the late Qing, contained a chapter named "Lecture on the Laws in Order to Warn the Ignorant and Obstinate." In this chapter, Xia focused on teaching the people about laws and punishments related to adultery, rape, homicide, and robbery. One of the laws taught in this lecture was the "Killing the Adulterous Lover" law. It read: "Whenever a husband catches his own adulterous wife and the adulterer at the place and immediately kills both of them, there is no punishment."[15] Although Xia significantly simplified the statute, the lecture conveyed clear and relatively accurate legal information. The three prerequisites for exoneration—"killing both of the adulterous lovers," "at the place of adultery," and "immediately," were reliably presented. When giving the community lecture based on the manual, the lecturer would read the statute aloud to his audience. Even if members of the audience were illiterate, they could still get the basic knowledge of the law.

The purpose of propagating the "Killing the Adulterous Lover" law in state-sponsored community lectures was to instill fear in people and deter them from committing adultery, so as to preserve family relations and social order. In practice, however, popular dissemination of the "Killing the Adulterous Lover" law usually led to chaos and destruction rather than order in local society. The late Qing jurist Shen Jiaben (1840–1913) noted the prevalence of knowledge about the "Killing the Adulterous Lover" law and observed that this knowledge significantly influenced people's actions and decisions to the extent that it greatly threatened family harmony and social stability. He wrote:

> As the old saying goes: You need to kill both when killing the adulterers (*shajian shashuang*). Therefore, when a husband kills the adulterer, he must kill his wife, too. When a husband catches the adulterer, his initial intention is usually just to beat him and vent his anger. If he

unintentionally beats him to death, he then has to kill his wife. Even though he does not want to kill his wife at the beginning, and even though his wife kneels on the ground in deep regret and swears not to commit adultery again, the husband is in the situation that he has no choice but to kill her.

To make the things even worse, sometimes there is someone who murders another man for other reasons. He then kills his own wife in order to be exonerated from the crime. There are countless people who have been murdered in this way after the promulgation of this law! People who die a wrongful death can also be found everywhere![16]

Shen harshly criticized the law and highlighted its disruptive effects. Instead of helping to preserve social order and family harmony, the law was widely abused and posed a threat to proper family relations. It encouraged husbands to kill their wives and provided a legal loophole that murderers could use to be exonerated. He moreover observed that evidence of adultery was often ambiguous (*aimei*), and fabrications were prevalent in "Killing the Adulterous Lover" cases. He noted: "Foolish villagers are ignorant and proud of such killings, and everyone feels that he is entitled to kill!"[17]

In murderer Du's case, Du was not the only person in his neighborhood who knew about the law. After Du killed his wife and his lover's husband, he notified his father and an uncle who lived next door. Upon learning that Du had killed the "adulterous lovers," the uncle comforted him and said: "Since he [Chen Wenxian] came to have illicit sex with your wife and you killed them, there's no problem. We'll just go tomorrow morning and report it to the magistrate."[18] Although the case report did not provide further information about where and how exactly they obtained this legal knowledge, we can see from other sources that information about the "Killing the Adulterous Lover" law circulated widely through a variety of channels, such as different editions of the Code, popular legal handbooks, popular literature, storytelling, and community lectures. Since legal information circulated in both textual and oral channels, people such as murderer Du had access to it regardless of whether they were literate or not. Knowledge about the "Killing the Adulterous Lover" law was powerful as well as dangerous—it strongly influenced people's actions and decisions. Based on his knowledge of the law, Du Huailiang made up his "perfect" murder plan, which led to a tragic end and the death of three people: both Mrs. Du and Chen

Wenxian were brutally murdered, and Du himself was sentenced to decapitation.

The case of murderer Du and, indeed, the many diverse examples contained in this study also make us reconsider who had the power to define the meaning and usage of law in late imperial China. The main purpose of popular legal knowledge, in officials' eyes, was to deter people from committing crimes. Officials hoped that people who knew about the "Killing the Adulterous Lover" law would not dare to commit adultery. Popular legal handbooks and folktales, however, often portrayed the law and legal information as instruments. Rather than instilling fear, the popular formats bearing information about the "Killing the Adulterous Lover" law in sample cases and stories usually focused on how people could use legal loopholes to achieve their own ends. In murderer Du's case, the popular perspective obviously had a much stronger influence on Du's decision than the official perspective did. Even though murderer Du clearly knew all about the law, he still dared to commit adultery with Mrs. Chen—and in fact used his knowledge of the law to seek exoneration for his immoral and violent deeds. The circulation in various media of the statute on "Killing the Adulterous Lover" vividly illustrates that the Qing state did not, or could not, control the popular dissemination of relatively accurate legal information. Nor could the state effectively shape how people viewed and used the law in local society. In the process of popular dissemination of legal information through both textual and oral channels, the meaning and application of law and legal knowledge were fundamentally transformed.

GLOSSARY

aimei 曖昧
anchashi 按察使
anji xuke 按季續刻
anlü chengban 按律懲辦

Balü kezui wenda 八律科罪問答
Bao Shichen 包世臣
Bao Shuyun 鮑書蕓
baojia 保甲
Baqi zeli 八旗則例
ben 本
benya cangban 本衙藏板
bianji zhijia 編輯之家
bianxiu 編修
bing 兵
bing'an zhi ke 秉案之客
Bo'an xinbian 駁案新編
Bo'an xinbian xubian 駁案新編續編
Botouzhen 泊頭鎮
bu 部
bushang lüli 補上律例
buzhengshi 布政使

Cai Fangbing 蔡方炳
caoben 草本
caomao 草茅
Changde 常德
chanming lüfa 闡明律法
Chen Bingzhi 陳秉直
Chen Hongmou 陳宏謀
Chen Ruolin 陳若霖
Chen Wenxian 陳文現
Chen Xun'an zhunsha jianfu 陳巡按准殺姦大

Cheng Xiangzhi 程祥芝
Cheng Xiuzhi 程秀芝
cheng'an 成案
chengren 成人
chengxiong ouda 逞兇毆打
chizhang 笞杖
Chu Ying 褚瑛
Chufen zeli 處分則例
Chun 春
Cisong zhinan 詞訟指南
cunzhong yumin 村中愚民
cusu 粗俗

da gan lü jiu 大干律究
Da Ming huidian 大明會典
Da Qing huidian 大清會典
Da Qing huidian bing zeli 大清會典併則例
Da Qing lü fuli zhujie 大清律附例注解
Da Qing lü jianshi 大清律箋釋
Da Qing lü jianshi hechao 大清律箋釋合鈔
Da Qing lü jijie fuli 大清律集解附例
Da Qing lü jizhu 大清律輯注
Da Qing lü xuzuan tiaoli 大清律續纂條例
Da Qing lü zhuzhu guanghui quanshu 大清律朱注廣匯全書
Da Qing lü zuanxiu tiaoli 大清律纂修條例
Da Qing lüli 大清律例
Da Qing lüli jizhu 大清律例集註
Da Qing lüli tongzuan jicheng 大清律例統纂集成
Da Qing lüli zhuzhu guanghui quanshu 大清律例朱注廣匯全書
Da Qing xinglü zeyao qianshuo 大清刑律擇要淺說
dagang 大綱
Dalisi 大理寺
dao 道
de 德
di 弟
dian 典
Dianshizhai huabao 點石齋畫報
diaojian 刁姦
Diaojian yin chuwai, ge zhang yibai zhi 刁姦引出外, 各杖一百止
diaosheng liejian 刁生劣監
Dichao 邸抄
Dingli cheng'an hejuan 定例成案合鐫
Dingli quanbian 定例全編

Dingli xubian 定例續編
Dongchang 東昌
Du Huailiang 杜懷亮
dubo 賭博
Dubu zeli 督捕則例
Duchayuan 都察院
dulü 讀律
Dulü Peixi 讀律佩觿
Dulü shuo 讀律說
Dulü suoyan 讀律瑣言
duyushi 都御史

eryu 珥語

fa 法
Fabi tianyou 法筆天油
Fajia toudan han 法家透膽寒
Fajia xinshu 法家新書
fajia zhi miji 法家之秘笈
falü zhishu 法律之書
Fan Huosheng 范火生
Fang Dashi 方大湜
fanjian 犯姦
Fanjian zongkuo ge 犯姦總括歌
fanke bijiu 翻刻必究
fanshang 犯上
fanyue 翻閱
Fashenju 發審局
fazheng xuetang 法政學堂
fazhong 發冢
Fengtian 奉天
fufu mingfen 夫婦名分
Fuhui quanshu 福惠全書
fumuguan 父母官
fuzhi 服制

gao 告
gao yayi taoyu zhaiju 告衙役套語摘句
gaoshi 告示
gejue 歌訣
gong 功
gongchen 功臣
gongju 公舉

gousong 搆訟
Gu Ding 顧鼎
Guan Heng 管蘅
Guangxun fulü cheng'an 廣訓附律成案
guanshuju 官書局
guanyu 官語
guanzhenshu 官箴書
guinie 圭臬

Haining 海寧
haoqiang shili zhi ren 豪強勢力之人
hejian 和姦
Hong Hongxu 洪弘緒
Hongdaotang 宏道堂
Hongloumeng 紅樓夢
houbu 候補
houbu yi dushu 候補宜讀書
Hu Qian 胡鈐
Hu Zhang 胡璋
Hu Zhaozhi 胡肇智
hua 化
hua bi shusu, tong wo Huafeng 化彼殊俗, 同我華風
huamin chengsu 化民成俗
Huang Ming zhusi gong'an 皇明諸司公案
Huangchao jingshi wenbian 皇朝經世文編
Huangyan 黃岩
Hui 回
Huibian 彙編
Huizuan 彙纂

ji chaoting chengxian zhicheng 集朝廷成憲之成
jiamai yu jianfu 嫁賣與姦夫
ji'an 積案
Jiang Chenxi 蔣陳錫
Jiang Tengjiao 江騰蛟
Jianghu Sanren 江湖散人
Jiangsu shuju 江蘇書局
jianshi hechao 箋釋合抄
Jianyang 建陽
jianyue 檢閱
jiao 教
jiaosuo cisong 教唆詞訟
jiaxun 家訓

jiewei 結尾

jiguan songgun 積慣訟棍

jijie 集解

Jin ping mei 金瓶梅

Jin Zhi 金植

jing 經

Jingbao 京報

Jingchang 經廠

jingshi zhi shu 經世之書

Jingtianlei 驚天雷

jingzhang 荊杖

jinke yicheng fu 金科一誠賦

Jinling 金陵

jinshenlu 搢紳錄

jinshenpu 搢紳鋪

jinshi 進士

Jishi tiaoli 祭祀條例

jishizhong 給事中

juan 卷

Juefei Shanren 覺非山人

Juhui 據會

Juwentang 聚文堂

kanfa fenyuan shu, jiandeng zhang jiushi 砍伐墳園樹, 減等杖九十

Kechang tiaoli 科場條例

kezidian 刻字店

lan 欄

Lejingtang 樂荊堂

Li Guanlan 李觀瀾

Li Laizhang 李來章

Li Nan 李柟

Li Rulan 李如蘭

Li Wei 李衛

Li Yuying 李玉英

Li Zhen 李珍

li 里 (mile)

li 理 (principles)

li 禮 (ritual)

li 例 (substatute)

Li shi 李氏

Li'an quanji 例案全集

Liang Maoxiu 梁懋修

liangchudao 糧儲道
Lianshan 連山
Liao shi 廖氏
Liaocheng 聊城
Liaozhai zhiyi 聊齋志異
Libu zeli 吏部則例
Lifanyuan 理藩院
liming 立命
lishen 立身
liu 流
Liu Heng 劉衡
Liu Jintang 劉錦棠
Liulichang 琉璃廠
Liuyu 六諭
Longyan zhenglue 龍巖政略
lü 律
Lu Fenglai 陸鳳來
lüji 律己
Lüli jianshi 律例箋釋
lüli quanshu 律例全書
lüli shanben 律例善本
lüli zongkuo ge 律例總括歌
Lüliguan 律例館
lümu 律目
Lunyu 論語
Luopu 洛浦
Lushan 魯山
Lüsutang 履素堂
lüyi 律意

mai 賣
Miao 苗
Mingxintang 銘心堂
minshi 民事
moufan 謀反
mudao 幕道
mufu 幕府
Muhan 穆翰
muyou 幕友

nannü hejian zhe, ge gai zhang bashi 男女和姦者，各該杖八十
neibu 內部
neiwai wenxing yamen 內外問刑衙門
neiyuan 內院

Ou Meicheng 歐美成

pan 判
Pingping yan 平平言
pozi qi 婆子氣

Qi Gong 祁墳
Qian Zhiqing 錢之青
Qiang 羌
qiangdao 強盜
qiangdao wei decai, yili ni liuzui 強盜未得財, 依例擬流罪
qianghun 強婚
qiangjian ruo weicheng, zhangbai liu sanqian li 強姦若未成, 杖百流三千里
qiangjian wu fuming, jianfu dangni jiao 強姦污婦名, 姦夫當擬絞
qiangzhan liangjia qi'nü 強佔良家妻女
qiedao 竊盜
Qin Ying 秦瀛
qinding 欽定
qing 情
Qingbai leichao 清稗類鈔
Qingbo Yisou 清波逸叟
Qinghefang 清河坊
Qinglaitang 清來堂
Qingtai 清泰
Qingyuan 慶元
qiongxiang pirang 窮鄉僻壤
Qiu 邱
quanben 全本
quanshu 全書
Quanti 筌蹄

Ren Pengnian 任彭年
renming 人命
riyong leishu 日用類書
Rongjintang 榮錦堂
ru lü fa jiu 如律法究

Sanchi dingheng fajia xinshu 三尺定衡法家新書
Sanliu daoli biao 三流道里表
Sanqi 三齊
sanren 散人
Sanshantang 三善堂
Saoye Shanfang 掃葉山房
sha 殺

shajian shashuang 殺姦殺雙
shanben 善本
Shanchengtang 善成堂
shangdeng ren 上等人
Shanghai Jinzhang Tushuju 上海錦章圖書局
Shanglinyuan 上林苑
Shangyu helü xiangyue quanshu 上諭合律鄉約全書
Shangyu shiliu tiao 上諭十六條
shanren 山人
shanshi 善世
sharen changming 殺人償命
shen han jia 申韓家
Shen Jiaben 沈家本
Shen Zhiqi 沈之奇
Sheng Fusheng 盛符昇
Shengjing 盛京
Shengyu shiliutiao fulü yijie 聖諭十六條附律易解
Shengyu tuxiang yanyi 聖諭圖像衍義
shengyu xuanjiang tai 聖諭宣講臺
Shengyu yanyi sanzige sujie 聖諭衍義三字歌俗解
shengyuting 聖諭亭
shiduan jin 十段錦
shixue 實學
shiyang 式樣
Shiyi xuzhi 事宜須知
Shuihu zhuan 水滸傳
Shuliao wenda 蜀僚問答
Shulin 書林
Shulin Xiyuan 書林西圍
Shuoping 朔平
shushen 樹身
si 死
Sibao 四堡
Sijingtang 思敬堂
songshi guobao 訟師果報
songshi miben 訟師祕本
sou 叟
sousuo 搜索
su 訴

Tang Huajing 唐化經
Tang shi 唐氏
tanghao 堂號
Tanglü shuyi 唐律疏議

Tao Jun 陶駿
Tao Nianlin 陶念霖
Tian Wenjing 田文鏡
tianxia dulüzhe 天下讀律者
tidu 提督
Tingsonglou 聽松樓
tongfang 通房
Tongwentang 同文堂
tongxing 通行
Tongxing Shuji Chu 通行書籍處
tongzhi zhuyou 同志諸友
tu 徒
Tuosuzhai 托素齋
tuyin 土音

Wan Weihan 萬維翰
Wang Dakui 王大奎
Wang Ding 王鼎
Wang Huizu 汪輝祖
Wang Kaitai 王凱泰
Wang Kentang 王肯堂
Wang Mingde 王明德
Wang Youhuai 王又槐
Wangjiang 望江
Wanping 宛平
Wei Yijie 魏裔介
weishi junzi 未仕君子
Wen Zhu 文柱
wenda 問答
wenmiao 文廟
Wenxing Deji 文興德記
Wenyuan Shanfang 文淵山房
Wu Tingchen 吳廷琛
Wu Xu 吳煦
Wu Yuan'an 吳元安
Wubentang 務本堂
wugao 誣告
Wuyingdian 武英殿
Wuyingdian tongxing shuji mulu
    qingce 武英殿通行書籍目錄清冊
Wuyingdian Xiushuchu 武英殿修書處
Wuyingdian Zaobanchu 武英殿造辦處
Wuyu 吳語
wuzhi 無知

xi fajiayan zhe 習法家言者
Xia Xin 夏炘
xiadeng ren 下等人
xian 陷
Xiangjue 相角
xiangyue 鄉約
xiao 孝
xiaobing 笑柄
xiaozhu 小注
xieban daxueshi 協辦大學士
xing 刑
Xing'an huilan 刑案匯覽
Xingbu 刑部
Xingbu xianxing zeli 刑部現行則例
xingming 刑名
Xingshi hengyan 醒世恆言
Xingshu 刑書
Xingtai Qinjing 刑台秦鏡
Xinke fajia xinshu 新刻法家新書
Xinqie falin jinjian lu 新鍥法林金鑑錄
Xinqie Xiao Cao yibi 新鍥蕭曹遺筆
xinzeng Da Qing lüli 新增大清律例
xinzeng suiyu 新增碎玉
xisha 戲殺
xiubing 修并
xiushen 修身
Xiyuanlu 洗冤錄
Xu Dong 徐棟
Xue Yunsheng 薛允昇
xuezheng 學政
Xuezhi shuozhui 學治說贅
Xunchao 訓鈔
xunfu 巡撫
xunqiu 尋求
Xunzhou 潯洲
Xuwanzhen 滸灣鎮

Yan Song 嚴嵩
Yanchang 延昌
yang 養
Yang Chong 楊寵
yangben 樣本
Yangshi 洋市
yanyu zhi zhinan 讞獄之指南

yanzheng 鹽政
Yao 瑤
Yao Run 姚潤
yi faling weishi 以法令為師
Yi Jingqing 易鏡清
yigai 移改
Ying Baoshi 應寶時
yinjian dangchan 因姦蕩產
yinjiuli 飲酒禮
yinqian 陰譴
Yizheng 儀徵
Yonghetang 永和堂
youfu ruo hejian, jiadeng zhang jiushi 有夫若和姦, 加等杖九十
Youyizhai 友益齋
youyong zhi shu 有用之書
yu lüli bubei 與律例不悖
Yu Zhi 余治
Yuan Liaofan 袁了凡
yuanban 原版
yuezheng 約正
Yugengtang 與耕堂
Yunhuitang 蘊暉堂
yushi 御史

Zaizitang 在茲堂
zang 贓
zaofan 造反
zeidao 賊盜
Zhan Sheng 詹昇
Zhang Guangyue 張光月
Zhang Guo 張國
Zhang Jixin 張集馨
Zhang Sichang 張嗣昌
Zhang Tianding 張添丁
Zhang Weichi 張惟赤
Zhang Yao 張曜
Zhang Yingji 張映璣
Zhang Youqing 張有情
Zhang Yutian 張玉田
Zhang Zhao 張照
Zhao Junying 趙俊英
zhaoxi 找洗
Zheng 鄭
Zheng Xuan 鄭玄

zhidao 治道
Zhihe 志和
zhinan zhiche 指南之車
zhisong zhidao 致訟之道
zhongdeng ren 中等人
Zhongshu zhengkao 中樞政考
Zhouli 周禮
Zhu Qingqi 祝慶祺
Zhu Tingzhen 朱廷禎
Zhu Yuanzhang 朱元璋
Zhuang 僮
Zhulin Langsou 竹林浪叟
zhushu 注疏
zhutu 諸圖
zhuyu 珠語
zhuzhu guanghui 硃註廣匯
zi 字
zixing 自省
zongmen 總門
Zongrenfu 宗人府
zongzhu 總註
zouben 奏本
Zuo Qiuming 左丘明
Zuozhi yaoyan 佐治藥言
Zuozhuan 左傳

NOTES

Introduction

1. Jones, *The Great Qing Code*, 271.
2. Hegel, *True Crimes*, 84. The case is cited from the same book, "Du Huailiang," 79–90.
3. Weber, *The Religion of China*, 120–21, 132.
4. Wejen Chang, "Legal Education in Ch'ing China," 292–302.
5. Sommer, "The Field of Qing Legal History," 113.
6. For these arguments, see Philip Huang, *Civil Justice in China*; Bernhardt and Huang, eds., *Civil Law in Qing and Republican China*; Bradly Reed, *Talons and Teeth*, "Money and Justice;" Macauley, *Social Power and Legal Culture*.
7. For the discussion on the Song and Ming print culture, see Ōki, *Minmatsu Kōnan*; Chia, *Printing for Profit*; Inoue, *Chūgoku shuppan bunkashi*; Chow, *Publishing, Culture, and Power*; Brokaw and Chow, *Printing and Book Culture*; Yuming He, *Home and the World*.
8. Brokaw, *Commerce in Culture*.
9. Xu and Du, *Chuanbo yu yuedu*; Fuma, "Songshi miben *Xiao Cao yibi* de chuxian"; Fuma, "Songshi miben de shijie"; Gong, *Ming Qing songxue yanjiu*; Will, *Official Handbooks and Anthologies*; Will, "Ming Qing shiqi de guanzhenshu"; Will, "Zai biaoge xingshi"; You, *Falü zhishi de wenzi chuanbo*; Chen Chongfang, "Qingdai jianyan"; Chen Chongfang, "*Xiyuanlu*"; Chen Chongfang, "Qianlong ba'nian."
10. For detailed discussions, see chapter 5.
11. These libraries include the National Library of China, Library of Congress, libraries of the University of Tokyo, Harvard-Yenching Library, Library of Waseda University, C. V. Starr East Asian Library of Columbia University, and HathiTrust Digital Library. This study also refers to several catalogs of Chinese legal books, such as Zhongguo zhengfa daxue tushuguan, *Zhongguo falü tushu zongmu*; and Will, *Official Handbooks and Anthologies*.

1. Qing Legislation and Imperial Editions of *The Great Qing Code*

1. For the history of Qing legislation, see Zheng, "*Da Qing lüli* kaoxi," 38–124; Zheng and Zhou, "Pursuing Perfection," 310–42.

2. Bodde and Morris, *Law in Imperial China*, 55–63.

3. Zhang Xiumin, *Zhongguo yinshua shi*, 195.

4. Miyazaki, "The Administration of Justice," 58. Due to the scarceness of relevant sources, whether the Song state effectively enforced the ban is still in question. There is no extant printed edition from the Song, which may suggest that the print run of the Song Code was small and that the ban was effective. See Xue Meiqing, *Song Xingtong yanjiu*, 155–60.

5. Miyazaki, "The Administration of Justice," 59; Zhang Xiumin, *Zhongguo yinshua shi*, 188–98, 334–39.

6. Farmer, *Zhu Yuanzhang*, 4. Jiang, *The Mandate of Heaven*, 55–58.

7. Zhang Xiumin, *Zhongguo yinshua shi*, 354–58. Wu Yanhong, "Guojia zhengce," 52–62; Wu Yanhong, "The Community of Legal Experts," 207–25.

8. This is an oversimplified description of the Qing judicial bureaucracy. For more details, see Bodde and Morris, *Law in Imperial China*, 113–43.

9. Ibid., 115–16.

10. Chiu, *Dang falü yushang jingji*, 103–8.

11. Bai Yang, "Qingdai cuo'an," 48–50.

12. Jones, *The Great Qing Code*, 396–97.

13. For sentencing legal cases at the county level, see Sommer, *Polyandry and Wife-Selling*, 341–75.

14. Bodde and Morris, *Law in Imperial China*, 30–31.

15. Ibid., 63.

16. Zheng and Zhou, "Pursuing Perfection," 317, 332.

17. Zheng, "*Da Qing lüli* kaoxi," 43, 95.

18. Yang Yifan and Liu Ducai, *Lidai likao*, 278–93.

19. Bodde and Morris, *Law in Imperial China*, 67.

20. Jones, *The Great Qing Code*, 74.

21. *Qing shilu*, 3:75.

22. Shen Jiaben, *Jiyi wencun*, juan 8, 2267–68.

23. *Da Qing lü jijie fuli* (1670), "Ganglin zhoushu," 1a–2b; and in Wudahai's memorial in 1646, collected in Shen Jiaben, *Jiyi wencun*, 2267–68. Also see Zheng and Zhou, "Pursuing Perfection," 313. For more information about *neiyuan*, see Hucker, *A Dictionary of Official Titles*, 348.

24. See Cao, "Kang Yong Qian," 14.

25. Shen Jiaben, *Jiyi wencun*, 2267–68.

26. *Da Qing lü jijie fuli* (1670), "Ganglin zhoushu," 2a.

27. Cao, "Kang Yong Qian," 14; Su, "Shunzhi lü kao," 139–78.

28. Zheng, "*Da Qing lüli* kaoxi," 43, 47. Some scholars argue that there were originally 458 statutes in the Shunzhi Code; see Su, "Shunzhi lü kao," 168–78.

29. *Qing shilu*, 3:699.

30. Cao, "Kang Yong Qian," 14; Xiao Li, "Qingdai Wuyingdian keshu chutan," 56.

31. Jin Zhi, *Buxiadai bian*, 65. Jin Zhi was commenting on the books printed by Yangzhou Poetry Bureau, a sub-branch of the Kangxi imperial publishing institutions

in Yangzhou. Books printed in the Song period were highly valued by Qing bibliographers for their beautiful printing and high quality.

32. *Qing shilu*, 3:913, 944, 1036, 1096.

33. *Qing shilu*, 4:368.

34. See Zheng, "Kangxi xianxing zeli kao," 88.

35. *Qing shilu*, 4:505.

36. Ibid., 195.

37. Zhang Weichi, *Rugao bian*, "xiabian," 15b.

38. Ibid., 16a.

39. Ibid., 16b.

40. *Da Qing lü jijie fuli* (1725), "Tuna zoushu," 6a–8a; "Zhang Yushu zoushu," 10b–11a; "Foge zoushu," 13a–b.

41. For Yongzheng's policies and reforms, see Zelin, *The Magistrate's Tael*, 72–220.

42. *Qing shilu*, 7:74–75.

43. *Da Qing lü jijie fuli* (1725), "Foge zoushu," 12a–14a; "Yuzhi xu," 3a–b.

44. Zheng and Zhou, "Pursuing Perfection," 328–30. See also *Da Qing lü jijie fuli* (1725), "Fanli."

45. *Da Qing lüli* (1999), 16.

46. Ibid., 27–28. See also Zheng and Zhou, "Pursuing Perfection," 332–33.

47. Yao Guan et al., *Da Qing lüli quanzuan*, "zoushu," 1a–4a.

48. *Qing shilu*, 12:539–40.

49. *Da Qing lüli* (1870), "Xingbu zoushu (1870)," 1a–3a.

50. Xiao Li, "Qingdai Wuyingdian keshu chutan," 56.

51. *Qinding Da Qing huidian shili, juan* 1173, 7b–9a; *juan* 1199, 1b–11a. Also see Yang Yuliang, "Wuyingdian xiushuchu," 31–36.

52. Weng, *Qing neifu keshu*, 422, 454, 621–24, 650–63.

53. Ibid., 484.

54. Yang Yuliang, "Qingdai zhongyang," 89–91; Cao, "Kang Yong Qian," 27–29.

55. Yang Yuliang, "Qingdai zhongyang," 90.

56. For example, see Qingshi Bianzuan Weiyuanhui, the *Zhupi zouzhe* database, No. 04-01-35-0912-038, No. 04-01-35-0918-056, No. 04-01-35-0920-009, No. 04-01-35-0898-30, and No. 04-08-35-0917-020; the *Nanbuxian dang'an* database, No.451242-Q1-08-01015 and No. 451242-Q1-09-00491. Chen Chongfang, "Qianlong ba'nian," 92–100.

57. Qingshi Bianzuan Weiyuanhui, the *Zhupi zouzhe* database, No. 04-01-38-0026-026.

58. For example, see the regulations of the Library of Zhongshan Academy in Tang Chunnian, *Zhongshan shuyuan zhi*, 39. See also Xiao Dongfa and Yuan Yi, "Luelun Zhongguo," 3; Fu Xuancong and Xie Zhuohua, *Zhongguo cangshu tongshi*, 798, 803–10.

59. *Qing shilu*, 3:699.

60. *Qinding Da Qing huidian shili, juan* 388, 10b–15b; and Yang Yuliang, "Qingdai zhongyang," 91.

61. Yang Yuliang, "Qingdai zhongyang," 89.

62. Ibid.

63. Xiang, "Qingdai dianben," 24.

64. Weng, *Qing neifu keshu*, 400, 689–721.

65. Ibid., 689–721.

66. For details about the price of commercial editions of the Code, see chapter 2.

67. Weng, *Qing neifu keshu*, 689–721, 738–51.

68. The process was based on Cao Zhenyong's memorial in 1820, which describes the general proofreading and printing procedures in the Wuyingdian. See Weng, *Qing neifu keshu*, 484.

69. *Qing shilu*, 10:922.

70. Ibid., 1032–33; Qingshi Bianzuan Weiyuanhui, the *Zhupi zouzhe* database, No. 04-01-01-0101-045; Weng, *Qing neifu keshu*, 484.

71. Zhongyang Yanjiuyuan Lishi Yuyan Yanjiusuo, the *Neige daku dang'an* database, No. 019667-001.

72. Chen Chongfang, "Qianlong ba'nian," 89–93.

73. Zhongyang Yanjiuyuan Lishi Yuyan Yanjiusuo, the *Neige daku dang'an* database, No. 018016-001.

74. Tao Xiang, *Qingdai dianbanshu shimo ji*, 2.

75. The analysis is based on the cover pages of the 1725, 1825, and 1870 imperial editions of the Code in the Library of Congress.

76. Needham, *Science and Civilisation*, 5 (1): 370; Chow, *Publishing, Culture, and Power*, 34; Kornicki, *The Book in Japan*, 137.

77. *Da Qing lüli quanzuan* (1796), "Zoushu," 8b–10b.

78. *Da Qing lü xuzuan tiaoli* (1743, 1746, 1750, 1795, and 1853).

79. *Da Qing lü xuzuan tiaoli* (1743), "fanli," 1a–1b.

80. According to Cynthia Brokaw's research on Sibao printing houses, the binding procedure was viewed as the work requiring little skill. Village women could do the work with needle and thread in their spare time. Brokaw, *Commerce in Culture*, 109–11.

81. Weng, *Qing neifu keshu*, 689–721.

82. *Da Qing lüli quanzuan* (1796), "Zoushu," 9b–10a, 15b.

83. *Da Qing lüli*, reprinted in *Jingyin Wenyuange siku quanshu*, Vol. 0672, 393–94. There are a number of financial reports submitted by Hubei provincial government on "the cost of printing regulations and substatutes," in Qingshi Bianzuan Weiyuanhui, the *Zhupi zouzhe* database: No. 04-01-35-0912-038, No. 04-01-35-0918-056, No. 04-01-35-0920-009, No. 04-01-35-0898-30, and No. 04-08-35-0917-020. The local archives in Nanbu County and Ba County in Sichuan also confirmed that the county magistrates did receive various printed updated regulations and substatutes from the provincial administrative commissioner's office. See Archive No. 451242-Q1-08-01015, No. 451242-Q1-09-00491 in the *Nanbuxian dang'an* database; Archive No. Qing6-04-00393, No. Qing6-04-01009-004, No. Qing6-04-01009-005, in the *Baxian dang'an* database in Qingshi Bianzuan Weiyuanhui.

84. Mokros, "Communication, Empire, and Authority," 29, 32, 160–63.

85. Rowe, *China's Last Empire*, 32.

86. Yao Run, *Da Qing lüli xing'an huizuan jicheng* (1859), "Wang Ding xu," 48b; "Changde xu," 47a.

87. Metzger, *The Internal Organization*, 130–31, 163–64.

2. Commercial Publications of the Code

1. See Wu Yanhong, "Guojia zhengce," 52–62; "The Community of Legal Experts," 207–25.

2. Most of these editions contain 30 chapters, bound into 10 volumes. Each page has 9 columns, and each column contains 20 characters. Su, "Shunzhi lü kao," 144–49.

3. Wanguzhai Zhuren, *Da Qing lüli zhuzhu guanghui quanshu* (1706), cover page.

4. *Mufu* literally means the "tent government." In the Qing period, it usually referred to (provincial) officials' private offices where their private advisors were working. See Folsom, *Friends, Guests, and Colleagues*, 34–57.

5. Sun Lun, *Dingli cheng'an hejuan*, cover page.

6. Li Zhen, *Dingli quanbian*, "Fanli," 1b.

7. Ibid., "Bianshu," 2a–b.

8. Here I follow Li Chen's argument and translate *muyou* as "legal advisor" instead of "legal secretary." Li Chen, "Legal Specialists," 4–5, 10–17.

9. Zhang Guangyue, *Li'an quanji*, "Zixu," 2a–b.

10. Sun Lun, *Dingli cheng'an hejuan*, cover page.

11. For example, see *Da Qing lüli zengxiu tongzuan jicheng* (1907), 49a–b.

12. Mokros, "Communication, Empire, and Authority," 2.

13. Li Zhen, *Benchao tibo gong'an*, "xu," 1a–2a; Liang Maoxiu, *Dingli xubian*, "Liang Maoxiu xu," 2b–3a.

14. *Qing shilu*, 7:513–14; *Da Qing lü xuzuan tiaoli* (1743), *juan* 2, 16a.

15. *Da Qing lüli jizhu* (1784), "Liyan," 2a.

16. Ibid., 1a.

17. *Da Qing lüli quanzuan* (1796), "Bianji tongren xingshi," 26a.

18. *Da Qing lüli quanzuan* (1796), "Qin Ying xu," 22a; *Da Qing lüli huizuan* (1792), "Qian Qi xu," 2b–3a; "Shen Shucheng zixu," 5a.

19. Li Chen, "Legal Specialists," 23–24; Cole, *Shaohsing*, 118–29.

20. *Da Qing lüli huizuan* (1792), "Canding tongren xingshi," 1a–1b; *Da Qing lüli chongding tongzuan jicheng* (1813), "Canding tongren xingshi," 40a.

21. *Da Qing lüli huizuan* (1792), "Shen Shucheng zixu," 2b–3a.

22. *Da Qing lüli quanzuan* (1796), "Qin Ying xu," 22a; "Zhang Yutian xu," 24b; "Zhang Yingji xu," 18a–b.

23. Li Chen, "Legal Specialists," 15.

24. *Da Qing lüli quanzuan* (1796), cover page; "Fanli," 33a–33b. *Huizuan* here refers to Shen Shucheng's *Da Qing lüli huizuan*, published in 1789 and reprinted in 1792. *Huibian* refers to Wang Youhuai's *Da Qing lüli huibian*, originally published in 1783 and revised in 1793 under a new title of *Da Qing lüli huizuan*.

25. *Da Qing lüli quanzuan jicheng* (1799), "Xu," 17a–b.

26. Ibid., cover page; "Xu," 18a.

27. *Da Qing lüli chongding tongzuan jicheng* (1813), "Zixu," 36b.

28. *Da Qing lüli quanzuan* (1796), "Zhang Yutian xu," 24b–25a.

29. *Da Qing lüli quanzuan jicheng* (1799), "Xu," 17b.

30. *Da Qing lüli huizuan* (1792), "Fanli," 1a–b; *Da Qing lüli quanzuan* (1796), "Fanli," 32a–b; *Da Qing lüli chongding tongzuan jicheng* (1813), "Zixu," 36a–b; "Fanli," 38a–b. These five "other commentaries" are *Dulü peixi, Dulü suoyan, Quanti, Xunchao,* and *Juhui.*

31. *Da Qing lüli huizuan* (1792), "Shen Shucheng zixu," 4a–b.

32. He Min, "Cong Qingdai sijia zhushi," 7.

33. Fu-mei Chang Chen, "The Influence of Shen Chih-Ch'i's *Chi-chu*," 171; He Min, "Cong Qingdai sijia zhushi," 8.

34. For a detailed discussion on the impact of private commentaries, see Fu-mei Chang Chen, "The Influence of Shen Chih-Ch'i's *Chi-chu*," 170–209; and Min Dongfang, *Da Qing lü jizhu yanjiu*, 107–249.

35. Zhang Guangyue, *Li'an quanji*, "Chen Ruji xu," 2b.

36. Qingshi Bianzuan Weiyuanhui, the *Zhupi zouzhe* database, No. 04-01-01-0031-005.

37. Yang Yifan and Liu Ducai, *Lidai likao*, 384–86. For the role of case precedents in the Qing legal system, see Wang Zhiqiang, "Qingdai cheng'an" 146–60; Koguchi, "Qingdai Zhongguo xingshi shenpan," 285–307.

38. *Da Qing lüli chongding tongzuan jicheng* (1813), "Zixu," 36a–b.

39. Fu-mei Chang Chen, "Private Code Commentaries," 73; *Da Qing lüli chongding tongzuan jicheng* (1813), "Qin Ying xu," 32a–33a.

40. *Da Qing lüli* (1870), "Guanxian," 70a; Zhao Erxun, *Qingshi gao, juan* 380:11609; *Da Qing lüli chongding tongzuan jicheng* (1815), "Chen Ruolin xu," 38a–39a.

41. *Da Qing lüli xinxiu tongzuan jicheng* (1826), "Wu Tingchen xu," 44b–45a.

42. Ibid., "Qi Gong xu," 45(1)b–45(2)b.

43. *Da Qing lüli xing'an huizuan jicheng* (1859), "Xu," 49a–b.

44. Ibid., "Ba," 54a–b.

45. *Da Qing lüli xing'an huizuan jicheng* (1859), "Fanli," 57b, "Xu," 50b–52a. *Xing'an huilan*, edited by Zhu Qingqi and Bao Shuyun in 1834 (four years before Hu Zhang's revision of *Comprehensive Integration*), was the most influential collection of case precedents in the late Qing. It consisted of about 5,640 legal cases from 1736 to 1834. See Bodde and Morris, *Law in Imperial China*, 144–47.

46. *Da Qing lüli zengxiu tongzuan jicheng* (1907), "Ying Baoshi xu," 60b–61a.

47. Yao Run's *Da Qing lüli xinxiu tongzuan jicheng* was originally published in 1823. Yao Run's revised editions of *Comprehensive Integration* were reprinted by various publishing houses in 1826, 1828, 1829, 1832, 1833, and 1843. Wu Xu did not point out exactly which edition he used for revision. Ibid., "Wu Xu xu," 56b–58a; "Wu Xu shuhou," 59a–b.

48. *Da Qing lüli zhengxiu tongzuan jicheng* (1891), "Xu," 9a; *Da Qing lüli zengxiu tongzuan jicheng* (1907), "Ying Baoshi xu," 61a–b.

49. *Da Qing lüli zengxiu tongzuan jicheng* (1907), "Wang Kaitai xu," 52b–53a; "Ying Baoshi xu," 60b.

50. *Da Qing lüli huiji bianlan* (1872), "Xiangwen," 42b; "Fanli," 51b–52a.
51. Wang Kentang, *Lüli jianshi*, "Chongbian baze," 2a–b.
52. *Da Qing lü jianshi hechao*, "Qian Zhiqing xu," 1a.
53. Liang Maoxiu, *Dingli xubian*, "Fanli," 1a.
54. *Da Qing lüli quanzuan jicheng huizhu*, "Li Guanlan ba," 1a.
55. Li Zhen, *Dingli quanbian*, "Bianshu," 1a–2b.
56. For example, see *Da Qing lü jianshi hechao*, "Qian Zhiqing xu," 1a; *Da Qing lü jizhu* (1745), "Zhang Sichang xu," 1a.
57. *Da Qing lüli jizhu* (1784), "Guan Heng xu," 2a.
58. For example, see *Da Qing lüli quanzuan jicheng*, "Li Guanlan ba," 1a.
59. *Da Qing lü jizhu* (1745), "Zhang Sichang xu," 3a–b.
60. *Da Qing lüli huizuan* (1792), "Qian Qi xu," 1b.
61. *Da Qing lü jizhu* (1745), "Jiang Chenxi xu," 1b.
62. For example, see Liang Maoxiu, *Dingli xubian* (1745), "Jiang Pu xu," 2b; *Da Qing lüli huizuan* (1792), "Qian Qi xu," 4a–b; *Da Qing lüli chongding tongzuan jicheng* (1815), "Chen Ruolin xu," 38a.
63. For example of the prices, see *Da Qing lüli chongding huitong xinzuan* (Diqisuo guanfang, 1829), cover page; *Da Qing lüli zhuzhu guanghui quanshu* (1706), cover page; *Da Qing lüli chongding tongzuan jicheng* (1823), cover page; *Da Qing lüli xing'an huizuan jicheng* (1859), cover page; *Da Qing lüli zengxiu tongzuan jicheng* (Juwentang, 1878 and 1907), cover page; *Da Qing lüli zengxiu tongzuan jicheng* (Qinglaitang, 1894), cover page; *Da Qing lüli zengxiu tongzuan jicheng* (Liulichang, 1864), cover page; *Da Qing lüli huitong xinzuan* (1873), cover page.
64. On average ordinary schoolteachers earned around twenty taels of silver per year. Jiang Wei, "Lun Qingdai shushi," 22. For officials' and legal advisors' salaries, see Ting Zhang, "Penitence Silver," 44; and Li Chen, "Legal Specialists," 18–20.
65. There are at least two extant editions of this book. One was sold by the Tingsonglou in Nanjing; the other was probably sold in a bookstore on the Liulichang Street in Beijing.
66. Liang Chufang, *Zhejiang jindai tushu*, 29–32; *Da Qing lüli zengxiu tongzuan jicheng* (1891), "Xihe yuyin xu,"1a.
67. *Da Qing lüli quanzuan* (1796), cover page.
68. Zhang Xiumin, *Zhongguo yinshua shi*, 547–58.
69. Sun Dianqi, *Liulichang xiaozhi*, 4–67; Liu Qiang, "Ronglutang yu Qingdai jinshenlu," 63–68.
70. See Christopher Reed, *Gutenberg in Shanghai*, 25–127, 161–202.
71. *Da Qing lüli xinxiu tongzuan jicheng* (1826), cover page; *Da Qing lüli zengxiu tongzuan jicheng* (1907), 90a.
72. Alford, *To Steal a Book Is an Elegant Offense*, 9–29; He Zhaohui, "Shilun Zhongguo gudai diaoban yinshua," 114–17.
73. Brokaw, *Commerce in Culture*, 398, 189–267; Ting Zhang, "Buying and Selling Law Books," 112–19. The Zaizitang book title was included in the publisher's book list. Unfortunately, the book does not survive. For Shanchengtang's bookselling network, see Brokaw, "Empire of Texts," 215–16.

74. Wang Jian, *Zhongguo jindai de falü jiaoyu*, 153–217. See chapter 3 herein for more on the new, stricter regulations on new officials' legal training and examination. For detailed discussion on legal imperialism and extraterritoriality in the late Qing, see Pär Cassel, *Grounds of Judgment*; and Li Chen, *Chinese Law in Imperial Eyes*.

75. Wu Yanhong, "The Community of Legal Experts," 207–25; Li Chen, "Legal Specialists," 1.

76. Li Chen, "Regulating Private Legal Specialists," 254–70; Li Chen, "Legal Specialists," 25.

3. Reading the Code

1. Zhang Jixin recorded this audience in his autobiography *Dao Xian huanhai jianwen lu*, which was not published until the 1980s. The information in Zhang's autobiography is likely trustworthy. In most cases, Zhang seems candid and sincere. Unlike most contemporary officials, Zhang did not write his autobiography for publication and did not brag about his own contributions. See Zhang Jixin, *Dao Xian huanhai jianwen lu*, "Xu," 1–13, 20–21; and Will, "Views of the Realm in Crisis," 135–37.

2. See Fang Dashi, *Pingping yan, juan* 1, 3a–7a, 48a; Zhang Zhidong, *Zhang Zhidong quanji*, 12:9793.

3. Zhang Jixin, *Dao Xian huanhai jianwen lu*, "Xu," 3, 16–20, 22, 44, 45, 60, 115, 475–78.

4. Ibid., 42, 115. For details of Fashenju, see Ocko, "I'll Take It All the Way to Beijing," 307.

5. Jones, *The Great Qing Code*, 89.

6. *Qinding Da Qing huidian shili, juan* 749, 18b–19a.

7. *Qing shilu*, vol. 44, *juan* 323, 782–83.

8. Qingshi Bianzuan Weiyuanhui, the *Lufu Zouzhe* database, No. 03-5017-033.

9. *Qing shilu*, vol. 49, *juan* 172, 109.

10. See *Shenbao*, "Jingbao quanlu," 1874.01.11, 4, 5; 1875.06.05, 4, 5; 1875.07.07, 3, 4; 1876.02.10, 4, 5; 1876.12.18, 3, 4; 1880.08.05, 3, 4, 5; 1880.09.01, 3, 4; 1880.12.10, 4, 5; 1881.04.08, 3, 4, 5; 1881.05.06, 3, 4, 5; and 1881.10.24, 3, 4.

11. Zhang Shiming and Feng Yongming, "Bao Shichen zhengyi de chengben," 7–12; Ocko, "I'll Take It All the Way to Beijing," 307.

12. Li Guilian and Hu Zhen, "Qingdai Fashenju yanjiu," 16, 22.

13. Qingshi Bianzuan Weiyuanhui, the *Zhupi zouzhe* database, No.04-01-12-0581-125. I found more than one hundred memorials submitted by governors-general and governors referring to retain newly appointed county magistrates in the *Lufu zouze* database and the *Zhupi zouzhe* database. The real number of new officials who had experience in the Fashenju was probably far beyond that.

14. Li Guilian and Hu Zhen, "Qingdai Fashenju yanjiu," 21; Zhang Shiming and Feng Yongming, "Bao Shichen zhengyi de chengben," 18, 19, 21.

15. Wejen Chang, "Legal Education in Ch'ing China," 294; *Qinding Da Qing huidian shili, juan* 331, 7b–8a. For details of the structure and content of the civil service examinations in the Qing, see Elman, *A Cultural History of Civil Examinations*.

16. For example, see Wejen Chang, "Legal Education in Late Imperial China," 294–96.
17. In fact, many failed candidates indeed became "litigation masters." For more details, see Macauley, *Social Power and Legal Culture*, 111–15.
18. Qingshi Bianzuan Weiyuanhui, the *Zhupi zouzhe* database, No. 04-01-38-0149-047.
19. Xu Dong, *Mulingshu jiyao*, juan 7, 1a.
20. Both authors and target readers of these handbooks were officials (including those who wanted to be officials) and private legal advisors. Based on their own experience, authors wrote and published these handbooks as guides for novices. For more details about official handbooks, see Will, "Ming Qing shiqi de guanzhenshu."
21. Tian Wenjing and Li Wei, *Qinban zhouxian shiyi*, 28a–29a.
22. Fang Dashi, *Pingping yan*, juan 1, 5b.
23. Chu Ying, *Zhouxian chushi xiaobu*, juan 2, 9a–b.
24. See Tian Wenjing and Li Wei, *Qinban zhouxian shiyi*, 28a–29a; He Changling, *Huangchao jingshi wenbian*, juan 21, 15a–b.
25. Liu Heng, *Shuliao wenda*, 2a; Wang Huizu, *Xuezhi shuozhui*, 8a–b.
26. See Bradly Reed, "Money and Justice," 345–79; Macauley, *Social Power and Legal Culture*, 18–145.
27. Bao Shichen, *Anwu sizhong*, juan 31 (shang), "Dulüshuo (shang)," 1a–b.
28. Ibid., 2a, 1b.
29. *Da Qing lü jizhu* (1745), "Jiang Chenxi xu," 1b; "Zhang Sichang xu," 2a.
30. Rowe, *Saving the World*, 3, 134–37.
31. He Changling, *Huangchao jingshi wenbian*, juan 21, 15b.
32. See Zhao Erxun, *Qingshi gao*, juan 479, 13082–83.
33. See Fang Dashi, *Pingping yan*, "Du Guichi xu," 1a–4a.
34. Ibid., *juan 1*, 3a–7a, 48a.
35. Liu Heng, *Shuliao wenda*, 15b–16a.
36. Yanchang, *Shiyi xuzhi*, juan 1, 9a–11a.
37. This genre of legal handbook was a new phenomenon in the Qing. For more details, see Will, "Zai biaoge xingshi," 33–48.
38. Wang Mingde, *Dulü peixi*, "Dulü bafa," 1.
39. Ibid., 1–2.
40. Wang Huizu, *Xuezhi shuozhui*, 8a–b.
41. Liu Heng, *Shuliao wenda*, 4a–b.
42. Muhan, *Mingxing guanjian lu*, 5b.
43. See Liu Heng, *Shuliao wenda*, 4b.
44. Wang Huizu, *Xuezhi shuozhui*, 8b; Liu Heng, *Shuliao wenda*, 3a.
45. Cavallo and Chartier, *A History of Reading*, 3.
46. *Da Qing lüli huitong xinzuan* (1873), juan 31, 3197–3224.
47. Shang Wei, "Jin Ping Mei," 204.
48. Yuming He, *Home and the World*, 77–78; Shang Wei, "Jin Ping Mei," 204, 217.
49. *Da Qing lüli huizuan* (1793), "Fanli," 1b.
50. *Da Qing lüli huizuan* (1792), "Fanli," 2a; *Da Qing lüli huizuan* (1793), "Fanli," 1b.

51. Jones, *The Great Qing Code*, article 107, 128.
52. *Da Qing lüli huitong xinzuan* (1873), *juan* 9, 1041–43.
53. Fu-mei Chang Chen, "The Influence of Shen Chih-Ch'i's *Chi-Chu*," 206, 209.
54. Jones, *The Great Qing Code*, 347–48.
55. *Da Qing lüli huitong xinzuan* (1873), *juan* 31, 3199.
56. Jones, *The Great Qing Code*, 132.
57. *Da Qing lüli huitong xinzuan* (1873), *juan* 9, 1061.
58. Wang Zhiqiang, "Qingdai cheng'an," 147; Su, *Ming Qing lüdian yu tiaoli*, 40.
59. *Da Qing lüli quanzuan*, "Zhang Yingji xu," 1b; "Fanli," 4b; *Da Qing lüli huiji bianlan* (1872), "Xiangwen," 42b, "Fanli," 52a; *Da Qing lüli quanzuan jicheng huizhu* (1804), "Fanli," 2a; *Da Qing lüli quanzuan jicheng* (1799), "Fanli," 2a.
60. See *Da Qing lüli huitong xinzuan* (1873), *juan* 25, 2527–31.
61. Li Yu, "A History of Reading," 8, 59, 94, 289.

4. Law and Legal Information in Popular Handbooks

1. For procedures of capital appeal, see Ocko, "I'll Take It All the Way to Beijing," 294–304.
2. For the Cheng brothers' case, see Guoli Gugong Bowuyuan, *Qingdai gongzhong dang ji Junjichu dang zhejian ziliao ku*, No. 404013144.
3. For example, see Li Rulan's memorial in Qingshi Bianzuan Weiyuanhui, the *Lufu zouzhe* database, No. 03-1195-009.
4. Fuma, "Songshi miben *Xiao Cao yibi* de chuxian"; Fuma, "Songshi miben de shijie"; Gong, *Ming Qing songxue yanjiu*; Macauley, *Social Power and Legal Culture*, 42–46.
5. I also refer to the research of Fuma Susumu, Gong Rufu and Sun Jiahong on many different editions of these handbooks in several leading Japanese and Chinese libraries. See Fuma, "Songshi miben *Xiao Cao yibi* de chuxian," 463–66; Gong, *Ming Qing Songxue yanjiu*, 120–28; Sun Jianghong and Gong Rufu, *Ming Qing songshi miben (shang)*, 1–7.
6. *Xinqie falin jinjian lu*; Zhulin Langsou, *Xinqie Xiao Cao yibi* (1595). See also Fuma, "Songshi miben *Xiao Cao yibi* de chuxian," 466–90; "Songshi miben de shijie," 213–14.
7. Fuma, "Songshi miben *Xiao Cao yibi* de chuxian," 471.
8. Gong, *Ming Qing songxue yanjiu*, 165–69.
9. This edition is Zhuyingxuan Zhuren, *Xinke fajia guanjian xingtai Qinjing* (1673).
10. For detailed policies, see Ocko, "I'll Take It All the Way to Beijing," 295.
11. As for the affordability of low-quality books in late imperial China, see Cynthia Brokaw, *Commerce in Culture*, 513–18.
12. The three editions are *Jingtianlei* (1915), *Xinke fabi jingtianlei* (1919), and *Jiaozheng jingtianlei* (1930). For civil law in the Republican period, see Philip Huang, *Civil Justice in China*, 9.

13. Gong, *Ming Qing songxue yanjiu*, 127. The hand-copied *Thunder* edition is *Fajia jingtianlei*, collected in the Digital Library of the Institute of Oriental Culture, University of Tokyo.
14. Jiang, *The Great Ming Code*, 201; Jones, *The Great Qing Code*, 325–26.
15. Wang Kentang, *Lüli jianshi*, "Yuanxu," 1a. Yuan Liaofan (1533–1606) was a famous scholar and an influential Buddhist moralist in the late Ming period.
16. For example, see Zhulin Langsou, *Xinqie Xiao Cao yibi, juan* 4, 36b; and Yunshui Letianzi, *Dingqie Jinling yuanban anlü bianmin zheyu qibian*, cover page.
17. Wu Tianmin and Da Keqi, *Xinke fajia xinshu* (1826). The other two Jianyang editions are Huhai Shanren Qingxuzi, *Heke minggong anduan falin zhuojian* (1612) and *Jingtianlei* (published by Shulin Xiyuan).
18. Xiangjian Buxiangzi, *Xinjuan fajia toudanhan*, cover page. For Sibao publishers, see Brokaw, *Commerce in Culture*.
19. For more detailed information on bookselling networks in late imperial China, see Brokaw, *Commerce in Culture*, 189–267; Brokaw, "Empire of Texts," 181–236; and Chia, *Printing for Profit*, 149–92.
20. *Xinke fabi jingtianlei* (1888), cover page; *Xinke fabi tianyou*, cover page.
21. Gong, *Ming Qing songxue yanjiu*, 127.
22. Qingshi Bianzuan Weiyuanhui, the *Lufu zouzhe* database, No. 03-1195-009.
23. Macauley, *Social Power and Legal Culture*, 4, 114; Fuma, "Songshi miben de shijie," 214. For example, see Zhulin Langsou, *Xinqie Xiao Cao yibi*, "Yibi fanli," 1b.
24. *Da Qing lü xuzuan tiaoli* (1743), *juan* 2, 16a.
25. See Fuma, "Songshi miben de shijie," 229.
26. I use the eight-chapter edition in Sun Jiahong and Gong Rufu's collections as the example when analyzing the text of *Thunder*. See *Xinke fabi jingtianlei*, in Sun and Gong, *Ming Qing songshi miben (shang)*, 219–394.
27. Feng Menglong, *Xingshi hengyan, juan* 27, 383.
28. Philip Huang, *Civil Justice in China*, 181–89; Bradly Reed, "Money and Justice," 345–82.
29. Sun Jiahong and Gong Rufu, *Ming Qing songshi miben (shang)*, 243.
30. Macauley, *Social Power and Legal Culture*, 61, 64.
31. Deng Jianpeng, "Songshi miben yu Qingdai suzhuang," 74.
32. Fuma, "Songshi miben de shijie," 225–27.
33. *Xinke fabi jingtianlei, juan* 1, 1a. The edition is collected in the Institute of Oriental Culture, University of Tokyo.
34. Sun and Gong, *Ming Qing songshi miben (shang)*, 245, 246.
35. These editions include Wu and Da, *Xinke fajia xinshu* (1826 and 1862); *Xinke fabi jingtianlei* (1888 and 1898), and three more editions without specific publishing dates; *Xinke fabi xinchun* (unknown publisher or publishing date).
36. The five statutes are article 366, "Fornication," article 367, "Facilitating and Tolerating the Wife's or Concubine's Fornication," article 368, "Fornication between Relatives," article 369, "Falsely Accusing the Father-in-Law of Fornication," and article 370, "A Slave or Hired Servant Who Engages in Fornication with the Wife of the Household Head." Sun and Gong, *Ming Qing songshi miben (shang)*, 227–28, 236–38.

37. Sun and Gong, *Ming Qing songshi miben (shang)*, 227.
38. Sun and Gong, *Ming Qing songshi miben (shang)*, 236; Jones, *The Great Qing Code*, 242–43, 246–47.
39. Sun and Gong, *Ming Qing songshi miben (shang)*, 232–36; Feng Wei, "*Tanglü shuyi wenda ti*," 120.
40. Sun and Gong, *Ming Qing songshi miben (shang)*, 234.
41. As for the detailed discussion on the laws and practices of family division in Qing China, see Wakefield, *Fenjia*, 34–63. *Da Ming huidian, juan* 19, 20a; *Da Qing lüli*, reprinted in *Jingyin Wenyuange siku quanshu*, Vol. 672, 535.
42. Sun and Gong, *Ming Qing songshi miben (shang)*, 253–55.
43. Sun and Gong, *Ming Qing songshi miben (shang)*, 252.
44. For the "civil laws" that Qing people frequently used in litigation, see Philip Huang, *Civil Justice in China*, 21–50, 76–109.
45. Sun and Gong, *Ming Qing songshi miben (shang)*, 227; Jiang, *The Great Ming Code*, 214; Jones, *The Great Qing Code*, 347.
46. Sun and Gong, *Ming Qing songshi miben (shang)*, 268; Jones, *The Great Qing Code*, 348.
47. Sun and Gong, *Ming Qing songshi miben (shang)*, 271.
48. *Da Qing lü jijie fuli* (1725), "Yuzhi xu," 1a–b.
49. Diyi Lishi Dang'anguan, the *Xingke tiben* database, No. 02-01-07-14078-007.
50. Xue Yunsheng, *Duli cunyi dianzhu*, 703.
51. The Dan-Xin Archives, No. 35104-1. See also Guanyuan Zhou, "Beneath the Law," 23–30.
52. The Dan-Xin Archives, No. 35104-3; Jones, *The Great Qing Code*, 324.
53. Sun and Gong, *Ming Qing songshi miben (shang)*, 237–38.
54. This was a common practice in land transactions in Taiwan in the late Qing. See Zhou Xianghe, "Qingdai Taiwan de diquan jiaoyi," 9–15.
55. The Dan-Xin Archives, No. 23103.1.
56. Jones, *The Great Qing Code*, 260; Sun and Gong, *Ming Qing songshi miben (shang)*, 322–24, 341–44.
57. The Dan-Xin Archives, No. 23103.1-10.
58. Guanyuan Zhou, "Beneath the Law," 146–209; Deng Jianpeng, "Qingdai zhouxian song'an," 70–76; Macauley, *Social Power and Legal Culture*, 140–42.
59. Gong Rufu, *Ming Qing songxue yanjiu*, 70.
60. Deng Jianpeng, "Songshi miben yu Qingdai suzhuang," 72.
61. Guanyuan Zhou, "Beneath the Law," 231–32.
62. Guoli Gugong Bowuyuan, *Qingdai gongzhong dang ji Junjichu dang zhejian ziliao ku*, No. 404013144.
63. Sun and Gong, *Ming Qing songshi miben (shang)*, 345–47.

5. Popular Legal Education

1. Rawski, *Education and Popular Literacy*, 22–23.
2. Wejen Chang, "Legal Education in Ch'ing China," 292–339.

3. Zheng Xuan and Jia Gongyan, *Zhouli zhushu, juan* 34, 19a.
4. *Da Qing lü jijie fuli* (1725), "Yuzhi xu," 1a–b, 4a–b.
5. For example, see *Qing shilu*, vol. 20, *juan* 933, 554.
6. *Analects*, 2.3, cited and modified from Bodde and Morris, *Law in Imperial China*, 21–22.
7. Durrant, *Zuo Tradition*, 1043, 1045.
8. *Qing shilu*, vol. 31, *juan* 258, 488–89.
9. Chang Jianhua, "Xiangyue de tuixing," 2; de Bary, *Asian Values and Human Rights*, 58–89; Übelhör, "The Community Compact," 371–88.
10. McDermott, "Emperor, Elites, and Commoners," 299, 310, 316; Chang Jianhua, "Xiangyue de tuixing," 2; Wang Sixia, "Ming Taizu," 31–32.
11. Mair, "Language and Ideology," 325–26.
12. Originally promulgated in 1397, the Six Edicts contained six moral maxims: (1) Be filial to your parents. (2) Be respectful to your elders. (3) Live in harmony with your neighbors. (4) Instruct your sons and grandsons. (5) Be content with your calling. (6) Do no evil. See Mair, "Language and Ideology," 327; and de Bary, *Asian Values and Human Rights*, 72.
13. de Bary, *Asian Values and Human Rights*, 72.
14. *Qinding Da Qing huidian shili, juan* 397, 3a–b.
15. Zhou Zhenhe, *Shengyu guangxun*, 585; *Qinding Da Qing huidian shili, juan* 397, 34b.
16. *Qinding Da Qing huidian shili, juan* 398, 1a–2a; *Qing shilu*, vol. 12, *juan* 264, 419–20; Zhou Zhenhe, *Shengyu guangxun*, 587–88.
17. For example, see *Qing shilu*, vol. 57, *juan* 449, 932.
18. McDermott, "Emperor, Elites, and Commoners," 306, 310–12.
19. Dai Zaochen, *Conggong sanlu*, 13a–14a.
20. The discussion on the language used in the late Ming lectures, see Wang Sixia, "Ming Taizu," 21–46; for the Qing, see Mair, "Language and Ideology," 326–56.
21. Chow, *The Rise of Confucian Ritualism*, 1.
22. Huang Liuhong, *The Complete Book*, 533–35; Zhou Zhenhe, *Shengyu guangxun*, 532–48; Chen Bingzhi and Wei Xiangshu, *Shangyu helü xiangyue quanshu*, 493–98; Wang Erh-Min, "Qingting *Shengyu guangxun*," 257–62; Mair, "Language and Ideology," 349–56.
23. See Zhou Zhenhe, *Shengyu guangxun*, 515, 534–35, and 543; Huang Liuhong, *The Complete Book*, 535.
24. For example, see Hsiao, *Rural China*, 184–201.
25. Mair, "Language and Ideology," 359; Zhou Zhenhe, *Shengyu guangxun*, 626; Wang Erh-Min, "Qingting *Shengyu guangxun*," 257–76. See also *Dianshizhai huabao*, "guibian," 51, "hengbian," 74.
26. Zhou Zhenhe, *Shengyu guangxun*, 626–28.
27. Among many examples, see Huang Liuhong, *The Complete Book*, 530–35; Chen Hongmou, *Xueshi yigui bubian, juan* 2, 1a–12a; Tian Wenjing and Li Wei, *Qinban zhouxian shiyi*, 7a–9b.
28. Meyer-Fong, *What Remains*, 30–34.

29. Sakai, *Zhongguo shanshu yanjiu*, 506–26; Dai Zaochen, *Conggong sanlu*, 15a–21a. See Zhou Zhenhe, *Shengyu guangxun*, 629; Mair, "Language and Ideology," 354–55.

30. Many scholars, such as Victor Mair, Zhou Zhenhe, and Sakai Tadao, have noticed that the legal education section of community lectures in their research. But what they have described is quite sketchy, and many only briefly mention that legal principles from the Code were introduced in the lectures. No details have been explored. See Mair, "Language and Ideology," 332–33; Zhou Zhenhe, *Shengyu guangxun*, 621–23; Sakai, *Zhongguo shanshu yanjiu*, 496; Wejen Chang, "Legal Education in Ch'ing China," 296–97.

31. Chen Bingzhi and Wei Xiangshu, *Shangyu helü xiangyue quanshu*, 268, 271–75; *Qinding Da Qing huidian shili*, juan 397, 3a–b.

32. Chen Bingzhi and Wei Xiangshu, *Shangyu helü xiangyue quanshu*, 268–69.

33. Ibid., 299–300, 418.

34. Ibid., 357–59. See also Jones, *The Great Qing Code*, 303, 311–12.

35. Chen Bingzhi and Wei Xiangshu, *Shangyu helü xiangyue quanshu*, 398–99; *Qinding Da Qing huidian shili*, juan 767, 6b; juan 815, 9b.

36. Chen Bingzhi and Wei Xiangshu, *Shangyu helü xiangyue quanshu*, 419.

37. Ibid., 405–6; *Qinding Da Qing huidian shili*, juan 397, 3a–b; Huang Liuhong, *A Complete Book*, 531.

38. For the detailed biographic information of Xia, see Yang Li, "Xia Xin de *Shi* xue sixiang yanjiu," 4–6.

39. *Qing shilu*, vol. 50, juan 247, 437; juan 266, 698; Weng, *Qing neifu keshu*, 711.

40. Luo Zhengjun, *Zuo Zongtang nianpu*, 380; Zhou Zhenhe, *Wan Qing yingye shumu*, 54.

41. Xia Xin, *Shengyu shiliutiao fulü yijie*, 552–53, 590–92.

42. In Xia's manual, only three regulations were not from the Code. One was a ban on parents forcing their children to become Buddhist monks or Daoist priests; one was a ban on providing shelter to Bannermen who were criminals; the last one was about drunk people who beat and robbed others. Ibid., 603, 606, and 612.

43. Zheng Qin, "*Da Qing lüli* kaoxi," 43, 95.

44. See Sommer, *Sex, Law, and Society in Late Imperial China*, 8–15, 96–101. Chen Bingzhi and Wei Xiangshu, *Shangyu helü xiangyue quanshu*, 436–39.

45. See Zhao Bingyi, *Guangxun fulü cheng'an* (1745), *Shengyu guangxun zhijie* (1857 preface), reprinted in Zhou Zhenhe, *Shengyu guangxun*.

46. Rowe, "Education and Empire," 417–20.

47. Zhou Zhenhe, *Shengyu guangxun*, 557–58.

48. Li Laizhang, *Lianyang bapai fengtuji*, juan 7, 1a; juan 8, 1a.

49. Ibid., juan 7, 5a–6b, 14a–15a, 20a–29a.

50. Zhou Zhenhe, *Shengyu guangxun*, 535, 558.

51. Ibid.

52. The statutes in Li's manual are articles 61, 78, 81, 82, 83, 84, 87, 88, 90, 97, 105, 112, 149, 162, 175, 178, 182, 272, 301, 316, 319, 329, 336, 338, 340, 365, 385, 386, 393, and 396. The substatutes belong to articles 4, 52, 54, 87, 90, 119, 162, 173, 175, 182, 278, 294, 299, 318, 332, 336, 360, and 374.

53. Zhou Zhenhe, *Shengyu guangxun*, 79–80.
54. Li Laizhang, *Lianyang bapai fengtuji, juan* 7, 6b; Zhao Erxun *Qing shigao*, vol. 43, *juan* 480, 13136–37.
55. Li Laizhang, *Lianyang bapai fengtuji, juan* 8, 12a–b.
56. Millward and Newby, "The Qing and Islam," 113–31; Liang Haixia, "Jindai Xinjiang Nanjiang sifa," 17–24; Millward, *Beyond the Pass*, 121–22.
57. There were some exceptions: some serious capital cases, such as rebellion and homicide, were sentenced according to *The Great Qing Code*, regardless of ethnicity. See Liang Haixia, "Jindai Xinjiang Nanjiang sifa," 23–25.
58. Jacobs, "Empire Besieged," ix, 23.
59. Luo Zhengjun, *Zuo Zongtang nianpu*, 380.
60. Cao Shangting, *Tulufan wuqiannian*, vol. 2, 575; Liang Haixia, "Jindai Xinjiang Nanjiang sifa," 47–53, 64–65.
61. Yang Pizhuo, *Luopu xian xiangtu zhi*, 708–9.
62. *Qing shilu*, vol. 12, *juan* 264, 419–20; vol. 32, *juan* 310, 115; vol. 36, *juan* 226, 379–80; *Qinding Da Qing huidian shili, juan* 398, 11b; Zhou Zhenhe, *Shengyu guangxun*, 509, 515–16, 519–20; Lipman, "A Fierce and Brutal People," 101.
63. *Qing shilu*, vol. 9, *juan* 37, 674; vol. 16, *juan* 625, 1020; vol. 20, *juan* 945, 794–95.
64. Zhihe, *Da Qing xinglü zeyao qianshuo*, 351.
65. Ibid., 374–75.
66. Ibid., 374.
67. Ibid., 412.
68. Ibid., 380–81.
69. Ibid., 352–53, 357, 361, 365, 370–71.

Conclusion: The Impact of Printing on Law and Legal Culture

1. Eisenstein, *The Printing Press*. For example, see Baker, "The Books of the Common Law," 430–32; Baker, "English Law Books," 474–503; Prest, "Law Books," 791–806; Baloch, "Law Booksellers and Printers," 389–90; Harvey, *The Law Emprynted and Englysshed*, 169–70, 194–206, 234–39, 241–53; and Henderson, "Legal Literature," 292–93.
2. Harvey, *The Law Emprynted and Englysshed*, 1–8, 10–11, 69–90, 202–6, 241–44, 253; Henderson, "Legal Literature," 290–93; Ross, "The Commoning of the Common Law," 326; Baloch, "Law Booksellers and Printers," 390.
3. Chow, *Publishing, Culture, and Power*, 1–89.
4. Printing also facilitated the circulation of some inaccurate or semi-accurate information about the law, such as legal information in novels, which is not the focus of this book but deserves further research. For some related research, see Hegel and Carlitz, *Writing and Law*, 189–260.
5. Harvey, *The Law Emprynted and Englysshed*, 16–68, 73–75, 91, 127.
6. Ibid., 2, 107–22; Ross, "The Commoning of the Common Law," 329–86.
7. Harvey, *The Law Emprynted and Englysshed*, 6, 202–6, 221; Wang Zhiqiang, "Zhongguo falüshi xushi zhong de 'panli,'" 144.

8. Chow, *Publishing, Culture, and Power*, 1–2, 189–240.

9. The Stationers' Company's control was probably more effective than the state's control on the law printing industry. Harvey, *The Law Emprynted and Englysshed*, 11–12, 16–68.

10. Baloch, "Law Booksellers and Printers," 389–421.

11. For example, see Wang Zhiqiang, "Qingdai cheng'an," 158–60; "Case Precedent in Qing China," 323–44.

Epilogue

1. The "Killing the Adulterous Lover" statute (article 285) had two parts. The first part is "killing the adulterous lover," which we saw in murderer Du's case. The second part is about adulterous wives or concubines who murdered their husbands. Here I only count the cases directly related to the first part. See Zhu Qingqi, *Xing'an huilan sanbian*, 31–36; Jones, *The Great Qing Code*, 271.

2. Zhu Qingqi, *Xing'an huilan sanbian*, 882, 894.

3. Chen Zhanbiao, "Qingdai 'shasi jianfu' de lifa," 7.

4. Jiang, *The Great Ming Code*, 171; Jones, *The Great Qing Code*, 271.

5. Shen Jiaben, *Jiyi wencun, juan* 2, 21b–22a.

6. Zhulin Langsou, *Xinqie Xiao Cao yibi, juan* 4, 30a.

7. Sun and Gong, *Ming Qing songshi miben (shang)*, 286.

8. Ibid., 233.

9. *Da Qing lüli* (1999), 424–25.

10. See Xiangjian Buxiangzi, *Xinjuan fajia toudanhan* (edition in the Library of University of Tokyo), *juan* 4, 4b–5a.

11. Yu Xiangdou, *Huang Ming zhusi gong'an*, 1785–86.

12. Qi Lianxiu, *Zhongguo gudai minjian gushi leixing yanjiu*, 1165–70.

13. Xu Ke, *Qingbai leichao*, 1192–93.

14. Ibid., 1195.

15. Xia Xin, *Shengyu shiliutiao fulü yijie*, 594.

16. Shen Jiaben, *Jiyi wencun, juan* 2, 23a.

17. Ibid., 22b.

18. Robert Hegel, *True Crimes*, 82.

SELECTED BIBLIOGRAPHY

See tables 1.1, 1.2, 2.2, and 3.1 for additional information on Chinese editions of *The Great Qing Code* and other law books.

The Qing Code and Commentaries

Da Qing lü jianshi. Edited by Li Nan and Cai Fangbing. 1689.
Da Qing lü jianshi hechao. Edited by Qian Zhiqing and Lu Fenglai. Zundaotang, 1705.
Da Qing lü jijie fuli. Unidentified publisher, 1670. Beijing: Wuyingdian, 1725.
Da Qing lü xuzuan tiaoli. Beijing: Wuyingdian, 1743.
Da Qing lü zhuzhu guanghui quanshu. Beijing: Liulichang, 1662–1722.
Da Qing lüli. Beijing: Wuyingdian, 1740, 1768, 1790, 1825, 1870. Proofread by Tian Tao and Zheng Qin, Beijing: Falü Chubanshe, 1999. Also reprinted in *Jingyin Wenyuange siku quanshu.* Taipei: Taiwan Shangwu Yinshuguan, 1983.
Da Qing lüli chongding huitong xinzuan. Beijing: Diqisuo Guanfang, 1829 and 1841.
Da Qing lüli chongding tongzuan jicheng. Edited by Hu Zhaokai and Zhou Menglin, revised by Tang Xun, 1813 and 1815. Edited by Wang Youhuai and Zhao Zuowen, 1814. Revised by Yao Guan, Hangzhou: Wubentang, 1823.
Da Qing lüli huiji bianlan. Edited by Hubei Yanju, Wuhan: Hubei Yanjiu, 1872. Hangzhou: Zhehang Dulü Shanguan, 1877 and 1885. Beijing: Shanchengtang, 1888. Beijing: Hongdaotang, 1898. Unidentified publishers, 1877, 1892, and 1903.
Da Qing lüli huitong xinzuan. Edited by Yao Guan and Hu Zhang, Beijing: Diqisuo Guanfang, 1873. Reprinted in *Jindai zhongguo shiliao congkan*, Series 3, Vol. 211. Taipei: Wenhai Chubanshe, 1987. Unidentified publishers, 1870 and 1875.
Da Qing lüli huizuan. Edited by Shen Shucheng, 1792. Revised by Wang Youhuai, 1793.
Da Qing lüli huizuan dacheng. Unidentified publishers, 1898 and 1903.
Da Qing lüli jiyao xinbian. Edited by Sun Zhaoji and Wang Weishu, 1819 and 1821.
Da Qing lüli jizhu. Edited by Wan Weihan and Teng Jingshan, Suzhou: Yunhuitang, 1769. Revised by Hu Qian and Wang Youhuai, Suzhou: Yunhuitang, 1784.
Da Qing lüli quanzuan. Edited by Yao Guan, Hangzhou: Mingxintang, 1796 and 1798.
Da Qing lüli quanzuan jicheng. Edited by Li Guanlan, revised by Wang Youhuai and Sun Guanglie, Hangzhou: Youyizhai, 1799 and 1801.
Da Qing lüli quanzuan jicheng huizhu. Edited by Wang Youhuai, Suzhou: Xieyunlou, 1803. Hangzhou: Youyizhai, 1804.

Da Qing lüli tongzuan. Edited by Hu Zhaokai and Zhou Menglin, Hangzhou: Youyizhai, 1807. Unidentified publishers, 1805 and 1816.

Da Qing lüli tongzuan jicheng. Edited by Hu Zhaokai and Zhou Menglin, Cenfeng Shuyuan, 1817. Edited by Wang Youhuai, unidentified publisher, 1871. Revised by Chen Junsheng, unidentified publisher, 1829.

Da Qing lüli xing'an tongzuan jicheng. Edited by Yao Run, revised by Hu Zhang, Nanjing: Zhihetang, 1855. Hangzhou: Sanshantang, 1859. Unidentified publishers, 1841, 1846, and 1855.

Da Qing lüli xing'an xinzuan jicheng. Edited by Wang Youhuai, revised by Hu Zhang, 1871.

Da Qing lüli xinxiu tongzuan jicheng. Edited by Yao Run, revised by Chen Junsheng, Hangzhou: Lüsutang, 1826.

Da Qing lüli zengxiu huizuan dacheng. Unidentified publishers, 1864, 1898, and 1903.

Da Qing lüli zengxiu tongzuan jicheng. Edited by Yao Run, revised by Lu Hanxian, 1832 and 1833. Revised by Zhang Yue and Shen Jiashu, Hangzhou: Tongwentang, 1843. Revised by Ren Pengnian, Hangzhou: Qinglaitang, 1871, 1875, and 1894. Revised by Hu Zhang, Beijing: Liulichang, 1865 and 1872. Revised by Tao Jun and Tao Nianlin, Hangzhou: Juwentang, 1878, 1890, 1898, and 1907. Shanghai: Saoye Shanfang, 1887. Shanghai: Yizhen Shuju, 1891. Shanghai: Wenyuan Shanfang, 1896, 1899, 1904, 1906, and 1908. Unidentified publishers, 1862, 1894, 1898, and 1901.

Da Qing lüli zhuzhu guanghu quanshu. Edited by Wanguzhai Zhuren. Nanjing: Tingsonglou, 1706.

Shen Zhiqi. *Da Qing lü jizhu*. 1715. Revised by Hong Hongxu, 1745. Proofread by Li Jun and Huai Xiaofeng, Beijing: Falü Chubanshe, 2000.

Wang Kentang. *Lüli jianshi*. Revised by Gu Ding. 1691 preface.

Wang Mingde. *Dulü peixi*. Beijing: Falü Chubanshe, 2000.

Other Primary Sources

Bao Shichen. *Anwu sizhong*. 1872 preface.

Chen Bingzhi and Wei Xiangshu. *Shangyu helü xiangyue quanshu*. 1679. Reprinted in *Gudai xiangyue ji xiangzhi falü wenxian shizhong*, edited by Yifan Cangshuguan Wenxian Bianweihui, vol. 1. Harbin: Heilongjiang Renmin Chubanshe, 2005.

Chen Hongmou. *Xueshi yigui bubian*. Reprinted in *Guanzhenshu jicheng*, edited by Guanzhenshu Jicheng Bianzuan Weiyuanhui, vol. 4. Hefei: Huangshan Shushe, 1997.

Chu Ying. *Zhouxian chushi xiaobu*. Reprinted in *Guanzhenshu jicheng*, edited by Guanzhenshu Jicheng Bianzuan Weiyuanhui, vol. 8. Hefei: Huangshan Shushe, 1997.

Dai Zaochen. *Conggong sanlu*. Reprinted in *Guanzhenshu jicheng*, edited by Guanzhenshu Jicheng Bianzuan Weiyuanhui, vol. 8. Hefei: Huangshan Shushe, 1997.

Dianshizhai huabao. Dianshizhai Shiyin Shuju, 1884–1898. Guangzhou: Guangdong Renmin Chubanshe, 1983.

Fajia jingtianlei. Unidentified publishers, 1644–1911.

Fang Dashi. *Pingping yan*. Reprinted in *Guanzhenshu jicheng*, edited by Guanzhenshu Jicheng Bianzuan Weiyuanhui, vol. 7. Hefei: Huangshan Shushe, 1997.

Feng Menglong. *Xingshi hengyan*. Beijing: Huaxia Chubanshe, 1998.

Guanzhenshu Jicheng Bianzuan Weiyuanhui, ed. *Guanzhenshu jicheng*. Hefei: Huang-shan Shushe, 1997.

He Changling, ed. *Huangchao jingshi wenbian*. Reprinted in *Jindai Zhongguo shiliao congkan*, edited by Shen Yunlong, vol. 731. Taipei: Wenhai Chubanshe, 1966–73.

Jin Zhi. *Buxiadai bian*. Beijing: Zhonghua Shuju, 1982.

Kungang, ed. *Qinding Da Qing huidian shili*. Shanghai: Shangwu Yinshuguan, 1908.

Li Laizhang. *Lianyang bapai fengtuji*. Reprinted in *Zhongguo fangzhi congshu*, Taipei: Chengwen Chubanshe, 1967.

———. *Shengyu xuanjiang tiaoyue*. Lianshan xianya, 1705.

Li Zhen, ed. *Benchao tibo gong'an*. Beijing: Rongjintang, 1720.

———. *Dingli quanbian*. Beijing: Rongjintang, 1715.

Liang Maoxiu, ed. *Dingli xubian*. Beijing: Rongjintang, 1745.

Liu Heng. *Shuliao wenda*. Reprinted in *Guanzhenshu jicheng*, edited by Guanzhenshu Jicheng Bianzuan Weiyuanhui, vol. 6. Hefei: Huangshan Shushe, 1997.

Muhan. *Mingxing guanjian lu*. 1847 preface.

Qinding liubu chufen zeli. Reprinted in *Jindai Zhongguo shiliao congkan*, edited by Shen Yunlong, vol. 34. Taipei: Wenhai Chubanshe, 1966–73.

Qing shilu. Beijing: Zhonghua Shuju, 1985.

Shen Shixing and Zhao Yongxian, ed. *Da Ming huidian*. 1587.

Su Shi. *Su Dongpo quanji*. Shanghai: Shijie Shuju, 1936.

Sun Jiahong and Gong Rufu, eds. *Ming Qing songshi miben bazhong huikan*. In *Lidai zhenxi sifa wenxian*, edited by Yang Yifan, vols. 11 and 12. Beijing: Shenghui Kexue Wenxian Chubanshe, 2012.

Sun Lun. *Dingli cheng'an hejuan*. Wujiang: Lejingtang, 1719.

Tang Chunnian. *Zhongshan shuyuan zhi*. Nanjing: Nanjing Chubanshe, 2013.

Tian Wenjing and Li Wei. *Qinban zhouxian shiyi*. Reprinted in *Muling quanshu*, edited by Ding Richang. Suzhou: Jiangsu Shuju, 1868.

Wang Huizu. *Xuezhi shuozhui*. Reprinted in *Guanzhenshu jicheng*, edited by Guan-zhenshu Jicheng Bianzuan Weiyuanhui, vol. 5. Hefei: Huangshan Shushe, 1997.

Wang Youfu. *Yide outan*. 1805 preface. Reprinted in *Zhongguo lüxue wenxian*, series 3, vol. 4, edited by Yang Yifan. Ha'erbin: Heilongjiang Renmin Chubanshe, 2006.

Weng Lianxi, ed. *Qing neifu keshu dang'an shiliao huibian*. Yangzhou: Guangling Shushe, 2007.

Wu Tan. *Da Qing lüli tongkao jiaozhu*. Beijing: Zhongguo Zhengfa Daxue Chubanshe, 1992.

Wu Tianmin and Da Keqi, eds. *Xinke fajia xinshu*. Shulin: Yugengtang, 1826 and 1862.

Xia Xin. *Shengyu shiliutiao fulü yijie*. Reprinted in *Zhongguo lüxue wenxian*, series 4, vol. 4, edited by Yang Yifan. Beijing: Shehui Kexue Wenxian Chubanshe, 2007.

Xiangjian Buxiangzi. *Xinjuan fajia toudanhan*. Liujingtang, 1812. Unidentified pub-lishers, 1368–1644, 1839.

Xinke fabi jingtianlei. Yonghetang, 1888. Shanghai: Jinzhang Tushuju, 1915, 1919, and 1930. Unidentified publishers, 1898, 1909, 1915, and 1644–1911.

Xinke fabi tianyou. Wenxing Deji, 1644–1911.

Xinke fabi xinchun. Unidentified publisher, 1644–1911.

Xinqie falin jinjian lu. Jinling Shushi, 1594.

Xu Changzuo. *Xinjuan dingbu zhushi Xiao Cao yibi.* Unidentified publisher, possibly 1583 or 1643.

Xu Dong. *Mulingshu jiyao.* Suzhou: Jiangsu Shuju, 1868.

Xu Ke. *Qingbai leichao.* Beijing: Zhonghua Shuju, 1984.

Yanchang. *Shiyi xuzhi.* 1885 preface. Reprinted in *Guanzhenshu jicheng,* edited by Guanzhenshu Jicheng Bianzuan Weiyuanhui, vol. 9. Hefei: Huangshan Shushe, 1997.

Yang Pizhuo. *Luopu xian xiangtu zhi.* 1907 preface. Reprinted in *Xinjiang xiangtu zhigao,* edited by Ma Dazheng, Huang Guozheng, and Su Fenglan. Urumqi: Xinjiang Renmin Chubanshe, 2010.

Yu Xiangdou. *Huang Ming zhusi gong'an.* Reprinted in *Guben xiaoshuo congkan,* edited by Liu Shide, Chen Qinghao, and Shi Changyu, series 6, vol. 4. Beijing: Zhonghua Shuju, 1990.

Zhang Guangyue, ed. *Li'an quanji.* Sijingtang, 1722.

Zhang Jinglu. *Zhongguo xiandai chuban shiliao.* Beijing: Zhonghua Shuju, 1959.

Zhang Jixin. *Dao Xian huanhai jianwen lu.* Beijing: Zhonghua Shuju, 2008.

Zhang Weichi. *Rugaobian.* Reprinted in *Congshu jicheng xubian,* vol. 58. Taipei: Xinwenfeng Chuban Gongsi, 1988.

Zhang Zhidong. *Zhang Zhidong quanji,* edited by Yuan Shuyi, Sun Huafeng, and Li Bingxin. Shijiazhuang: Hebei Renmin Chubanshe, 1998.

Zhao Erxun, ed. *Qingshi gao.* Beijing: Zhonghua Shuju, 1977.

Zheng Xuan and Jia Gongyan. *Zhouli zhushu.* Beijing: Wuyingdian, 1739. Guangzhou: Gongdong shuju, 1871 reprint.

Zhihe. *Da Qing xinglü zeyao qianshuo.* Huiwen Shanfang, 1864. Reprinted in *Zhongguo lüxue wenxian,* series 4, vol. 4, edited by Yang Yifan. Beijing: Shehui Kexue Wenxian Chubanshe, 2007.

Zhu Qingqi, ed. *Xing'an huilan sanbian.* Beijing: Guji Chubanshe, 2004.

Zhulin Langsou. *Xinqie Xiao Cao yibi.* Unidentified publisher. 1595 preface.

Zhuyingxuan Zhuren, ed. *Xinke fajia guanjian huiyu xingtai Qinjing.* Unidentified publisher. 1673 preface.

Secondary Sources

Alford, William P. *To Steal a Book Is an Elegant Offense: Intellectual Property Law in Chinese Civilization.* Stanford: Stanford University Press, 1995.

Bai Yang. "Qingdai cuo'an zhuize zhidu yunxing zhong de kunjing ji yuanyin tanxi." *Zhejiang shehui kexue* 7 (2019): 48–55.

Baker, J. H. "The Books of the Common Law." In *The Cambridge History of the Book in Britain, Vol. 3, 1400–1557,* edited by Lotte Hellinga and J. B. Trapp, 411–32. Cambridge, UK: Cambridge University Press, 1999.

———. "English Law Books and Legal Publishing." In *Cambridge History of the Book in Britain, Vol. 4, 1557–1695,* edited by John Barnard and D. F. McKenzie, 474–503. Cambridge, UK: Cambridge University Press, 2002.

Baloch, Tariq A. "Law Booksellers and Printers as Agents of Unchange." In *Cambridge Law Journal* 66, no. 2 (2007): 389–421.

Bernhardt, Kathryn, and Philip Huang, eds. *Civil Law in Qing and Republican China*. Stanford: Stanford University Press, 1994.

Bodde, Derk, and Clarence Morris. *Law in Imperial China: Exemplified by 190 Ch'ing Dynasty Cases*. Cambridge, Mass.: Harvard University Press, 1973.

Brokaw, Cynthia. *Commerce in Culture: The Sibao Book Trade in the Qing and Republican Periods*. Cambridge, Mass.: Harvard University Press, 2007.

———. "Empire of Texts: Book Production, Book Distribution, and Book Culture in Late Imperial China." In *The Book Worlds of East Asia and Europe, 1450–1850: Connections and Comparisons*, edited by Joseph P. McDermott and Peter Burke, 181–236. Hong Kong: Hong Kong University Press, 2015.

Brokaw, Cynthia, and Kai-Wing Chow, eds. *Printing and Book Culture in Late Imperial China*. Berkeley: University of California Press, 2005.

Brokaw, Cynthia, and Christopher A. Reed, eds. *From Woodblocks to the Internet: Chinese Publishing and Print Culture in Transition, circa 1800 to 2008*. Leiden: Brill, 2010.

Cao Hongjun. "Kang Yong Qian sanchao zhongyang jigou keyin shu yanjiu." PhD dissertation, Nanjing Shifan Daxue, 2006.

Cao Shangting. *Tulufan wuqiannian*. Urumqi: Xinjiang Daxue Chubanshe, 2007.

Cassel, Pär Kristoffer. *Grounds of Judgment: Extraterritoriality and Imperial Power in Nineteenth-Century China and Japan*. Oxford: Oxford University Press, 2012.

Cavallo, Guglielmo, and Roger Chartier, eds. *A History of Reading in the West*. Oxford, UK: Blackwell, 1999.

Chang, Wejen. "Legal Education in Ch'ing China." In *Education and Society in Late Imperial China, 1600–1900*, edited by Benjamin Elman and Alexander Woodside, 292–339. Berkeley: University of California Press, 1994.

Chang Jianhua. "Xiangyue de tuixing yu Mingchao dui jiceng shehui de zhili." In *Ming Qing luncong*, vol. 4, edited by Zhu Chengru and Wang Tianyou, 1–36. Beijing: Zijincheng Chubanshe, 2003.

Chen, Fu-mei Chang. "The Influence of Shen Chih-Ch'i's *Chi-chu* Commentary upon Ch'ing Judicial Decisions." In *Essays on China's Legal Tradition*, edited by Jerome Alan Cohen, Fu-mei Chang Chen, and R. Randle Edwards, 170–221. Princeton: Princeton University Press, 1980.

———. "Private Code Commentaries in the Development of Ch'ing Law, 1644–1911." PhD dissertation, Harvard University, 1970.

Chen, Li. *Chinese Law in Imperial Eyes: Sovereignty, Justice, and Transcultural Politics*. New York: Columbia University Press, 2015.

———. "Legal Specialists and Judicial Administration in Late Imperial China, 1651–1911." *Late Imperial China* 33, no. 1 (2012): 1–54.

———. "Regulating Private Legal Specialists and the Limits of Imperial Power in Qing China." In *Chinese Law: Knowledge, Practice and Transformation, 1530 to 1950s*, edited by Li Chen and Madeleine Zelin, 254–86. Leiden: Brill, 2015.

Chen, Li, and Madeleine Zelin, eds. *Chinese Law: Knowledge, Practice and Transformation, 1530 to 1950s.* Leiden: Brill, 2015.

Chen Chongfang. "Qianlong ba'nian *Da Qing lüli* de banxing." *Fazhishi yanjiu* 29 (2016): 77–124.

———. "Qingdai jianyan zhishi de changgui yu shijian." *Qingshi yanjiu* 3 (2018): 33–49.

———. "*Xiyuanlu* zai Qingdai de liuchuan, yuedu, yu yingyong." *Fazhishi yanjiu* 25 (2014): 37–94.

Chen Zhanbiao. "Qingdai 'shasi jianfu' de lifa ji sifa shijian." *Faxue yanjiu* 8 (2013): 7–10.

Chia, Lucille. *Printing for Profit: The Commercial Publishers of Jianyang, Fujian (11th–17th Centuries).* Cambridge, Mass.: Harvard University Press, 2002.

Chiu Peng-sheng. *Dang falü yushang jingji: Ming Qing Zhongguo de shangye falü.* Taipei: Wu'nan Tushu Chuban Gongsi, 2008.

Chow, Kai-wing. *Publishing, Culture, and Power in Early Modern China.* Stanford: Stanford University Press, 2004.

———. *The Rise of Confucian Ritualism in Late Imperial China: Ethics, Classics, and Lineage Discourse.* Stanford: Stanford University Press, 1994.

Ch'ü, T'ung-Tsu. *Law and Society in Traditional China.* Paris: Mouton, 1961.

———. *Local Government in China under the Ch'ing.* Cambridge, Mass.: Harvard University Press, 1988.

Cohen, Jerome Alan, Fu-mei Chang Chen, and R. Randle Edwards, eds. *Essays on China's Legal Tradition.* Princeton: Princeton University Press, 1980.

Cole, James H. *Shaohsing: Competition and Cooperation in Nineteenth-Century China.* Tucson: University of Arizona Press, 1986.

Crossley, Pamela K., Helen F. Siu, and Donald S. Sutton, eds. *Empire at the Margins: Culture, Ethnicity, and Frontier in Early Modern China.* Berkeley: University of California Press, 2006.

de Bary, William Theodore. *Asian Values and Human Rights: A Confucian Communitarian Perspective.* Cambridge, Mass.: Harvard University Press, 1998.

de Bary, William Theodore, and John W. Chaffee, eds. *Neo-Confucian Education: The Formative Stage.* Berkeley: University of California Press, 1989.

Deng Jianpeng. "Qingdai zhouxian song'an he jiceng de sifa yunzuo: yi Huangyan susong dang'an wei yanjiu zhongxin." *Fazhi yanjiu* 5 (2007): 70–80.

———. "Songshi miben yu Qingdai suzhuang de fengge: yi 'Huangyan susong dang'an wei kaocha zhongxin." *Zhejiang shehui kexue* 4 (2005): 71–75.

Durrant, Stephen, Wai-yee Li, and David Schaberg. *Zuo Tradition: Commentary on the "Spring and Autumn Annals."* Seattle: University of Washington Press, 2016.

Eisenstein, Elizabeth. *The Printing Press as an Agent of Change: Communications and Cultural Transformations in Early-Modern Europe.* Cambridge, UK: Cambridge University Press, 1979.

———. *The Printing Revolution in Early Modern Europe.* New York: Cambridge University Press, 1983.

Elman, Benjamin A. *A Cultural History of Civil Examinations in Late Imperial China.* Berkeley: University of California Press, 2000.

Elman, Benjamin A., and Alexander Woodside, eds. *Education and Society in Late Imperial China, 1600–1900*. Berkeley: University of California Press, 1994.

Farmer, Edward L. *Zhu Yuanzhang and Early Ming Legislation: The Reordering of Chinese Society following the Era of Mongol Rule*. Leiden: Brill, 1995.

Feng Wei. "*Tanglü shuyi* wenda ti shuzheng tezhi wenju tanxi." *Changchun shifan xueyuan xuebao* 29, no. 6 (2010): 120–23.

Folsom, Kenneth E. *Friends, Guests, and Colleagues: The Mu-fu System in the Late Ch'ing Period*. Berkeley: University of California Press, 1968.

Fu Xuancong and Xie Zhuohua, eds. *Zhongguo cangshu tongshi*. Ningbo: Ningbo Chubanshe, 2001.

Fuma Susumu. "Songshi miben de shijie." Translated by Li Li. *Beida falü pinglun* 11, no. 1 (2010): 210–38.

———. "Songshi miben *Xiao Cao yibi* de chuxian." Translated by Zheng Minqin. In *Zhongguo fazhishi kaozheng (bingbian)*, vol. 4, edited by Yang Yifan, 460–90. Beijing: Zhongguo Shehui Kexue Chubanshe, 2003.

Gong Rufu. *Ming Qing songxue yanjiu*. Beijing: Shangwu Yinshuguan, 2008.

Harvey, David. *The Law Emprynted and Englysshed: The Printing Press as an Agent of Change in Law and Legal Culture, 1475–1642*. Oxford, UK: Hart, 2015.

He, Yuming. *Home and the World: Editing the "Glorious Ming" in Woodblock-Printed Books of the Sixteenth and Seventeenth Centuries*. Cambridge, Mass.: Harvard University Press, 2013.

He Min. "Cong Qingdai sijia zhushi kan chuantong zhushi lüxue de shiyong jiazhi." *Faxue* 5 (1997): 7–14.

He Zhaohui. "Shilun Zhongguo gudai diaoban yinshua banquan xingtai de jiben tezheng." *Tushu yu qingbao* 3 (2008): 113–18, 125.

Hegel, Robert E. *True Crimes in Eighteenth-Century China: Twenty Case Histories*. Seattle: University of Washington Press, 2009.

Hegel, Robert E., and Katherine Carlitz, eds. *Writing and Law in Late Imperial China: Crime, Conflict, and Judgment*. Seattle: University of Washington Press, 2007.

Henderson, Edith G. "Legal Literature and the Impact of Printing on the English Legal Profession." *Law Library Journal* 68, no. 3 (1975): 288–93.

Hsiao, Kung-chuan. *Rural China: Imperial Control in the Nineteenth Century*. Seattle: University of Washington Press, 1960.

Hsu, Stephen C., ed. *Understanding China's Legal System: Essays in Honor of Jerome A. Cohen*. New York: New York University Press, 2003.

Huang, Liuhong. *A Complete Book concerning Happiness and Benevolence*. Translated by Djang Chu. Tucson: University of Arizona Press, 1984.

Huang, Philip C. C. *Civil Justice in China: Representation and Practice in the Qing*. Stanford: Stanford University Press, 1996.

Hucker, Charles O. *A Dictionary of Official Titles in Imperial China*. Taipei: Southern Materials Center, 1988.

Inoue, Susumu. *Chūgoku shuppan bunkashi: shomotsu sekai to chi no fūkei*. Nagoya: Nagoya Daigaku Shuppankai, 2002.

Jacobs, Justin. "Empire Besieged: The Preservation of Chinese Rule in Xinjiang, 1884–1971." PhD dissertation, University of California, San Diego, 2011.

Jiang, Yonglin, trans. *The Great Ming Code*. Seattle: University of Washington Press, 2005.

———. *The Mandate of Heaven and the Great Ming Code*. Seattle: University of Washington Press, 2011.

Jiang Wei. "Lun Qingdai shushi de zhiye shouru ji xiangguan wenti." *Lishi jiaoxue* 675, no. 14 (2013): 17–23.

Johnson, David, Andrew J. Nathan, and Evelyn S. Rawski, eds. *Popular Culture in Late Imperial China*. Berkeley: University of California Press, 1985.

Jones, William C., trans. *The Great Qing Code*. Oxford: Oxford University Press, 1994.

Koguchi, Hikota. "Qingdai Zhongguo xingshi shenpan zhong cheng'an de fayuanxing." Translated by Zheng Minqin. In *Zhongguo fazhishi kaozheng (bingbian)*, vol. 4, edited by Yang Yifan, 285–307. Beijing: Zhongguo Shehui Kexue Chubanshe, 2003.

Kornicki, Peter. *The Book in Japan: A Cultural History from the Beginnings to the Nineteenth Century*. Leiden: Brill, 1998.

Li Guilian and Hu Zhen. "Qingdai Fashenju yanjiu." *Bijiao fa yanjiu* 4 (2006): 15–26.

Liang Chufang, Zhu Xiaojun, Hu Xueyan, and Chen Houyang, eds. *Zhejiang jindai tushu chubanshi yanjiu*. Beijing: Xuexi Chubanshe, 2014.

Liang Haixia. "Jindai Xinjiang Nanjiang sifa zhidu yanjiu." PhD dissertation, Shaanxi Shifan Daxue, 2010.

Lipman, Jonathan N. "A Fierce and Brutal People: On Islam and Muslims in Qing Law." In *Empire at the Margins: Culture, Ethnicity, and Frontier in Early Modern China*, edited by Pamela K. Crossley, Helen F. Siu, and Donald S. Sutton, 83–110. Berkeley: University of California Press, 2006.

Liu Junwen, ed. *Riben xuezhe yanjiu Zhongguoshi lunzhu xuanyi*. Beijing: Zhonghua shuju, 1992.

Liu Qiang. "Ronglutang yu Qingdai jinshenlu zhi chuban." *Tushuguan zazhi* 27, no. 10 (2008): 63–68.

Luo Zhengjun. *Zuo Zongtang nianpu*. Changsha: Yuelu Shushe, 1983.

Macauley, Melissa A. *Social Power and Legal Culture: Litigation Masters in Late Imperial China*. Stanford: Stanford University Press, 1998.

Mair, Victor H. "Language and Ideology in the Written Popularizations of the Sacred Edict." In *Popular Culture in Late Imperial China*, edited by David Johnson, Andrew J. Nathan, and Evelyn S. Rawski, 325–59. Berkeley: University of California Press, 1985.

McDermott, Joseph P. "Emperor, Elites, and Commoners: The Community Pact Ritual of the late Ming." In *State and Court Ritual in China*, edited by Joseph P. McDermott, 299–351. New York: Cambridge University Press, 1999.

McDermott, Joseph P., and Peter Burke eds. *The Book Worlds of East Asia and Europe, 1450–1850: Connections and Comparisons*. Hong Kong: Hong Kong University Press, 2015.

Metzger, Thomas A. *The Internal Organization of Ch'ing Bureaucracy: Legal, Normative, and Communication Aspects*. Cambridge, Mass.: Harvard University Press, 1973.

Meyer-Fong, Tobie. *What Remains: Coming to Terms with Civil War in 19th Century China*. Stanford: Stanford University Press, 2013.

Millward, James A. *Beyond the Pass: Economy, Ethnicity, and Empire in Qing Central Asia, 1759–1864*. Stanford: Stanford University Press, 1998.

Millward, James A., and Laura J. Newby. "The Qing and Islam on the Western Frontier." In *Empire at the Margins: Culture, Ethnicity, and Frontier in Early Modern China*, edited by Pamela K. Crossley, Helen F. Siu, and Donald S. Sutton, 113–34. Berkeley: University of California Press, 2006.

Min Dongfang. *Da Qing lü jizhu yanjiu*. Beijing: Shehui Kexue Wenxian Chubanshe, 2013.

Miyazaki, Ichisada. "The Administration of Justice during the Sung Dynasty." In *Essays on China's Legal Tradition*, edited by Jerome Alan Cohen, R. Randle Edwards, and Fu-mei Chang Chen, 56–75. Princeton: Princeton University Press, 1980.

Mokros, Emily. "Communication, Empire, and Authority in the Qing Gazette," PhD dissertation, Johns Hopkins University, 2016.

Needham, Joseph, ed. *Science and Civilisation in China*, vol. 5, *Chemistry and Chemical Technology*, part 1, "Paper and Printing." Contributed by Tsien Tsuen-Hsuin. New York: Cambridge University Press, 1985.

Ocko, Jonathan K. "I'll Take It All the Way to Beijing: Capital Appeals in the Qing." *Journal of Asian Studies* 47, no. 2 (1988): 291–315.

Ōki Yasushi. *Minmatsu Kōnan no shuppan bunka*. Tokyo: Kenbun Shuppan, 2004.

Prest, Wilfrid. "Law Books." In *The Cambridge History of the Book in Britain, Vol. 5, 1695–1830*, edited by Michael F. Suarez and Michael L. Turner, 791–806. Cambridge, UK: Cambridge University Press, 2009.

Qi Lianxiu. *Zhongguo gudai minjian gushi leixing yanjiu*. Shijiazhuang: Hebei Jiaoyu Chubanshe, 2007.

Rawski, Evelyn S. *Education and Popular Literacy in Ch'ing China*. Ann Arbor: University of Michigan Press, 1979.

Reed, Bradly W. "Money and Justice: Clerks, Runners, and the Magistrate's Court in Late Imperial Sichuan." *Modern China* 21, no. 3 (1995): 345–82.

———. *Talons and Teeth: County Clerks and Runners in the Qing Dynasty*. Stanford: Stanford University Press, 2000.

Reed, Christopher A. *Gutenberg in Shanghai: Chinese Print Capitalism, 1876–1937*. Vancouver: University of British Columbia Press, 2004.

Ross, Richard J. "The Commoning of the Common Law: The Renaissance Debate over Printing English Law, 1520–1640." *University of Pennsylvania Law Review* 146, no. 2 (1998): 323–461.

Rowe, William T. *China's Last Empire: The Great Qing*. Cambridge, Mass.: Harvard University Press, 2009.

———. "Education and Empire in Southwest China: Ch'en Hung-mou in Yunnan, 1733–38." In *Education and Society in Late Imperial China, 1600–1900*, edited by Benjamin A. Elman and Alexander Woodside, 417–57. Berkeley: University of California Press, 1994.

———. *Saving the World: Chen Hongmou and Elite Consciousness in Eighteenth-Century China*. Stanford: Stanford University Press, 2001.

Sakai Tadao. *Zhongguo shanshu yanjiu*. Translated by Liu Yuebing, He Yingying, and Sun Xuemei. Nanjing: Jiangsu Renmin Chubanshe, 2010.

Shang, Wei. "'Jin Ping Mei' and Late Ming Print Culture." In *Writing and Materiality in China: Essays in Honor of Patrick Hanan*, edited by Patrick Hanan, Judith T. Zeitlin, Lydia H. Liu, and Ellen Widmer, 187–238. Cambridge, Mass.: Harvard University Press, 2003.

Shen Jiaben. *Jiyi wencun*. Taipei: Taiwan shangwu yinshuguan, 1976.

Shimada Masao. "Qinglü zhi chengli." In *Riben xuezhe yanjiu Zhongguoshi lunzhu xuanyi*, edited by Liu Junwen, 461–521. Beijing: Zhonghua shuju, 1992.

Sommer, Matthew H. "The Field of Qing Legal History." In *A Scholarly Review of Chinese Studies in North America*, edited by Haihui Zhang, Zhaohui Xue, Shuyong Jiang, and Gary Lance Lugar, 113–32. Association for Asian Studies, open access e-book. www.asian-studies.org/Publications/Chinese-Studies.

———. *Polyandry and Wife-Selling in Qing Dynasty China: Survival Strategies and Judicial Interventions*. Oakland: University of California Press, 2015.

———. *Sex, Law, and Society in Late Imperial China*. Stanford: Stanford University Press, 2002.

Su Yigong. *Ming Qing lüdian yu tiaoli*. Beijing: Zhongguo Zhengfa Daxue Chubanshe, 1999.

———. "Shunzhi lü kao." In *Zhongguo fazhishi kaozheng (jiabian)*, vol. 7, edited by Yang Yifan, 125–78. Beijing: Zhongguo Shehui Kexue Chubanshe, 2003.

Sun Dianqi. *Liulichang xiaozhi*. Beijing: Beijing Chubanshe, 1962.

Tao Xiang. *Qingdai dianbanshu shimoji*. In *Taoshi shumu shierzhong*. Wujin Taoshi, 1936.

Übelhör, Monika. "The Community Compact (*Hsiang-yüeh*) of the Sung and Its Educational Significance." In *Neo-Confucian Education: The Formative Stage*, edited by William Theodore de Bary and John W. Chaffee, 371–88. Berkeley: University of California Press, 1989.

Wakefield, David. *Fenjia: Household Division and Inheritance in Qing and Republican China*. Honolulu: University of Hawaii Press, 1998.

Wang Erh-min. "Qingting *Shengyu guangxun* zhi banxing ji minjian zhi xuanjiang shiyi." *Zhongyang yanjiuyuan jindaishi yanjiusuo jikan* 22 (1993): 255–76.

Wang Jian, *Zhongguo jindai de falü jiaoyu*. Beijing: Zhongguo Zhengfa Daxue Chubanshe, 2001.

Wang Sixia. "Ming Taizu 'Shengyu liuyan' yanyi wenben yanjiu." MA thesis, Dongbei Shifan Daxue, 2011.

Wang Zhiqiang. "Case Precedent in Qing China: Rethinking Traditional Case Law." *Columbia Journal of Asian Law* 19, no. 1 (2005): 323–44.

———. "Qingdai cheng'an de xiaoli heqi yunyong zhong de lunzheng fangshi." *Faxue yanjiu* 3 (2003): 146–60.

———. "Zhongguo falüshi xushi zhong de 'panli.'" *Zhongguo shehui kexue* 5 (2010): 137–53.

Weber, Max. *The Religion of China: Confucianism and Taoism*. Glencoe: Free Press, 1951.

Will, Pierre-Étienne (Wei Pixin). "Ming Qing shiqi de guanzhenshu yu Zhongguo xing-zheng wenhua." Translated by Li Bozhong. *Qingshi yanjiu* 1 (1999): 3–20.

———. *Official Handbooks and Anthologies of Imperial China: A Descriptive and Critical Bibliography*. Manuscript in progress.

———. "Views of the Realm in Crisis: Testimonies on Imperial Audiences in the Nine-teenth Century." *Late Imperial China* 29, no. 1, supplement (2008): 125–59.

———. "Zai biaoge xingshi zhong de xingzheng fagui he xingfadian." Translated by Zhang Shiming. *Qingshi yanjiu* 4 (2008): 33–52.

Wu Yanhong. "The Community of Legal Experts in Sixteenth- and Seventeenth-Century China." In *Chinese Law: Knowledge, Practice and Transformation, 1530 to 1950s*, edited by Li Chen and Madeleine Zelin, 207–30. Leiden: Brill, 2015.

———. "Guojia zhengce yu Mingdai de lüzhu shijian." *Shixue yuekan* 1 (2013): 52–62.

Xiang Xuan. "Qingdai dianben shoumai liutong kaoshu." *Shixue yuekan* 10 (2018): 22–32.

Xiao Dongfa and Yuan Yi. "Luelun Zhongguo gudai guanfu cangshu yu sijia cangshu." *Tushu qingbao zhishi* 1 (1999): 2–6.

Xiao Li. "Qingdai Wuyingdian keshu chutan." *Tushu yu qingbao* 2 (1983): 56–60.

———. "Qingdai Wuyingdian keshu chutan (xu)." *Tushu yu qingbao* 3 (1983): 48–51.

Xu Zhongming and Du Jin. *Chuanbo yu yuedu: Ming Qing falü zhishi shi*. Beijing Daxue Chubanshe, 2012.

———. "Qingdai sifa guanyuan zhishi jiegou de kaocha." *Huadong shifan xueyuan xuebao* 48, no. 5 (2006): 69–90.

Xue Meiqing. *Song Xingtong yanjiu*. Beijing: Falü Chubanshe, 1997.

Xue Yunsheng. *Duli cunyi dianzhu*. Edited by Hu Xingqiao and Deng Youtian. Beijing: Zhongguo Renmin Gong'an Chubanshe, 1994.

Yang Li. "Xia Xin de *Shi* xue sixiang yanjiu." MA thesis, Anhui Shifan Daxue, 2006.

Yang Yifan, ed. *Zhongguo fazhishi kaozheng*. Beijing: Zhongguo Shehui Kexue Chuban-she, 2003.

Yang Yifan and Liu Ducai. *Lidai likao*. Beijing: Shehui Kexue Wenxian Chubanshe, 2012.

Yang Yuliang. "Qingdai zhongyang guanzuan tushu faxing qianxi." *Gugong bowuyuan yuankan* 4 (1993): 87–92.

———. "Wuyingdian xiushuchu ji neifu xiushu geguan." *Gugong bowuyuan yuankan* 1 (1990): 28–40.

You Chenjun. *Falü zhishi de wenzi chuanbo: Ming Qing riyong leishu yu shehui richang shenghuo*. Shanghai: Shanghai Renmin Chubanshe, 2013.

Yu, Li. "A History of Reading in Late Imperial China." PhD dissertation, Ohio State University, 2003.

Zelin, Madeleine. *The Magistrate's Tael: Rationalizing Fiscal Reform in Eighteenth Century Ch'ing China*. Berkeley: University of California Press, 1984.

Zhang, Ting. "Penitence Silver and the Politics of Punishment in the Qianlong Reign, 1736–1796." *Late Imperial China* 31, no. 2 (2010): 34–68.

Zhang Shiming and Feng Yongming. "'Bao Shichen zhengyi' de chengben: wan Qing Fashenju de falü jingji xue kaocha." *Qingshi yanjiu* 4 (2009): 1–34.

Zhang Xiumin. *Zhongguo yinshua shi.* Shanghai: Shanghai Renmin Chubanshe, 1989.

Zheng, Qin, and Guangyuan Zhou. "Pursuing Perfection: Formation of the Qing Code." *Modern China* 21, no. 3 (1995): 310–44.

Zheng Qin. "*Da Qing lüli* kaoxi." In *Zhongguo fazhishi kaozheng (bingbian)*, vol. 7, edited by Yang Yifan, 38–124. Beijing: Zhongguo Shehui Kexue Chubanshe, 2003.

———. "Kangxi xianxing zeli kao—lüli zhiwai de tiaoli." *Lishi dang'an* 3 (2000): 87–92.

———. *Qingdai falü zhidu yanjiu.* Beijing: Zhongguo Zhengfa Daxue Chubanshe, 2000.

Zhongguo Zhengfa Daxue Tushuguan, ed. *Zhongguo falü tushu zongmu.* Beijing: Zhongguo Zhengfa Daxue Chubanshe, 1991.

Zhou, Guangyuan. "Beneath the Law: Chinese Local Legal Culture during the Qing Dynasty." PhD dissertation, University of California, Los Angeles, 1995.

Zhou Xianghe. "Qingdai Taiwan de diquan jiaoyi—yi dianqi wei zhongxin de yige yanjiu." *Zhongguo jingjishi yanjiu* 2 (2001): 9–15.

Zhou Zhenhe. *Shengyu guangxun: jijie yu yanjiu.* Shanghai: Shanghai Shudian Chubanshe, 2006.

———. *Wan Qing yingye shumu.* Shanghai: Shanghai Shudian Chubanshe, 2005.

Zhu Saihong. "Wuyingdian keshu shuliang de wenxian diaocha ji bianxi." *Gugong bowuyuan yuankan* 3 (1997): 25–32.

Zhu Shijia. *Guanshuju shumu huibian.* Beijing: Zhonghua Tushuguan Xiehui, 1933.

INDEX

Lightning Source UK Ltd.
Milton Keynes UK
UKHW041252290320
361016UK00012B/204